THE
FRAGRANT
HEAVENS

Valerie Ann Worwood

BANTAM BOOKS

London • New York • Toronto • Sydney • Auckland

THE FRAGRANT HEAVENS
A BANTAM BOOK : 9780553505795

Originally published in Great Britain by Doubleday,
a division of Transworld Publishers Ltd

PRINTING HISTORY
Doubleday edition published 1999
Bantam Books edition published 1999

7 9 10 8

Set in 11/13pt Century Schoolbook by Falcon Oast Graphic Art

Bantam Books are published by Transworld Publishers,
61–63 Uxbridge Road, London W5 5SA,
A Random House Group Company.

Addresses for Random House Group Ltd companies outside the UK
can be found at: www.randomhouse.co.uk
The Random House Group Ltd Reg. No. 954009.

The Random House Group Limited supports The Forest Stewardship
Council (FSC®), the leading international forest certification organisation.
Our books carrying the FSC label are printed on FSC® certified paper.
FSC is the only forest certification scheme endorsed by the leading
environmental organisations, including Greenpeace. Our
paper procurement policy can be found at
www.randomhouse.co.uk/environment

Printed and bound in Great Britain by Clays Ltd, St Ives PLC

Also by Valerie Ann Worwood
and available from Bantam Books

THE FRAGRANT PHARMACY
THE FRAGRANT MIND

DEDICATION

For Nan and Pop who would remind me that
'there are more things betwixt heaven and earth than we will
ever know about', and Uncle Will who understood the
spiritual importance of fragrant plants.

ACKNOWLEDGEMENTS

A book of this nature involves a great deal of research in many areas of spiritual experience. In particular I would like to thank Sheila Beber, Lita de Alberdi, Khadija, Zaneta B. Matkowska, Lily Cornford and Maria Phylactou.

Many people within the religious community have been extremely helpful in providing me with information. I am particularly grateful to Gregorios Archbishop of Thyateira and Great Britain, Revd Allen Morris, Dr Richard Mortimer, Rabbi Jonathan Magonet, Malcolm Thomas, Revd Brian Woodcock, W. Tomlinson, Richard J. B. Willis, Revd Geoffrey H. Roper, Revd David M. Chapman, Revd A. Ward Jones, Revd Angela Robinson, Revd T. R. Barker, Revd M. H. Burden, Gillian Crow, Sarah Cohen, Ani Lhamo, Andrew Fergusson, David Coffey and Jane Clements.

Three special people were involved on this journey, and to them I am most thankful. In my search for the truth I was assisted by Julia Stonehouse, who helped me to wade through the literature and with the research into the energy of essential oils. As the fragrant threads and aromatic clues came together, we both felt the impact of enquiring into the spiritual and vibrational realms of fragrance. Lily, Julia's daughter, helped by always having the smile of innocence. And I'm grateful to my daughter, Emma, who offered her unique perspective when we experienced sweat lodges and sacred plant journeys together, and for her patience and love.

PLEASE NOTE:

The material in this book is not meant to take the place of diagnosis and treatment by a qualified medical practitioner. Since the actual use of essential oils by others is beyond the author's control, no expressed or implied guarantee as to the effects of their use can be given, nor liability taken. Essential oils are to be used at the user's own discretion.

Any application of the recommendations set forth in the following pages is at the reader's sole risk. The author and publishers disclaim any liability arising directly or indirectly from the use of this book.

There are eighty myriads of trees in every corner of Paradise, the meanest among them choicer than all the spice trees. In every corner there are sixty myriads of angels singing with sweet voices, and the tree of life stands in the middle and shades the whole of Paradise. It has fifteen thousand tastes, each different from the other, and the perfumes thereof vary likewise. Over it hang seven clouds of glory, and winds blow upon it from all sides, so that its odor is wafted from one end of the world to the other.

LOUIS GINZBERG,
Legends of the Bible

CONTENTS

INTRODUCTION   1

CHAPTER ONE: LET THERE BE LIGHT   13
The Singing Forest   15
Plants that Feel and Speak   21
The Sanctity of Plants   29
Essential Oils: The Unseen Energies   32

CHAPTER TWO: USING ESSENTIAL OILS FOR
SPIRITUAL CONNECTION   38
Thought, Intent and Purpose   40
Purification   44
Handling and Storage   46
Making the Spiritual Connection   47
  The Heavenly Atmosphere   47
Anointing   52
  The Sacred Waters   57
  Body Oils   59
Spiritual Blending   60
  Blending with Prayer and Affirmations   61
Methods of Use   61
Carrier Oils   68
  Pregnant or Lactating Women   69
  People on Medication   70
  People Using Homeopathy   70
  Tranquillizer Addiction   70

Substance Addiction   70
Alcohol Addiction   71
Safety and Precautions   71

CHAPTER THREE: PRAYER AND MEDITATION   73
Prayer   74
  'Dear God . . .'   79
  Taking the Pathway to Heaven   80
Blocks in the Flow   85
  Fear   85
  Guilt   86
  Unworthiness   87
  Receiving and Accepting   87
  Giving and Letting Go   88
Creating Your Spiritual Haven   89
Heaven Scent   92
Meditation   97

CHAPTER FOUR: ON PERFUMED
ANGELS' WINGS   101
Angelic Aromas   115
  The Angelic Vibrations; the Attractants of
    Fragrances   115
  The Angelic Fragrances: 62 Profiles   117

CHAPTER FIVE: FRAGRANT TRANSITION   129
The Fragrance of the Spirit   135
Making the Transition   136
Using Essential Oils for Making the Transition   139
  Spritzers   140
  Hydrolats   140
Fragrance and Transition – The Long Tradition   141

CHAPTER SIX: REMEMBRANCE OF
FRAGRANCE PAST   145

CHAPTER SEVEN: FRAGRANT CLOUDS OF
PURITY AND PROTECTION   157
   The Beneficent Home   162
   Clearing the Atmosphere   164
   Cleansing Blends   167
     Misters and Sprayers   167
     Water Bowls   167
     Essential Oil Cleansing Bundles   168
     Salt   168
   Energy-Cleansing Baths   168
     Energy-Cleansing Bath Blends   171
     The Elements   172
   Holy Smoke – for Purification   173
     Smudge Sticks   175
     Decorative Bundles   179
     Herbal Smoke Bowls   179

CHAPTER EIGHT: MULTIDIMENSIONAL BODIES   180
   The Subtle Bodies   184
     To Feel Your Own Aura   188
     To See Your Own Aura   188
     Aura Fluffing   189
   Essential Oils and the Human Auric Field   190
     Choosing Essential Oils for Subtle Energy Work   191
     Chart: *Evaporation Rates within the Auric Field*   195
     Using Essential Oils in the Auric Field   196
     Chart: *Collective Data Regarding Auric Colours*   198

CHAPTER NINE: VIBRATIONAL AROMATHERAPY   199
   The Chakras   202
   Body Scanning   203
     Chart: *Chakras and their Related Vertebrae and
     Physical Body Areas*   207
     Chart: *Essential Oils for the Chakras*   212
   Using Vibrational Aromatherapy in Treatment   213
     Music   213
     Sounds   213
     Colour   214

Aromas	214
Accessories	215
Treatment	215
Miasms	218
Energies	218
Healing the Spiritual Crisis	219
Charts: *The Seven Main Chakras*	222
The Fragrant Symphony	228

CHAPTER TEN: ENERGETIC AROMATHERAPY   231

Essential Oils and Spiritual Healing	235
The Room	236
In the Auric Field of the Client	237
On the Healer	238
Essential Oils and Distant Healing	238
Healing Lists	241
Essential Oils and Energy Workers	241
Essential Oils and Reiki	243
Essential Oils and Crystal and Gem Therapy	245
Chart: *General Guidelines to the Physical Colours of Essential Oils*	249
Essential Oils and Channelling	251
Essential Oils for Channelling	256
Essential Oils and Colour Healing	257
Chart: *The Colours of Essential Oil Plants and Oils – Physical and Etheric*	263

CHAPTER ELEVEN: THE ESSENTIAL OIL
SPIRITUAL PROFILES   274

What are Essential Oils?	275
Capturing the Fragrance of our Favourite Flowers – What to do if You Don't Have the Essential Oils	276
Glossary of Therapeutic Properties as Itemized Under the Heading 'Physical Healing'	277

Amber; Angelica Root; Angelica Seed; Aniseed;
Balsam de Peru; Basil; Bay Laurel; Benzoin;
Bergamot; Birch (White); Black Pepper;
Camphor; Cardamom; Carnation (Absolute);

Cedarwood; Chamomile German; Chamomile
Roman; Cinnamon; Clary Sage; Clove (Bud);
Coriander; Cypress; Dill; Elemi; Eucalyptus
Radiata; Fennel (Sweet); Fir (White Spruce);
Frankincense; Galbanum; Geranium; Ginger;
Grapefruit; Helichrysum; Hyacinth (Absolute);
Hyssop; Jasmine (Absolute); Juniper; Labdanum
(Rock Rose); Lavender; Lemon; Lemongrass;
Linden Blossom (Absolute); Mandarin;
Marjoram (Sweet); Melissa; Myrrh; Myrtle;
Narcissus (Absolute); Neroli; Nutmeg; Orange;
Ormenis Flower (Chamomile Maroc); Palma
Rosa; Patchouli; Peppermint; Petitgrain; Pimento
Berry; Pine; Rose Absolute; Rose Otto; Rosemary;
Sage; Sandalwood; Spikenard; Storax (Styrax);
Thyme (Red and chemotype linalol); Tuberose
(Absolute); Vetiver; Violet Leaf (Absolute);
Yarrow; Ylang Ylang; Yuzu

CHAPTER TWELVE: THE AROMATIC
TRADITIONS   369
   The Goddess of the Sacred Trees   370
   Ancient Egypt   372
   Mesopotamia   376
   The Hebrew Tradition and the Kabbalah   379
   The Christian Tradition   384
   Ancient Greece and Rome   389
   The Vedic Scriptures   393
   Islam and Arabia   396
   Buddah of the Sacred Tree   398
   Taoism and Chinese Tradition   402
   Shinto and the Japanese Tradition   403
   The Native American Nations   405

Bibliography   409
Index   422

INTRODUCTION

To see a world in a grain of sand
And heaven in a wild flower,
Hold infinity in the palm of your hand
And eternity in an hour

WILLIAM BLAKE, 'Auguries of Innocence'

The omnipresent divine has been put through the prism of human experience, and is expressed in many different ways. Some people focus their ideas of the divine on an original Creator, God, and venerate prophets of that God. Some spiritual traditions pay reverence to the whole living environment; others turn inward, and use specific mental exercises to connect with the oneness of the universe. Whether we pray to God, whether we pay homage to Mother Earth, Father Sky or the spirit of the sage, whether we look to the stars, or seek the stars within, spirituality is about making connections. We may take different routes, but the destination is the same.

Although spiritual practices differ greatly, there's no coincidence in the fact that so many use fragrance. Every evening in India, the air is rich with the aroma

1

of incense burning at home shrines. Smoke fragrant with the aroma of the smouldering resins, frankincense and myrrh, fills the air in Ethiopian Coptic and Orthodox Christian churches. Muslims use lavish quantities of sweet-smelling rose water to impart fragrance to mosques and other holy places. In Native American sweat lodges, for ritual purification and spiritual connection, the fragrant herbs of sage, cedar and sweetgrass are put on the hot rocks to release their aroma molecules into the humid atmosphere. Clouds of fragrant smoke rise from handfuls of incense sticks, placed at Chinese Buddhist shrines. In the *havdallah* ceremony held in Jewish homes at the close of the sabbath every Saturday night, blessings for light and fragrance are recited over the candle and spice box. Each dawn, Tibetans go up on the roofs of their houses and light stoves in which they burn bundles of juniper – to force the sky door open. As plumes of smoke rise from the houses and fragrance fills the air, prayers can be heard.

It's the essential oils in fragrant plant materials, the aroma molecules, that are released by these various practices – they are what gives incense its aroma, just as the essential oil in pine needles gives a pine forest its uplifting quality. Essential oils exude from plants into their 'headspace', where we smell them when walking amongst nature, and humans have devised many methods to capture this essence of the plant, the molecules so many people have chosen to help them connect with and feel the divine.

Fragrance has been said to alert the gods to our presence, and act as a sign that the human mind is focused and receptive to spiritual guidance. In many cultures sweet-smelling aroma was, and still is, associated with divinity – with gods, heavens, angels and saints all being attributed a delightful fragrance. By being oneself fragrant, or burning fragrant material, a link or bridge could be formed to the divine. In *Legends of the Bible* Louis Ginzberg tells us that the Tabernacle had two altars: one brass, and used for food offerings, corresponding to the body; and one of gold, used for offering spices and sweet incense – 'for the soul takes delight in perfumes only.'

Fragrance and spirituality mingle as one in the spiritual traditions of the world. The heavens are redolent with exquisite aroma, the gods are sweetly fragrant, as are angels, saints, and those touched by the divine. The odour of sanctity has impressed many nations, and the people, in turn, make offerings of sweet-smelling aroma to the deity.

The Polynesian god, Urutaete, carried souls of the dead to Rohutu noanoa, a garden paradise perfumed with exquisite odours, known as 'Fragrant Rohutu' or 'Perfumed Rohutu'. Buddhists will pass to the fragrant mountain known as 'gandhamadana'. The gods of the ancient Greeks lived on the fragranced Mount Olympus, while Elysium, the pre-Hellenic paradise, was reserved for human heroes and heroines. They passed there without dying, and found the Elysian Fields suffused with delicious aroma. According to Homer, those favoured by the gods had their body and soul made immortal in this land of perfect happiness. Lucian spoke of the 'scented Isles of the Blessed', and a golden city beside a river of myrrh, while Plutarch wrote about the intoxicating fragrance rising from the River Lethe where 'souls were imbibing these delicious scents aglow with pleasure and engaging in concourse with the other'.

The exhalations of the Muslim paradise have been described as of 'musk, ginger, amber and from the very ground of Eden'. The French Christian saint, Gregor, around AD 310, apparently after a brief sojourn there, said paradise was a 'prairie from which rises at all times an extraordinary perfume'.

In the last book of the New Testament, Revelations 5:8, we hear of the twenty-four elders in Heaven, who fell down before the Lamb, 'having every one of them harps, and golden vials full of odours, which are the prayers of saints'. Heaven is fragrant indeed. In 8:3–4, an angel came to the altar holding a golden censer and was given much incense 'that he should offer it with the prayers of all saints upon the golden altar which was before the throne. And the smoke of the incense . . . ascended up before God'.

The presence of the Holy Spirit is often said to be made known by a mystical fragrance, while so many Christian saints were said to be sweet-smelling or to produce fragrant relics that the idea of an 'odour of sanctity' has likewise continued through the aeons of time. Homer described the Greek god Zeus as 'wreathed in a fragrant cloud', and the ancient Greeks and Romans recognized they were in the presence of a deity when they smelled an especially powerful fragrant odour. Artemis appeared in this way, as did Bacchus – who smelt of saffron and myrrh. The garments of Demeter were said to be fragrant, while Aphrodite/Venus had fragrant robes and hair, and a fragrant temple. Plato wrote of Eros, 'Love will not settle on body or soul or aught else that is flowerless or whose flower has faded away.'

Gods were often said to have been born from various scented parts of plants – the resin that exuded from a cut in a tree, the fragrant bark that was so often used for making incense, or a flower that was, and still is, used for making perfume. The ancient Egyptian god

4

Amon Ra emerged from a lotus, as did the Indian God, Brahma, while Adonis was born from a myrrh tree. The Egyptians called the incense resin that exuded from certain trees, 'the tears' or 'sweat of the gods'.

Egyptian hieroglyphics tell the story of the holy conception of Queen Hatshepsut. Her mother, Queen Ahmose, was awakened from her sleep in her beautiful palace by the majestic aroma of the god Amon. 'All his odours were from Punt', the inscription says, which is perhaps why his daughter, Hatshepsut, felt driven to organize a trade delegation to the land of Punt (probably present-day Somalia) with orders to bring back incense trees, which she had planted in the garden in front of her palace.

Shamans across the world today, as ever, use fragrance to invite the ancestral, animal or nature spirits into this world, and sometimes spirits are recognized as being present by their fragrance alone. So it is with the Chewong, of the Malay peninsula, who have a group of female spirits they call the 'leaf people' – they are recognized by non-shamans as being present in the meeting house only by their fragrance. Nearby, the Batek Negrito say their spirits live in a land that is perpetually fragrant with the aroma of fruit blossoms, and that they love incense and the scent of flowers, while the Warao of Venezuela believe that fragrance originates in the refreshing land of the God of Life.

Places of worship were often fragrant because of the building material used. The temple of Solomon where Jesus taught in Jerusalem was made with the magnificent, fragrant cedars that once covered Lebanon. Indian sandalwood temples are called 'houses of fragrance', *gandhakuti*, and at the Spiritual Grove Temple in Hangzhou, China, an aromatic effigy of

5

Buddha stands fifty feet tall and emits the aroma of its seventy-four blocks of camphor wood.

When the Dalai Lama was a young boy, Tibetans still walked, and prostrated themselves on the earth, along the long circuitous processional route to the monastery at Lhasa, past endless fires of burning juniper. Today, sadly as refugees in Ladakh, Kashmir, the Drokpa Tibetans in particular burn huge amounts of juniper in offering to the minor deities and gods of place – a tradition that pre-dates Buddhism and denotes purification, atonement, and hope for rebirth.

The aromatic tradition is often hidden in symbols, the origins of which we have long since ceased to question. The word 'rosary', for example, stems from the fact that early Christian priests wore garlands of roses around their necks on feast days. The first rosaries were made from 165 rosebuds or rolled up rose petals, sometimes held in place with lampblack. And the famous Jewish candlestick with seven arms, the menorah, the emblem of Israel for over 3,000 years, is a material replica of the fragrant healing plants of the *Salvia* species that not long ago still covered Mount Moriah in Jerusalem.

At Jesus' birth, the kings brought gifts of gold, frankincense and myrrh – gold, perhaps, to help financially; frankincense and myrrh as incense material and medicine. Two days before the Crucifixion Mary Magdalene took 'a pound of ointment of spikenard, very costly, and anointed the feet of Jesus, and wiped his feet with her hair: and the house was filled with the odour of the ointment' (St John 12:3). Spikenard is related to the valerian plant; its aroma is earthy yet sweet and its effect is sedative. Jesus was going to need it, and when Judas Iscariot complained at the waste of such a quantity of precious

6

oil, saying the cost could be given to the poor, Jesus said, 'Let her alone: against the day of my burying hath she kept this.' (St John 12:7)

The word 'messiah' means 'the anointed one'. Kings had from very early times been anointed as a sign of their kingship, and Jesus was a king in the line of David. Shakespeare describes the spiritual and irreversible nature of the anointing of Richard II: 'Not all the water in the rough rude sea; Can wash the balm from an anointed king; The breath of worldly men cannot depose; The deputy elected of the Lord.'

The ingredients of the royal anointing oil have changed little over hundreds of years. At the coronation of Queen Elizabeth II in June 1953, it was composed of the essential oils of neroli, rose, cinnamon and jasmine, together with benzoin, musk, civet and ambergris, blended in sesame oil. This differs from the oil used at the coronation of Charles I in 1626 only in that sesame replaced 'oil of been'. Charles was anointed on the breast, between the shoulders, on both shoulders, in the angle of both arms and on the head – seven places in all. Elizabeth was anointed on the palms, the breast and on the head.

The coronation oil has historically been prepared by the royal physicians, in 1953 by the Surgeon-Apothecary, but it is applied in a spiritual context. The oil for anointing Elizabeth was consecrated – set apart as sacred to God – by the Bishop of Gloucester in the chapel of St Edward the Confessor, in Westminster Abbey, before it was laid on the altar, with the crown, ready for the ceremony. It was contained in a gold ampulla in the shape of an eagle, which was used at the coronation of Henry IV in 1399. The precious holy oil was poured from the beak of the eagle into an elaborate golden spoon dating from around 1200 which, with the ampulla, is now part of the crown jewels at the Tower of London. The act of anointing hallowed and dedicated Queen Elizabeth II in her office – it set the seal of God's approval.

The first English king to be anointed was Egforth of Mercia, in 785, in a ceremony derived from the Jewish tradition described in the Old Testament. The aromatic traditions go far back in time, and are continuing into the future throughout the world. Until recently we did not require an explanation as to why aroma was used in spiritual practice. Fragrance simply drifted between supplicant and deity, joining the two by the shared olfactory experience. A connection was made and more hoped for. Today, we want to know how everything works, including the spiritual use of fragrance.

Unfortunately, we have yet to figure out exactly how aroma works. We can see that two olfactory bulbs protrude from the front of the brain, and have nerves extending down into the top of the nose, where they come into contact with aroma molecules. We also know that aroma is made up of molecules with particular configurations, vibration and light-refraction qualities, and that they 'lock' with receptors, sending messages to the brain. Aroma evokes memory and we can identify the part of the brain involved, but nobody has any idea how the aroma of jasmine, say, can make a picture of a garden on a warm starlit night jump into your head.

Bliss, superconsciousness and even transcendence may prove easier to explain, as opiate and other interesting receptors are most highly concentrated in the limbic system, which is the part of the brain immediately stimulated into action by aroma molecules. Aroma molecules get as close to the brain as it is possible to get, without actually *being* the brain. They stimulate the brain, that is their job, and the olfactory bulbs reach out to meet them.

Aroma evokes emotions, as well as memory, and often the two are connected. Emotions run deep, to the very core of our being. But aroma can reach them, instantaneously. Time means nothing to aroma. Although aromatic functioning is so often accidental and unconscious, within a spiritual context it is deliberate and conscious. We choose particular fragrant materials, and use them in a particular way.

The fragrance molecules, the essential oils, come from plants, to which people are inextricably linked. Plants make the air we breathe, and provide the food for all living beings, on land or in water. Without them life comes to a stop. Because of them, we live; that is the humble relationship we have with them. We think we know about plants and even fiddle with their genes. But the fact is, we could not *make* one plant cell from scratch. We can clone, but not create nature – because we don't know how it works. From an energetic and informational point of view, there is more to life than we know.

Essential oils contain this mystery of life; they have powerful inexplicable energies too. Standing in an ancient forest, under a thick canopy of stars, I have felt the energy of the universe. Plants are the interface between cosmic energies and the earth upon which we depend. They capture the sun in photosynthesis, that much we know. Their aura can be caught by Kirlian photography, and, even when a leaf has been cut, the otherwise invisible outline remains. What this energy is, we do not know, but we see it also emanating from humans. Here is an energy field that connects us, and the likelihood is, it is one of many.

9

If neither nature, nor aroma, has yet been fully explained, how can we hope for science to pin down spirituality? And do we even need it to? Spirituality has its own 'proof', in experience. And if the scientific secret of spirituality *is* to be 'discovered', it will probably be through experience of it!

Twenty years ago in aromatherapy, there was an unwritten rule that we would not be too open about the spiritual side of the essential oils we worked with. We talked about their anti-infectious qualities, their beautifying effects on the skin, and about any number of benefits to body and mind. The positive spiritual changes were recognized, but silently. It seemed far too bold to suggest that the strength and confidence of nature was carried in the essential oils, or that the light and wisdom of the universe flowed through them, their fragrance like messengers from heaven, aromatic angels that come and touch us with the positivity and love of the deity.

All this is a long way from 'anti-bacterial agents'. But being able to talk about spirituality has gone hand in hand with scientific developments which have forced us to open our minds. Quantum physics and chaos theory turn everything topsy-turvy, while the insistence of physicists that the influence of an observer must be put into the experimental equation really focuses the mind. It seems the flutter of a butterfly wing on one side of the world affects events on the other side, and that what we think makes a difference to the universe. The idea that there is a division between body and mind has been put well and truly to rest by the latest discoveries in psychoneuro-immunoendocrinology: it appears that, because there are receptors to brain chemicals throughout the whole body, mind and body are in fact one. On a molecular level, there are striking similarities between parts of humans and plants, and we can see our evolution was deeply entwined. So many connections can now be made, between people and plants, mind and body, the observer and the observed, that it is difficult to see sharp divisions. Indeed, it's now logical to state 'all is one', or agree with the inscription found on the first known picture of a distillation unit, from first-century Alexandria: 'It is towards oneness that all phenomena tend.'

We all have spiritual experiences; it's a question of degree. We all love, and, as they say, 'God is love'. Love transcends time and place, so we feel that loving connection whether the loved one is with us or not. Some people hear the forest sing and are moved to their very core. Others stand in their garden in the morning and feel the unity of the universe in every shaking leaf. Many people have had instant, spiritual experiences, which change their lives for ever.

Whatever form it takes, it is the depth and strength of the spiritual experience which carries conviction forward. More than just 'tradition', spirituality puts us in touch with the cosmic network which permeates all time and space.

From a brain biochemistry point of view, the pursuit of spirituality through aroma makes a great deal of sense, as the mechanics of smell are but one short biological step away from consciousness, including higher consciousness. Thinking of it in terms of light, essential oils *are* captured light, passed from the heavens by plants to us. From a vibrational electromagnetic and energetic point of view, essential oils are in harmony with life. They resonate with us, as the vibration in one violin string can cause vibration in another. We hear the message they have to bring. On a molecular level, natural plant aroma molecules touch cells' receptors with the lightest of contact, then retreat, their job of instigating a series of reactions having been done.

With an etheric quality, essential oils activate the receptors of love, compassion and empathy. They are an information network, carrying messages and crossing boundaries; operating on many different levels. Through them, we can contact the wisdom of nature, the power of the light, the energy of the universe, and the love in our hearts.

What is remarkable about essential oils is that they influence the whole being. Just as they are the catalyst that can make a wound heal, or a mind relax, so they can transport a soul. I know of no other substances that can do that. They are flexible, adaptable, multifaceted, deep, complex, light, subtle, etheric, and all in a positive way. If molecules could be angels, they would surely be essential oils.

The fragrant molecules that are essential oils have been the vehicle for many spiritual journeys. Weaving in and out of the body, as they weave silently through the atmosphere, ethereal but real and deep, essential oils can put us on a wavelength, a network, a web, something which connects the whole. It may be that the experience is brief, but it is never forgotten. Indeed, it is imprinted on the very soul.

Journeys often need guides, and *The Fragrant Heavens* is such a guide – to the spiritual aromatic adventure. I will point out landmarks, introduce aromas and show the view. I can even take you to visit 'museums of spiritual aroma', and to futuristic research labs. Beyond that, I cannot go, because spirituality is always a personal journey.

Chapter One

LET THERE BE LIGHT

> The scientist's religious feelings take
> the form of a rapturous amazement at
> the harmony of natural law, which
> reveals an intelligence of such superi-
> ority that, in comparison with it, the
> highest intelligence of human beings is
> an utterly insignificant reflection.
>
> ALBERT EINSTEIN

As each day dawns, pure sunlight sparkles in dew drops, shimmering on the grass, and on the leaves and flowers of the world. Walking through the woods, light filters through the leaves, creating a green haven of peace. The plant world is full of beautiful sights; there isn't a tree or flower that doesn't look good.

Although we might think so sometimes, providing aesthetic pleasure is not the most important thing about plants. By taking carbon dioxide and water from the air and, with light, converting it into carbo-hydrates, plants are the ultimate production machine, purifying the air and providing food and medicine for humans and animals alike. Plants are both the lungs and the larder of the earth. They are the conduit between the light of the heavens, and the dark of the earth, channelling energy from the sky into the crystalline structures of mother earth, to be reflected throughout the planet.

Plants are magnificent. The tallest tree in Redwood National Park, California, is the height of twenty-six London double-decker buses stacked on top of one another. These trees can live over 1,000 years, but even one only 800 years old has stood through the coronations and reigns of thirty-five kings and queens of England. The size and longevity of these master-pieces of creation is humbling, but to actually walk amongst the immense trees of an ancient forest is more humbling still.

The smallest seed is awesome in its capacity to create another plant, perfect in every detail, including its store of seeds for future generations. Plant seeds have been found in archaeological sites and germin-ated, thousands of years after they were dropped – testament to the monumental capacity of tiny seeds to hold life.

Most of us live not in a living, breathing jungle but in a concrete one. We can redress this balance some-what, by bringing the essence of plants – essential oils – into our homes, but to understand these fully we need to reacquaint ourselves with their heritage, their source – plants in their natural habitat.

THE SINGING FOREST

The trees are the teachers of the law.

Brooke Medicine Eagle

In the 1950s something happened in an ancient North American forest. The event was so poignant that it went down in folklore but, because of the 'Chinese whispers' effect over the years, there are now two versions. In one, the central character was a US Forest Service employee, and in the other he was a Ph.D. student conducting research for his thesis on the age of trees in a bristlecone pine forest.

The man walked deep into the forest for many days until he found a tree he thought might be the oldest. He planned to extract a sample using a core drill, to enable him to count its rings and date it, but the drill didn't work. For some days he tried to fix it, without success. He also had a saw. He looked at the saw and he looked at the tree; he thought about the long walk back to get another core drill, and about the importance of his research. So he cut down the tree and dated it. It was 4,000 years, old enough to have lived through most of known human history. When Moses was a baby, this tree was already five hundred years old.

People have different relationships with nature. Some, like the man in this story, don't treat it with the respect it deserves, making it a sacrifice to the human ego. Others claim that plants have intelligence, soul and the capacity to communicate, and would no more cut down an ancient tree than cut down a grand-mother. Attitudes differ. Some people hear the forest sing, some don't.

15

One hundred and forty million years ago most of the northern hemisphere was covered in redwood and other trees. Mankind made its appearance maybe 200,000 years ago and has, especially in the last 200 years, remorselessly cut the forest down. As early as 1905 American congressman William Kent and his wife Elizabeth recognized the potential ecological danger, and bought 295 acres of redwood forest in California, for $45,000, naming it 'Muir Woods' after the conservationist John Muir. He wrote to the Kents, 'You have done me great honor, and I am proud of it.' We owe thanks to them all because today Muir Woods is one of the few remaining enclaves where you can stand amongst these magnificent trees without hearing the sound of a distant saw indicating that clear-cut logging is heading your way.

It is a humbling experience to stand under ancient redwood trees. In Muir Woods I felt like a three-year-old in the presence of very large, old and wise men, in awe yet certain I would be completely protected. I did not want to leave their presence. Leaning on a redwood that extended too high into the sky for me to see its top, I felt the energy flooding into me, a cosmic river of refreshment for the soul.

I heard the drone of a distant saw but knew in this protected forest island it must only be someone cutting dead wood and undergrowth, to clear the ground. Even so, it reminded me of other areas of the world where international logging consortiums are destroying huge areas of precious forest, and I felt an overwhelming emotion of sadness and guilt. I apologized to the trees on behalf of human beings. Strange as it may seem, the trees spoke to me, directly, without voice, from their heart to mine. They conveyed to me their resignation, deep sadness and incomprehension as to why we should want to do such things.

To someone living in a large city, a long way away from trees, having a conversation with a tree might seem an odd thing to do. But when you are actually out amongst them it seems the most natural thing in the world. I can fully understand why traditional Native Americans, when planning to cut down a tree to make a totem pole or boat, asked permission, and gave thanks directly to the tree making the sacrifice.

My love of trees started when I lived in Switzerland and used to take my dog for a walk in the forest late at night. When the moon and stars illuminated our path we walked on and on, for my pleasure rather than for the dog's convenience, as the silence and majesty of the forest filled me with feelings of reassurance and gratitude. It was there, high in the mountains, that I first sensed the living connection between the night sky, the trees and the earth. Many years later, in ancient redwood and cedar forests in North America, this impression was reinforced. Standing under a thick canopy of stars illuminating the sky, I sensed that trees, particularly very tall, ancient trees, act in some way as planetary antennae. The very tops of the trees seem to attract starlight and other cosmic energies, 'earthing' that energy as it travels down through the trunk, into the roots and the earth. I also wonder if the trees don't also transmit information back into the sky, sending vibrational energy, including human thought energy, out into the cosmos. I have no scientific proof, of course, but the thought remains: these giant trees are receivers and transmitters of energy, crucial even to cosmic balance and human spiritual growth.

Anyone who studies trees knows that there is still a great deal to learn about them, especially in terms of energy and communication. Even in terms of mechanics and chemistry, areas we think we know so much about, new discoveries are being made all the time. Scientists of the British Columbia Ministry of Forests only recently found that certain tree species can share resources by using an underground network of fungal threads. Seedlings of Douglas fir, paper birch and western red cedar were subjected to carbon dioxide containing different carbon isotopes. Two years later, 10 per cent of the carbon-type fed to the birch was found in the fir. Both species share mycorrhizal fungi, which created the network of threads between them, and the carbon travelled along this complex connection. Because this same fungi does not connect with cedar, its particular experimental carbon composition was unaffected. Meanwhile, in Kenya, scientists have discovered that as well as sucking water up from the deep earth a 'substantial' amount of water is transported downward by trees, to the dry sub-surface. These are pretty fundamental discoveries, which tell us a great deal about the working of trees we did not know before, in an area – the mechanical – we thought we already understood.

In British Columbia, Canada, the drive to harvest large-dimension lumber is in full swing, as logging companies race to bring down the last remaining trees before politicians accept what environmentalists have been telling them for years and bring the harvest to an end. Standing in these forests is scary. You can hear the drone of mechanical saws and you know you're standing among doomed giants. These magnificent trees are silently performing crucial ecological tasks for the whole living planet; they have lived through so much of human history and yet are helpless to stop our saws cutting through them. This helplessness, coming from such powerful, massive living things, is infinitely sad.

I was intrigued to hear about a woman who claims to have heard the forest sing. Living deep in a forest in British Columbia, where the loggers cut 1,000-year-old trees, Gladys McIntyre earns a living planting seedling trees. In June 1990, in a part of the cedarwood forest called Howser Creek, Gladys found herself thinking about the 'immense verticality' of the trees when 'a profound vertical alignment took place in me in response; and suddenly I felt about twelve feet tall. I wondered for a moment if this was soulic consciousness, then I was struck in my solar plexus by an impact of sound. It grew to an upwelling, crescendoing symphony of sound, in range and tone unlike anything I had ever heard before! Emanating from the forested hillsides across the valley, it was unquestionably a great hymn of adoration, of joy in Creation and praise to the Creator! Words cannot possibly express the magnitude of this joyous sound, nor my absolute awe at witnessing it.'

But from being a song in praise of the Creator, the song abruptly changed from 'overwhelming joy to abject sorrow'. Gladys writes: 'My cognitive mental faculty seemed to be translating information received by my soul from that incredible presence at worship over there.' It said, 'O noble and worthy, exploiters and conquerors, have mercy, have mercy, do not end our singing which allows the conditions necessary to all life on the planet as you know it.'

Reports as powerful as this can easily be dismissed as the workings of an overactive imagination, so I went to visit Gladys, to try to get closer to the truth. I found her living with her husband Vince, growing organic vegetables that are exquisitely formed, massive, and with a delicious, vibrant taste. Those

19

vegetables positively vibrated and shone in pure, verdant, colourful perfection, well-loved and content. Gladys is a person clearly in touch with the laws of nature, and as sane as you or I.

I came away thinking that if the forests do communicate, Gladys is the right person to hear it. But she is not the only one. In another ancient forest a young woman and her boyfriend went to sit on a splendid mountain ridge to admire the forest view. But instead of feeling glad to be in the splendour the girl became overcome with a sense of panic and fear coming from the forest. Sick with anguish, she had to return home. Days passed, but the sadness wouldn't go. The girl felt driven to return to that part of the forest, to try to understand why she had been so affected. When she arrived she was horrified and stunned to discover the whole area had been clear-cut to the ground.

Although to 'civilized' people communicating with trees may sound bizarre, it is in fact something that's been going on for a very long time. Indeed, trees have long been central to spiritual culture. In ancient Egypt the 'world tree' was associated with a 'sycamore', possibly the sycamore fig that gave shade to the goddess worshippers in their 'groves'. Kabbalah, the mystical aspect of Judaism, has its 'tree of life' and has traditionally been taught to men over forty while they sat under trees. In the last book of the New Testament, Revelations 22:2, we hear that the tree of life is in 'the midst of the street' in Heaven. Buddha received enlightenment while sitting under a tree. The ancient Assyrians had many tree cults, with the tree of life sometimes depicted as a cedar, fir, date or pomegranate. The Chinese associated the tree of life with the peach, and in later times the cassia, while in Norse mythology it was the ash. A Polynesian legend says 'out of this magic breadfruit tree a great goddess was made'. The sacredness of trees is universal, and this may not simply be because they routinely offer up their bounty, but because they have a spirit we can feel.

PLANTS THAT FEEL AND SPEAK

When we suddenly remember to water our plants, is it because the plants sent us a message across the room – 'hey, don't forget about us'? Why shouldn't they talk to us, we talk to them. People in their high-rise apartment blocks, or in their gardens, say to their plants, 'You look lovely today,' or, 'What's up? You're looking a bit off-colour', and then fuss around them, administering love and fertilizer – organic, of course. Chatting to plants is a regular occurrence, even for royalty, and some plant aficionados play them music, taking care to choose something they like.

Edward Bach, famous for his Flower Remedies, attributed certain medicinal qualities to plants because the plants themselves told him what they were. An entire Western healing system is thus based on plant communication, and has inspired further plant-human exploration. Meanwhile, in many cultures it is considered quite wrong to become a healer without first having had dreams or visions relating to the plants to be used. In other words, the spiritual realm is seen as the source of accurate information. Cultures that are very much in touch with the earth and all that grows in it believe unreservedly that plants have a spirit. Obviously a plant is unable to speak, so to communicate with it we have to get into the spiritual 'space' we share with it. If you want to know what a plant can do, go to the source and ask it. To indigenous peoples, that's the logical thing to do. There are variations on this cultural theme; with some people believing the spirit of the individual plant conveys the information; or that each species of plant has a kind of 'overall' spirit which communicates; or that there are a variety of nature spirits; or that it is the voice of the Creator who speaks. These are all variations on a theme: you can speak to, or through, a plant.

The Yaqui people of northwestern Mexico have an oral tradition going back 4,000 years, to 2000 BC. Around AD 1500, because of the oppressive actions of the Spanish conquistadors, the Yaqui were forced to make their sacred traditions secret. Seven lineages were chosen to preserve them, through sacred oral and family traditions. Through many subsequent generations the sacred way of the Yaqui was kept alive, underground, as the bullets flew overhead. Now that we are older and wiser, hopefully, the knowledge can re-emerge. Indeed, it is time for us to know it.

Cachora Guitemea is a man who carries this knowledge, passed to him by his father and mother. A Yaqui traditional spiritual healer, Cachora is a highly respected Native American elder. It was, then, a great privilege for me to be privately invited to spend a few days in the Mexican desert with Cachora to learn about sacred plant medicine. We were accompanied by both our daughters and the mutual friend who introduced us. Although Cachora is over eighty and has white hair, you would never guess his age – either from his appearance or from his extraordinary energy. His face is lit up with a joy that defies time. And, despite his boyish love

22

of jokes, you never forget that you are in the presence of great wisdom and positive intent.

Cachora teaches that we must respect plants. Permission must be sought from the plant before picking it, and if the plant is required for ceremonial purposes sacred chants and mantras are said aloud, in honour of the plant or tree. All plants have souls and spirits that guard and protect the species. It is not that every individual plant has its own, but that there is a species-spirit, which has a place within plant hierarchy, depending on the sacredness of the purpose the plant is put to.

Many plants also have animal spirits attached to them, says Cachora. The connection may be derived from the fact that an animal eats from the plant and thus distributes the seeds; or because the animal eats smaller animal pests upon the plants; or because the animal uses the plants as a food and medicine.

Cachora is quite plain about the underlying principle of healing herbs. He says that healing takes place when a person connects into the plant spirit, becoming the plant, and understanding its personality. Using spirit as the method of transference, the plant's energy or healing properties are transmitted to the person. Once the spirit of a particular species has come to be known, and its use and purposes memorized, its strengths and weaknesses understood, then in times of ill-health, as body, mind and spirit are one, by calling on the spirit and taking into one's mind the spiritual essence of the plant, healing can take place.

Plant life must be respected and spoken to, says Cachora, for it is part of the universe, part of ourselves, our heritage. I understand this to mean that everyone evolved through the plant, and through the plant cycle of crystalline life – we are all part of the same consciousness pool. Getting to know plants involves looking at them closely, communicating with them with honesty and integrity, and with gentleness. Human thought is the greatest obstacle to plant communication. You have to get beyond thought, into empathy and feeling, through focus and concentration.

On this amazing journey I encountered a magnificent six-feet-high white sage bush, a grandfather of the species which, having seeded many generations of plants, was an elder in its own right. So vibrant was it that the leaves seemed to send out showers of sparks, but I was rather taken aback when the large bush bowed its body to greet us. As there was not a hint of a breeze I turned to my friend beside me to verify what had happened. I could tell from her wide-open eyes that she could! Then the sage spoke to me, in a silent block of communication, clear and precise.

There are many indigenous peoples in the world who feel the spirit in nature, and work with it. Certain themes emerge. One such idea is that some plants should not be picked because they are too sacred – too old and valuable to their 'tribe'. Just like us, plants need their wise elders. They say you should ask a plant if it is OK to pick it. A plant may say no, it may agree – and it is respectful to explain who the plant is for, and what is wrong with them. The plant will then know it is not being needlessly sacrificed. Another is the general idea that the spirit of the plant is a communal one, shared by the species as a whole, so that when you communicate with a plant you communicate with its species-spirit. When I spoke to the large sage bush I spoke to the spirit of the species, but *through* the wise old bush who happened to hold a great deal of communal species wisdom and could express more information more clearly.

24

When you think about it, this is not dissimilar to the way horticulturists and gardeners view the plants in their care. Older plants possess an authority that seedlings do not. Also, each species has its own nature, and individuals within the species have their particular character. We speak of animals in much the same way, describing a breed of dog as being generally 'good with children', but individuals within the species may not be good, with children in general, or with a particular child.

Many Western gardeners 'tune in' to their plants in essentially the same way as do indigenous peoples. Looking at a bed of roses, next to a bed of hollyhocks, we might perceive each species to have a different emotional tone. Each species looks different, grows differently, with different kinetic qualities and character – in much the same way as people have different characters. The more species we grow, and the longer we work with them, so our 'instinct' about plants develops (as instinct develops over time when using essential oils).

The difference between our approach and that of indigenous peoples is the way we learn about plants. We spend time reading gardening books, while they sit with a plant for hours, days even, getting to *know* it. They'll respectfully bring it little presents, in gratitude for what it offers and to let the plant know they *care*. They go to plants as a pupil goes to a wise person, *to learn*. Western horticulturists, on the other hand, often feel that *they* are the holders of information, and that it is their job to control the plant, which they see as their property.

We know, of course, from 'companion gardening' that plants can influence each other in terms of preventing pests and disease. This is often accomplished through scent, as aroma molecules from one plant waft over another, exerting their beneficial influence. Stephen

Harrod Buhner relates an interesting anecdote on this subject in *Sacred Plant Medicine*. He was sitting with a lichen called usnea, which has powerful antibiotic qualities, when suddenly the usually subtle 'feeling tone' of the usnea increased in intensity, Buhner felt his 'personal boundaries' dissolving, and the plant appeared as a youngish man. The plant-man told him that usnea's primary role is to keep the earth's lung system healthy, by being an antibiotic for the trees on which it grows, adding that as a by-product of this intended role, usnea can also be used to treat individual human lung infections. Imagine how much more we could learn about plant interaction, and how many new medicines we could discover, if more of us could hear what plants have to say.

Plants are sensitive, sentient beings. There has been a great deal of research in this area, starting in 1966 with the work of Cleve Backster, then a New York expert in the field of lie-detection working for law-enforcement agencies. One classic Backster experiment involved plant murder. He put two plants next to each other in a room, along with six of his students, who each picked a piece of paper from a hat; one of the pieces of paper carried instructions for the murder. The people with the five 'blank' papers left the room with Backster. In the room the 'murderer' ripped one of the plants to shreds. Backster then returned, attached the remaining plant to a polygraph machine, and called the students into the room, one by one. There was no response on the machine to the five innocent students, but when the murderer entered the pen flew across the paper as the silent 'witness' recognized the guilty party.

The implications of Backster's work on plants are staggering enough, but he has also done experiments with other life forms, including eggs, shrimps and human mouth cells – the implications of which are equally amazing. Backster had to conclude that all nature is essentially unified, not separate.

The planet earth hums. It emits a low-frequency radio signal, the earth's 'vibration', which is known as the Shumann resonance, and it can be detected coming off trees. Researchers in America were curious to know whether this vibration could be altered with human thought and feeling, and connected an oak tree to a machine described as being not unlike those used to measure brainwaves in humans. A group of people circled the tree and, saying a traditional Native American prayer, sent it love. The charts reportedly went off the scale. Although the measurements couldn't indicate whether the tree was happy to receive this love, or whether it wanted everyone to go away, clearly some form of interaction was taking place.

Plants respond to human thought, and to the human energy field. You can prove it for yourself in the following thought experiment devised by Marcel Vogel. Pick three leaves from the same tree or plant and place them by the side of your bed. (Vogel put them on glass, presumably so that he could view the underside without touching the leaves, but a sheet of paper will do.) Each morning when you wake, concentrate on just two of the leaves, sending them love and pleading with them to live. Imagine them green and healthy-looking. Ignore the third leaf. Don't touch any of them. After seven days the two chosen leaves should still look fresh, while the ignored leaf should be shrivelled. Do the experiment when you wake because that's when you're most physically and mentally relaxed. It's absolutely vital to approach this with a pure heart, because plants know what you think. Don't try to fool them because you'll only be fooling

27

yourself. *Expect* the experiment to work.

Another classic experiment was originally devised by mathematician and healer Daphne Beall. Fill a container with water and energize the water by putting both hands around the container, without touching it. Relax, and visualize white-light energy coming out of your hands into the container. Imagine the water becoming bright white; do this for ten minutes. Then put an organic, non-genetically manipulated tomato in the water. Fill a second container with water, and put another similar tomato in that container without giving it any thought. Leave both containers overnight and in the morning take the tomatoes out of the water and place them somewhere where they can sit for two weeks without being moved. Make sure you have a way of remembering which is which. The tomato placed so briefly in the energized water will prove to have a much greater lifespan.

An energy connects us to plants. In some people the energy is very obvious, when they transform a neglected piece of earth, with fairy dust, into a resplendent garden. We call this 'having a green thumb'. Almost everybody, natural gardeners or not, has empathy for the glory of nature.

Human–plant interaction involves the study of light, physics, astrophysics, metaphysics, botany, biology, harmonics, electromagnetics, hydrology, mineralogy, and a dozen other things including neurology, philosophy, spirituality, theology and psychology, to name but a few. Perhaps that is why it is so little researched – we don't know whose academic territory it is! The answer may be of course that it is everyone's territory, because there is only one territory, in that we are all part of the connecting whole.

THE SANCTITY OF PLANTS

People have always been spiritual, at least we can say so from looking at palaeolithic cave art and the many images and objects people have created since that time, say 30,000 years ago. Indeed, spirituality has been the drive of much, if not most, culture and art throughout time – think of the temples, sculpture and paintings. People used to believe so sincerely in an afterlife that they made sure their relatives were buried with goods they would need there, including sometimes a fortune in gold jewellery. Today we may question the existence of an afterlife, and any jewellery goes in the will. Sometimes, we don't seem very spiritual at all. Yet, even *we* feel it strongly – there must be something else . . .

Where does this spirituality come from? Put another way – what has made people think there is a life after death, and an intelligence that embraces the universe? Some sceptics would say that spirituality is just an ongoing tradition of superstition – that people don't have spiritual experiences, they just *think* they do. These people can point to certain evidence. For example, the crystals in granite, being radioactive, cause brain stimulation including hallucinations, which may explain why it was used to build the neolithic dolmens (shelters) and to cover the walls of important rooms, like the King's Chamber in Cheops pyramid in Egypt. People sat in these places and 'tripped out' – more or less like an acid trip (LSD). They thought they were having spiritual experiences, but may have been playing with their own minds.

The same sceptical attitude could be taken towards the spiritual use of sound, dance and plants. Sound, in the form of chanting, singing, or the repetition of mantras, sets up a vibration which changes brain functioning and could cause a 'spaced out' feeling. Dance can do the same thing. Certain plants are psychoactive – they have an effect on the mind or psyche – and have been used by shamans for millennia, from South America to Siberia, to facilitate a state of trance, and another perception of reality. Some say these activities gave a false impression of 'spirituality', and fear and superstition did the rest.

This is a very one-sided point of view, for there are many other types of spiritual experience which involve neither stones, sound, dance nor plants. The basic spiritual experience is love, with some people falling in love after a very long time of knowing each other, or instantly – seeing a stranger across a crowded room. When that loved-one is far away, they can be thought about, scanned for on the distant horizon, located, and their spirit bought into the heart. We seem connected in a way that defies the laws of place. Love is spiritual. Also, nature is spiritual, with many people saying their strongest feeling of spirituality is when out amongst nature, on a mountain top perhaps, admiring the view, overcome with a strong sense of there being a beneficent intelligence watching over us all. Many people have spontaneous spiritual experiences, when they suddenly 'get it', and become devout. Others have near-death experiences, see the other side, and come back certain of an afterlife. People hear voices – including some of the central characters in the Old Testament – when they're just walking along, not expecting revelation. And people have been bumping into angels for millennia.

It's because the spiritual realm is there that we have this thing called 'spirituality'. When people use stones, sound, dance and plants, they are *seeking* to make the connection with something they already know is there. These things are not *the reason for* spirituality, but *a means to* spirituality. People want to reconnect, and they feel they need help.

When Aaron burnt incense every morning and evening, it was not to create two little pockets of 'spiritual experience' within the day. Aaron felt the spirit all day long. He burned incense to concentrate his mind on the subject . . . and because God had told him to. Likewise, Buddhists don't burn incense to receive the enlightenment of Buddha's words, they already know them, and believe them to be the right path to follow in life: incense is burnt to experience the enlightenment directly, to connect with something they know is there.

Certain plants have been chosen as spiritual aids by people living thousands of miles apart, on different continents, in different millennia. Cedar is a case in point. The temple of Solomon in Jerusalem was built with cedars from Lebanon, and it is possible the Hebrews extracted an oil from the wood. In India, cedar is used to induce trance, while in Native American culture it is said to have the ability to counteract negative forces. Why should these, and other peoples, choose cedar? Is it because it *smells* good; or because it *does* something in the spiritual realm; or because it does both?

Plant materials have long been used in spiritual practice, and the more fragrant they were, the more spiritual they were considered. This may be because fragrance transports. You can be in a place feeling very uncomfortable, with chaos and noise all around, then close your eyes, inhale a particular fragrance, and bypass it all, reconnecting with the great cosmic whole, and peace. It's like a private vehicle silently and instantaneously whisking you away to reconnection; fragrance can be a ticket to the divine.

ESSENTIAL OILS: THE UNSEEN ENERGIES

In the usual light photographs of the Milky Way, the shape seems obvious – it's a spiral disc, a basically flat circular shape made up of countless white stars – but when you get on the Internet and look at some of the photographs that have come back from space, you can see that the reality is much more complex. The web sites to visit are the Goddard Space Flight Center, NASA, and the University of Illinois, which display photos of the Milky Way taken using X-ray, infra-red and radio equipment. When the frequency is changed, further levels of reality are exposed. Using computer enhancement and colour, different swirls of energy are highlighted, and 'bipolar outflows' are revealed as emerging from the centre, like two trumpets, perpendicular to the disc of stars. These exciting new pictures illustrate how much more there is to life than we can see with our eyes.

Life on our planet certainly seems more benevolent than on the other planets in our solar system, and more vibrant, but what do we know of its invisible energies? Human energy fields have been recognized in most, if not all, spiritual traditions. Eastern traditions talk of *prana* and *ch'i* – the energies that are vital to health. In Western terminology, we hear of the 'aura', or the 'etheric body', 'astral body', 'mental body' and 'spiritual body', and a 'golden web' that connects us all. It is likely that we are dealing with several energy fields that interact with each other, and our physical selves, and they are said to be the means by which we connect with the divine.

According to Dr Valerie Hunt, a physiological scientist and author of *Infinite Mind, the Science of Human Vibrations*, although the electrons existing in humans and inactive matter are the same, the human field absorbs and throws off energy, while inert matter is passive. In addition to the electrical frequencies of muscle, brain and heart there is 'another field of energy, smaller in amplitude and higher in frequency'. Apparently this energy is electromagnetic, and eight to ten times faster than the other electromagnetic energy recorded on the body's surface. Dr Hunt has done much research on the human aura: taking measurements when subjects were in the mountains and near the sea; or after having a swim, a shower, or a barefoot walk on grass; and in special scientific study environments, such as the Mu and Anechoic rooms at the University of California in Los Angeles. The Mu room, located in the physics department, is an environment in which the electromagnetic energy in air can be altered. The Anechoic room is designed to take out sound and light, and thus these sources of electromagnetism; and subjects lose their sense of time and became unable to operate the instruments taken in there for research study.

There are few people in the Western world who have carried out as much scientific research on the human aura as Dr Hunt, and she writes:

> *The human field looms as primary to life.*
> *Resonating frequencies are primary physical bonds in nature. For every frequency or frequency band, there exists natural or created resonators.*

33

In other words, a field's frequency pattern at a given time is a resonating structure that determines the energy it will absorb or by which it will be affected. Theoretically, all frequency vibrations exist in the universe (which includes the body) – from sub herzian to as high as modern instruments can measure – billions and trillions of cycles per second. Nonetheless, each material substance, living or inert, mineral or chemical, has its own vibratory signature carried in the structure of its field. There are dominant and recessive vibrations in each field, giving it character. Field interactions result from the strength and pattern of these field vibrations. These constitute windows, or thoroughfares for transactions.

A sound general principle states that interaction between fields occurs when there are compatible harmonic frequencies.

I believe essential oils are 'thoroughfares for transactions' – they have their own vibrations which connect with the frequencies in the human energy field, causing effects in the physical, emotional and spiritual body. Essential oils have different electrical qualities, and different molecular shape and vibration. Interesting though all the data is, it does not explain what one might rather vaguely call 'the energy' of a particular essential oil. New methods of recording are required.

With this in mind, I went to see Harry Oldfield, who co-authored *The Dark Side of the Brain* with Roger Coghill in 1988, at the time a seminal work on unseen energies. Harry has invented an energy field imaging system which records the invisible aura of energy around all living things, and I was interested to know

34

what it could reveal about essential oils. According to Harry, the images produced show interference patterns with light, as light rays and photons get 'interfered with by the subtle energy effects emanating from the object or space point. I say "space point" because there are atmospheres and places that give off emanations too.'

Using this new equipment, which produces moving images on a computer monitor, colourful and dynamic patterns emerge in the air around the end of the smelling strip, on which the essential oils are placed. With some, such as jasmine and ginger, the end of the strip appeared bright white, with all the colour spectra in that spot. In others, the whole strip appeared energized, while yet others showed no change. The background is generally green but each essential oil makes it explode into different colours and shapes. We saw either magenta, predominantly purple, orange, turquoise, or blue circles and squares: all actually layers of colour, rather like a rainbow. With eucalyptus citriodora a yellow haze appeared; while with frankincense a sudden rocket of energy flew out from the end of the strip; and with neroli a blue circle appeared at a distance and started beating like a heart, getting slightly smaller then larger – a flashing light of life – pulsating seven times before dispersing. The individuality of these essential oil energy patterns is amazing, and the more you see, the more amazing they are!

What we are seeing, Harry believes, is the etheric energy in the fabric of space itself, going beyond the molecules themselves, an energy that is in a buffer zone between the physical and higher energies. Some of the essential oils made little impression, and some were very dramatic, and the differences were not related to when the image was taken. It cannot be said, then, that as the aroma molecules built up in the atmosphere, things got more dramatic. Sometimes, towards the end of a session, there would be an essential oil that showed very little activity altogether. Also, some of the energy fields were very small and remained close to the end of the strip, while others immediately shot out all around and took up much space. In some, the energy field seemed to hover above the smelling strip, then in others it hung below. Some fields seemed to come towards us, some went out, some stayed where they were, while others leaped! The kinetic nature of these events is not of course captured by the still images reproduced here. In some essential oil recordings, the energy was slow to build up, in others it was instant.

Discussing the images observed on the computer screen with the other people in the room, I realized that we were using the same vocabulary as I use when describing essential oil fragrances in other contexts. Someone would say it's 'round', or 'sharp', 'sparkly', 'heavy', 'light', 'soft', 'dynamic', or that it 'has direction'.

It was also very interesting to watch the energy field of the essential oil mingle with and affect the aura emanating from a person, if they held the smelling strip, or stood near by. I was reminded of Hunt's phrase, 'a thoroughfare for transactions'. When the energy fields from the essential oil and the person gently connected, we saw an expansion of the human aura. Harry's words were emphatic: 'They definitely interact in the human energy field, there's no doubt about it.' The mystery of 'the life force' of essential oils was looking less mysterious by the minute.

Essential oils are crystalline structures that carry light. They vibrate, and cause selective synchronous vibration; they are electromagnetic, as we are ourselves. They are thought to travel through the interstitial fluid and the extra-cellular spaces – the space between the cells, where the molecules of emotion may also travel, as described by psycho-immunologist Candace Pert in *Molecules of Emotions*. It's no wonder that fragrance has been used since time immemorial to connect people with the divine, lifting us to finer, higher vibrations, in touch with wider consciousness.

Chapter Two

USING ESSENTIAL OILS FOR SPIRITUAL CONNECTION

To wonder at nothing when it happens:
to consider nothing impossible before it
comes to pass.

MARCUS TULLIUS CICERO

The spiritual connection could be said to take place within the dynamic energy which permeates the entire universe. It is a space of light and high vibration, and anything used for subtle healing – the reconnection of body to spirit – needs to be in harmony with it.

Essential oils carry the light, and that light potential is activated by positive thought. Even physicists now accept that thoughts are a form of energy, saying the human observer has to be taken into account as part of the experiment: what they are thinking changes the outcome. Thought is part of scientific equations, even though we can't grab a thought and put it under the microscope!

When working with essential oils for first aid, or for physical ailments such as rheumatism, although the energetic aspects of essential oils are important, they are not as important as choosing an essential oil with the chemical properties to do the job then required of it. When choosing an essential oil for subtle healing or spiritual connection, however, the chemical constituents are less important because they are not being required to act on the physical, chemical matter of the human body. What *is* most important is the energy of the essential oil, its vibrational note, which interacts with our own spiritual harmonic note as part of the universal symphony.

Any essential oil distilled from a plant lovingly grown in unsullied soil, under an unpolluted sky, by caring people, and distributed by a company working with integrity and respect, is going to have a good energy. Nature vibrates with its own joy of life in which we can share and, indeed, essential oils produced under such favourable conditions appear to have a more beneficial effect on the sick or wounded than those distilled from plants subjected to polluted growing conditions, chemical adulteration or negative thought-forms. When considering using essential oils for subtle healing and spiritual purposes, the energetic aspects of production are equally important.

The first step, then, is to consider the question of supply. Ultimately, after the various mechanical means of purity analysis, there is one judge of aroma: the nose, the most direct pathway to the mind and spirit. The way to train a nose is by comparison – opening the tester bottles of the various brand-named essential oils and taking a sniff. After a while, you'll find outlets that carry oils with a purity, clarity and energy that stand out. Take your time though, make it a mission, it's worth the effort. Talk to the shopkeepers and find out about their sources. That won't tell you the whole story, but it might give you a clue here and there. Seek, as they say, and you shall find.

THOUGHT, INTENT AND PURPOSE

Thoughts are very powerful things, and I say 'things' because, although they're invisible, they're almost tangible. They seem sometimes to fill the space around a person, so you can know what they're thinking even when their back is turned. Some people even believe thoughts get impregnated into the fabric of buildings or objects, and that their energy can be felt centuries later. Thoughts certainly travel across space very quickly, with people often knowing what someone else is thinking at that instant, no matter where in the world they are.

When it is *we* who are having the thoughts, they can also seem to fill the whole space around us. Sometimes we may feel people can read our thoughts because they are so obvious and extended from ourselves. They seem to have a power, an energy of their own; even transmitting to other people, sometimes when we wish they wouldn't.

There have now been many studies on what is termed 'non-local quantum thought phenomena' – how one person's thoughts can somehow instigate an effect in another person. Research also shows that this phenomenon is instantaneous and isn't affected by distance – it doesn't matter whether the two people are standing right next to each other or on different continents. Although such a concept seems unbelievable, it actually mirrors a phenomenon known by science to occur with subatomic particles. If two subatomic particles that have been in contact with each other are separated, a change to one also occurs, in exactly the same way and instantaneously, in the other, no matter how distant the particles are from each other. So, if there is a correspondence between one human's thought and another human's thought, and between subatomic particle and subatomic particle, why not between humans and essential oils?

We have at this point to bring in a few scientific facts. First, as I have written in *The Fragrant Mind*, scientists have established that the chemical composition of the DNA in a moose – the animal – and a spruce – the tree – is essentially identical. Both DNAs are encased in cells, which are structurally the same and like ours. Moreover, the only chemical difference between chlorophyll in plants and red haemoglobin in human blood is that a magnesium atom in one replaces an iron atom in the other. As Richard Thompson so eloquently puts it in *The Brain: A Neuroscience Primer*, 'The similarity of the genetic material in all forms of life that exist in the world today, including bacteria, plants, animals, and people, indicates that all living organisms descended from the same single cell-line.' In other words, human beings and plants come from the same familial line and have a relationship. It is that fundamental relationship that can be activated by thought. (How poignant it is that all Lakota North American ceremonies end with the words *mitakuye oyasin*, meaning 'we are all related': a prayer recognizing every living thing – every person, animal and plant – as part of the same family.)

Of course, essential oils are not living plants; and, although some might be prepared to accept that we can communicate with plants, they might say we can't communicate with essential oils, as they are 'only' the

41

essence of a plant. I'm reminded now of some work carried out by Cleve Backster, who became famous as the man who proved that plants respond to human thought. He also discovered, however, that if he ground up a leaf he could get the same emotional-electrical results as he did with live plants.

I talked to many people while researching this book and each time the subject of thoughts came up, everyone was emphatic – yes, the energy of essential oils varies depending on the mind-frame of those handling them. Whether I spoke to scientists who take measurements of essential oils, religious leaders or medicine men, all were in agreement: essential oils have a vibration which is altered by the person handling them. This fact throws light on a strange (or not so strange) phenomenon: two people using the same species of essential oil can elicit two different responses – one that has the desired effect and one that doesn't. It almost seems as if, in the latter case, the oil has been sapped of its energy; however, it's more the case that the light potential in the oil has been switched off – and, thankfully, it can be rekindled.

The first thing I say to students or people attending workshops, is that the most important element of handling essential oils is encapsulated in three words – thought, intent and purpose. 'Thought' motivates the action of picking up a particular essential oil, 'intent' is about having positive intentions, and the objective, what you are trying to achieve, is the 'purpose'.

Basically, we need to stop and think about what we are doing; why we are doing it; and apply our head and heart to it. We want to *attain* a good result, and use the appropriate essential oils to achieve it. Smile, and *visualize* the recipient in a completely abundant way: in spirit, mind and body, their positive qualities enhanced. Don't dwell on any minor irritating aspects they may have, or impose any private thoughts on the essential oils – such as 'this will calm him down'. It is not for us to impress our will or ego on the oils; we merely facilitate the joining of the harmonious energies between them and human beings.

Medical therapists have to do more research than casual aromatherapy users, and will be knowledgeable in the therapeutic values of essential oils. They know the potential of any particular species, and may invoke that potential as they blend their oils. For example, if a client has an inflammatory condition, as they roll the bottle between their hands, the therapist could think of the anti-inflammatory qualities of the essential oil, and ask that energy to come to the aid of the client – not forgetting to kindly thank it. This is energetic blending to a purpose. Sometimes that purpose may be limited; a sports-damaged knee and a healthy knee can be the purpose in mind. At other times, the purpose may be larger, encompassing spiritual health too, and therapists will want to blend for positivity and happiness.

When using the essential oils at home, say when taking a bath, make a conscious decision to do it in a certain way. Don't let your mind ruminate on whatever is bothering you at the time. When picking up a bottle of essential oil, think instead of the source of it: if it's sandalwood, think of the thirty-feet-high tree with its inner core, the heartwood that is used in the production of this oil; if it's rose, think of the many-petalled delicate flower. Or take a deep breath and focus your whole mind on a picture you enjoy, a view of nature or something else that brings a smile to your face. Pamper yourself spiritually. Or think of yourself at your most glorious best, as you would wish to be.

PURIFICATION

Nature is remarkably resilient. Think of a little seed lying in the earth, and along comes this massive machine, shaking the ground, moving inexorably towards it, and then it dumps a whole load of bitumen right on top of the seed, to make a path or driveway. You might think, That's the end of that! But no, time passes, and a tiny green shoot pops its head through a hairline crack in the hardened bitumen, into the light, and grows into a plant. We come along and say, 'Look at that, another weed,' and pull it out! But more plants grow in its place and despite everything we do nature still has that profound drive to live. Essential oils, too, appear to have that life quality, despite whatever human negativity they get subjected to.

Thoughts are vibratory, and essential oils are too. If the vibration of the thought is light or heavy, the essential oil will respond accordingly. Perhaps even the earth in which the essential oil plant grows is affected by thought. Finding out about the mind-set of the growers, distillers, bottlers and sellers, however, can be difficult. Going to the fields in which the crop is grown, and meeting with the people involved in the process, all the way down the line, is impossible for most essential-oil users. Some aromatherapists do spend a fair amount of their time sourcing, and will drop or adopt different suppliers depending on their attitude of mind, be it negative or positive. For the casual user, however, the most practical way to approach the problem is to spend some time clearing the oils. Let me say here that I do not believe essential oils can do harm energetically; it's just that they may not be able to realize their light potential if any negative thought-forms have been around them.

Some people invoke the help of God, through prayer, to cleanse their essential oils, or they use the classic decontamination material, salt. Reference is made to it in the Bible (2 Kings 2:20–21) when Elisha 'healed' the spring water at Jericho: 'And he said, Bring me a new cruse, and put salt therein. And they brought it to him. And he went forth unto the spring of the waters, and cast the salt in there, and said, Thus saith the Lord, I have healed these waters; there shall not be from thence any more death or barren land.' At Shinto shrines in Japan, piles of salt are often placed on either side of the Torri arch, to clear negativity from the people entering. Salt is certainly cleansing, which is why a dentist may tell you to rinse your mouth with it, but that does not explain why it is so universally used for spiritual decontamination. Perhaps it is because the crystalline structure of salt makes it an attractor. There was a time when sea-salt was usually preferred for these purposes, but since the seas are now so polluted, rock salt is probably best. Salt deposits are found all over the world, with some of the largest being between 250 and 2,000 feet thick.

Making sure the top is tightly shut, put the bottle of essential oil in a glass and cover it with salt. Leave it there for twenty-four hours, then rinse the bottle in spring water and wipe it dry. At this point, if you wish, the bottle can be surrounded by rock crystals, which have themselves been washed in salty spring water and left to dry in the sun. This should be done with a completely clear mind, as there is absolutely no reason to impose your mind, or even your love and good intentions, on the essential oils at this point. They have their own love and good intent – pure, egoless energy. By carrying out this process, we clear the way for that loving energy to shine through.

HANDLING AND STORAGE

The most important thing about handling essential oils is to treat them with respect, for these are living things and wise healers. At home, keep them somewhere that intuitively feels right, where you feel peaceful and relaxed perhaps, or near a sacred picture, a religious symbol or on a shrine. Many people keep their most precious spiritual articles together, and the essential oils could be kept with them. There are other considerations though. Essential oils don't like light or heat and should be kept in dark glass bottles, stored away from both artificial and natural light and heat sources. They should also be stored away from sources of radiation and electromagnetism such as microwaves, computers, radios, CD players and TVs. It is quite difficult to find a place that fits all these requirements in a typical modern home, but, with a bit of thought and ingenuity, a suitable place can be found. Also, there are various devices on the market designed to counteract these energies. If your usual sacred area is too light, simply store the essential oils in a box, or make a space for the essential oils in a shaded place – a cupboard for example – perhaps putting around them some of your other precious and sacred things, whatever it is that means 'sacred' to you. Above all, think of the essential oils as living things which deserve to be treated with reverence, because the power of nature, of creation, of light, of love is within them.

MAKING THE SPIRITUAL CONNECTION

> And there appeared unto him an angel
> of the Lord standing on the right side
> of the altar of incense.

> St Luke 1:11

When using essential oils specifically for subtle healing or spiritual enhancement, create a special time to link with the divine energy of the universe. You may plan this, or intuitively decide 'this is the time', but whichever it is, approach it as sacred and special. Mark it out in your mind as qualitatively different from the rest of the day. What you do in that time – in terms of it being a ceremony or ritual of some sort – is not as important as approaching it with right intention. Empty your mind of negativity, focus on the positive, and recognize the divinity in the energy that pervades all living things. Breathe deeply, slow down, and rest in infinite peace within yourself.

The Heavenly Atmosphere

> . . . among the ten thousand rites, the burning of incense has the primacy . . .

> Taoist Liturgical Text

In the Eastern spiritual traditions of Hinduism, Buddhism, Shinto and Taoism, the burning of incense is commonplace both during public worship at temples or shrines and at home. The earliest evidence for the burning of incense in China comes from the Shang dynasty, which was 1500–1066 BC. Islam has also been very positive about the use of fragrance, partly because of these words ascribed to the prophet Mohammed: 'It has been given to me to love three things in your base world: women, perfume and prayer, but the apple of my eye is prayer.' In Pakistan, Muslims use incense during the ceremonies of circumcision and marriage, and it's burnt from the moment a person dies until they are buried.

The Western spiritual traditions of Judaism and Christianity, on the other hand, have historically been ambivalent about the religious use of fragrant materials, with different branches of the religions, at different times, being for or against it. The early antipathy to the burning of incense, other than for priestly use, comes from the fact that the religious opposition – goddess worshippers – burnt incense in some profusion. In Ezekiel 8:9–14, for example, we hear how 'abominations' were taking place in the form of idol worship, with seventy elders, '. . . every man his censer in his hand; and a thick cloud of incense went up', with women weeping for Tammuz, lover of the goddess Ishtar, the 'Queen of Heaven'. These practices were already ancient at the time, having been imported from Babylon. The early Hebrews were also, of course, familiar with the burning of incense, which was an important aspect of Egyptian spiritual practice. Incense-burning became central to Jewish ritual, but was controlled by the priests, starting with Moses and Aaron. In Exodus 30:34–37, God ordered Moses to make an incense:

> Take unto thee sweet spices, stacte, and onycha, and galbanum; these sweet spices with pure frankincense: of each shall there be a like weight:

And thou shalt make it a perfume, a confection
after the art of the apothecary, tempered together,
pure and holy:

And thou shalt beat some of it very small, and
put of it before the testimony in the tabernacle of
the congregation, where I will meet with thee: it
shall be unto you most holy.

And as for the perfume which thou shalt make,
ye shall not make to yourselves according to the
composition thereof: it shall be unto thee holy for
the Lord.

At the Temple in Jerusalem, incense was offered twice a day on the Golden Altar in the Holy of the Sanctuary, and once a year before the Ark of the Covenant in the Holy of Holies – on Yom Kippur. The ingredients are listed in the daily Siddur, in the early section on offerings: stacte, *onycha*, galbanum, frankincense, myrrh, cassia, spikenard, saffron, costus, aromatic bark and cinnamon. Each component of the incense is said to represent part of the community of Israel, and none may be ignored.

In the Christian tradition there has been, over the millennia, much argument about the use of incense. Adverse associations may in part have derived from the fact that Christians were forced to burn incense before images of Roman Emperors as evidence of imperial loyalty, or face execution. By the fifth century it was accepted as a symbol of prayer, but fell into disfavour after the Reformation began in 1517, when Martin Luther nailed his complaints against the theological establishment to a church door in Wittenberg, Germany. Since then, there has been a great deal of debate, not to say division, between different Christian groups on the question of the use of incense, as well as other practices. Incense is today burnt in some Anglican churches, and is of course much used in Catholic churches. Revd Allen Morris kindly told me, on the subject of incense, that, 'There is no attempt to lay down "recipes" by the Church. The requirement simply is that when burnt, the incense should be able to symbolize the sweetness of Christ's sacrifice, as well as the prayers of the Church rising to the throne of God.'

Let my prayer be set forth before Thee
as incense.

Psalm 141:2

Greek Orthodox Churches offer up incense every day, as well as at Eucharistic and sacramental worship. 'On a less formal level', explains Gregorios Archbishop of Thyateira and Great Britain, 'incense is used in the homes in a simple ritual in the morning and at sunset when a member of the household (usually the lady of the house) will offer prayers and incense in front of the family's icons and will then take the incense into each room of the house and also incense the members of the family. Even in those households where the daily offering of incense has less emphasis, the incense will be offered at sunset on Saturday and great festivals – sunset being the beginning of the new day in the Orthodox Church and therefore the beginning of the feast.'

There are many types of incense used in homes around the world, such as incense sticks or cones and aromatic plant material placed on burning charcoal. People have had different reasons – secular as well as sacred – for burning fragrance in their environment. It's been used to 'fumigate' against insects and disease; simply as perfume; for helping focus during meditation and when offering prayers. Whatever form it comes in, incense gets its aroma from the aromatic molecules of the plant materials from which it is derived – essential oils. When incense is burnt, there can be a great deal of smoke, which some people enjoy. For those who don't, essential oils provide another option.

There are many ways of using essential oils in an enclosed environment, but the most usual means is by diffuser. How much essential oil you use will depend on the strength of aroma required, the size of the area, and the power of the essential oil(s) being used. Bearing these things in mind, use between 6–12 drops for an average-size room, or more if you wish.

It brings communication with the transcendent.
It purifies mind and body.
It removes uncleanliness.
It keeps you alert.
It can be a companion in the midst of solitude.
In the midst of busy affairs, it brings a moment of peace.
When it is plentiful, one never tires of it.
When there is little, still one is satisfied.
Age does not change its efficacy.
Used everyday, it does no harm.

Ten Virtues of Koh (Incense)
compiled in sixteenth-century Japan

ANOINTING

Then the Lord said to Moses. 'Take the following fine spices: 500 shekels of liquid myrrh, half as much (that is, 250 shekels) of fragrant cinnamon, 250 shekels of fragrant cane, 500 shekels of cassia – all according to the sanctuary shekel – and a hint of olive oil. Make these into a sacred anointing oil, a fragrant blend, the work of a perfumer. It will be the sacred anointing oil.'

The Holy Bible: New International Version
Exodus 30:20–25

By anointing with the oil, the sick are strengthened and healed, the catechumens are empowered to resist Satan and to reject sin and evil, the baptized are sealed with the gifts of the Spirit, and the ministers of the Church are sanctified in God's service.

Through the use of these holy oils may God's grace be poured forth always upon the Church.

Rite for blessing the repository in which anointing oils are kept (Catholic Church)
Book of Blessings 1985

Anointing was practised by the ancient Mesopotamians, Egyptians, Syrians and Persians, as well as by the Hebrews. In Egypt, according to Eugene Rimmel, author of *The Book of Perfumes*, 'Besides incense, ointment was also offered to the gods, and formed an indispensable part of what was considered a complete oblation. It was placed before the deity in vases of alabaster or other costly material, on which was frequently engraved the name of the god to whom it was offered. Sometimes the king or the priest took out a certain portion, and anointed the statue of the divinity with his little finger ... No king could be crowned without being anointed: this was done privately by the priests, who pretended that the ceremony had been performed by a god, in order to convey to the people a more exalted notion of the benefits conferred on their monarchs.' Even mummies were anointed, several times a year, with 'sweetly scented oil' which 'was poured over their heads and carefully wiped off with a towel carried on the shoulder for the purpose. A priest was generally called in to officiate on these occasions.'

Mary Magdalene is sometimes called 'the patroness of aromatherapy' because she famously anointed Jesus with a great deal of spikenard in St John 12:3–7 and St Mark 14:3–8. Jesus sent his disciples out 'by two and two', to spread the word, and in Mark 6:13, 'they cast out many devils, and anointed with oil many that were sick, and healed them.' According to Martin Dudley and Geoffrey Rowell, authors of *The Oil of Gladness, Anointing in the Christian Tradition*, during the early Church years '. . . there was a good deal of "do-it-yourself" anointing during this period. Phials of oil are passed from holy man to distressed woman, from monk-bishop to the terminally sick.' Ideally, the anointing oil should have been blessed by a bishop, a presbyter, or even a holy man of the desert, but 'if absolutely stuck', the oil from a lamp in the church would have to do. Around AD 405, Pope Innocent I told a bishop that oil consecrated by him 'is lawful not for the priests only but for all Christians to use for anointing in their own need or in the need of members of their household'.

The significance of the act of anointing in the Christian tradition is perhaps best made clear by the words used during the holy rites. The following are extracts from the rites of various traditions; where there is a '+' symbol, that indicates that a cross is made with the fingers at that point. The first two extracts are from the consecration of the Holy chrism rite, and are very similar although they're from two

Churches – the contemporary Anglican and the Reformed Roman.

And so, Father, by the power of your love, bless to our use this mixture of oil and perfume as a sign and means of your heavenly grace. Pour out the gifts of your Holy Spirit on those who are anointed with it. Let the splendour of your holiness shine on the world from every place and thing signed with this oil.

Contemporary Anglican rite –
Consecration of the Holy chrism

And so, Father, by the power of your love, make this mixture of oil and perfume a sign and source + of your blessing. Pour out the gifts of your Holy Spirit on our brothers and sisters who will be anointed with it. Let the splendour of holiness shine on the world from every place and thing signed with this oil.

Reformed Roman rite –
Consecration of the Holy chrism

Oh, Lord, the Creator of all things, by your servant Moses you commanded the hallowing of ointment made with the mixture of aromatic herbs; we humbly implore your mercy that you would bestow the grace of your Spirit and the fullness of + consecration on this ointment, drawn from a growing plant . . .
May this mingling of liquids bring to all anointed with them mercy and safe protection for ever and ever. Amen.

Pre-Vatican II Roman rite –
Consecration of the Holy chrism

*Lord God, you bring healing
to the sick through your son,
Jesus Christ, our Lord. May
your blessings come upon all
who are anointed with this
oil, that they may be freed
from pain and illness and be
made whole. Amen.*

Lutheran Church in America and Canada
Prayer for the laying on of hands and
anointing the sick, using olive oil blended
with aromatic ingredients

*... and we pray that we may
receive your hallowing, like
the chrism which is poured
upon our heads, since the
chrism which is poured out
is the Name of your only-
begotten Son, Christ our
God, through whom the
whole world, visible and
invisible, is sweetly scented.*

The Byzantine Rite
Blessing of the Holy chrism

The Byzantine chrism is made by combining olive oil
with between thirty-eight and fifty-seven aromatic
substances, making it one of the most complex synergistic blends ever devised. Different Christian
traditions apply holy chrism in differing circumstances, which may include some, or all, of the
following: baptism, confirmation, anointing of
the deceased, ordination of bishops and priests, consecration and blessing of churches, altars, chalices and
bells. In the Roman Catholic Church, the only requirement is that 'some aromatic substance' is added, so
there is a fair amount of variation in the constituents.
In a private communication, Revd Allen Morris has
said that, 'It would be proper only for natural
fragrances to be used.'

In the Christian tradition, in years gone by, the use
of fragrance by women for cosmetic purposes was
sometimes frowned upon because it seemed to indicate
a certain frivolity, or because it diverted aromatic
resources from their more important, spiritual, use.
These days, fragrant materials are much more widely
available – especially in synthetic form, but we have

forgotten that fragrance is inextricably linked with spiritual practice. Yet, what does a woman do when she dabs perfume on her wrist but anoint herself? It seems a profoundly secular act, the height of indulgence, yet it finds echoes in our spiritual past, when people made themselves fragrant to make themselves more acceptable to God.

Although fragrance has got itself a bit of a bad name because of 'the fallen woman' syndrome, it was originally used to attract God and the angels, rather than any potential suitor. If we can get past any self-indulgent or even lascivious connotations, and understand the spiritual nature of fragrance, then 'anointing' in this sense can assume again some of its original purpose and meaning.

In the traditional use of the word 'anointing', oil is always taken as the basic substance used. But if fragrance is the key substance of interest, it can be carried in a water-alcohol solution as well as by oil. We can make our own spiritual blends of essential oils, and use them within an oil-based 'perfume', or within a water-based spray, like an eau de Cologne. The aroma in these circumstances is intended to attract the messengers of Heaven, and help us become closer to the universal whole as we carry out our spiritual practice, such as prayer, meditation or affirmations.

> *Thou lovest righteousness, and hatest wickedness: therefore God, thy God, hath anointed thee with the oil of gladness above thy fellows.*
> *All thy garments smell of myrrh, and aloes, and cassia, out of the ivory palaces, whereby they have made thee glad.*
>
> Psalm 45:7–8

56

The Sacred Waters

*And Aaron and his sons thou shalt bring
unto the door of the tabernacle of the congregation, and shalt wash them with water.*

Exodus 29:4

Water was used by the early Hebrews for cleansing
and purifying. Due to a commandment given by God to
Moses, in the city of David, Jerusalem, pilgrims went
daily in a big procession to the spring, Shilock, the
waters of which were said to cleanse and sanctify. The
priests had to sanctify their hands and feet with water
poured from a golden flask before they could go to the
altar or do anything of spiritual significance.

Baptism is a Christian sacrament of spiritual
rebirth by which the recipient is cleansed of original
sin through the symbolic application of water – by
immersion, pouring or sprinkling. Muslims, five times
a day, obey these words of the Koran: 'When ye prepare for prayer, wash your faces, and your hands (and
arms) to the elbows; rub your heads (with water); and
(wash) your feet to the ankles. If ye are in a state of
ceremonial impurity, bathe your whole body.' (Sura
5:7) If water is not available, 'clean sand or earth' is to
be used instead.

The spiritual nature of water is also recognized in
India, where the fondest wish of devout Hindus is to
bathe in the River Ganges at least once in their lifetime and have their ashes scattered on it after death.
The river is referred to as *Ganga Ma*, Mother Ganga,
and each day countless worshippers can be seen on her
shore, chanting prayers and offering flowers.

Those who bathe devoutly once in the pure currents of the Ganga, their tribes are protected by Her from hundreds of thousands of dangers. Evils accumulated through generations are destroyed. Just by bathing in the Ganga one gets immediately purified.

The Brahmandapurana

The tradition of ritual bathing may go back over 4,000 years on the Indian subcontinent, to the city of Mohenjo Daro in present-day Pakistan. The city was built on a grid system, with each house having a bathroom and toilet – with a clay-pipe drainage system – and a 'Great Bath' measuring 39 by 23 feet, and 8 feet deep, which was probably used for ritual purification purposes.

Bathing has two meanings from a spiritual point of view. It can denote cleansing before taking part in religious observance, or a spiritual transformation as in baptism. Immersion in water induces a state of relaxation which quite often leads to moments of inspiration, spiritual and otherwise.

When creating your own sacred waters, run the warm bathwater, then add the essential oil – with the bathroom door closed to ensure the aroma molecules remain in the room. The essential oils are inhaled with the steam, and absorbed through the skin by osmosis. As a general rule, use 4–6 drops of essential oil per bath. This may not seem a great deal, but just one drop of essential oil will infuse the entire body of water with its aromatic impact. Lie there for at least ten minutes, inhaling the precious fragrance.

Bathrooms sometimes have electrical fans installed in them, often integral to the light fitment. When using essential oils for spiritual purposes, the noise and vibration of these fittings may disturb the energy or atmosphere you wish to create, so candlelight would be more appropriate. Some people like total silence as they lie in water – the amniotic fluid of the universe – while others may prefer the sound of gentle music to help them reach the higher realms. Bathing always allows a certain detachment from the hubbub of daily life, but, with a little extra thought and preparation, and the fragrance of the heavens, the inner core of spirtuality can more easily be experienced.

Body Oils

In many Arabian countries, a bride's body is massaged in preparation for the sacred marriage ceremony with oils including orange blossom (neroli), rose, jasmine and other exquisite perfumes. Her dress is often perfumed, while the bridegroom might be anointed with rose and *oud* (also known as aloeswood). These aromatic extravagances have a very long tradition, and their purpose is not only to purify, but to deter the evil spirits, the *jinn*, from coming to the ceremony.

There is a special sacredness about using essential oils directly on the body. The human being is physical, mental, emotional and spiritual, and all are precious. As a general rule, to one ounce of carrier oil (30 ml) add between 10–20 drops of essential oil.

In clinical aromatherapy – the use of essential oils for therapeutic purposes – the choice of carrier oil can be very important to the outcome. This is not necessarily the case with subtle healing. In Western spiritual traditions, two oils stand out as well-established and loved, olive oil and almond oil, no doubt because these trees grew in the Holy Land.

Olive oil is too heavy for all-over body oils; almond oil is thus a good option when choosing a carrier oil. The words 'carrier oil' are interchangeable in aromatherapy with 'base oil' or 'vegetable oil'.

When making a body oil, put the essential oils into the empty bottle first, and swish them around the bottom of the bottle to allow them to act synergistically with each other. Only when they are blended, and have become something more than their individual parts, should the carrier oil be added. Put the top on the bottle, turn it upside down a couple of times, then gently roll the bottle between your hands. This action not only ensures complete mixing of the ingredients, but energizes the blend.

SPIRITUAL BLENDING

Aromatherapists choose which essential oils to use for a particular client by an informed diagnosis of the condition presented, the decision on how it can best be treated, and an extensive knowledge of essential oils – as they may affect the physical, mental and emotional. The good intent of the therapist or person applying the oils activates the light potential in essential oils.

Just before blending, I look at the client and in that instant know whether another element should be added, the spiritual. As the essential oils are joined together, their colours glow, their voices sing. When they have been synergistically blended, the carrier oil is added, and the bottle is whirled around in the hands. At that most energetic point, concentrate with love on the plants from which these essences came, on the sacredness of the fragrance and the joy they bring. Those thoughts will be transmitted into the blend.

At this point, my mind goes empty: with no thoughts, just a feeling of complete peace and oneness with the oils. I see the energy of the oils, and dwell in them for a microsecond, luxuriating in the universal energies of which we are all a part. Then I return to the client and continue in a clinical way, not thinking again about the essential oils, nor imposing any thoughts upon them. The blend performs its own mission, transporting the precious molecules, which connect with receptors throughout the body. We are the go-betweens, carrying the catalyst – the essential oils – which will help the mind, body and spirit to heal itself.

Blending with Prayer and Affirmations

Prayer and affirmations are positive thought patterns, vibrations that can be transmitted to essential oils, especially when blending. Prayer is not something tangible – something you can hold in your hand or measure in a laboratory – although its effects are. Many miraculous healings have been accomplished through the power of prayer. However, when praying for another person, and particularly when blending essential oils for other people, it is crucial to be quite sure what it is they wish for. In my experience people are very complex and may *think* they want a particular outcome when, in their heart of hearts, they don't. By all means, make a blend of essential oils to give to others, which may help them find peacefulness.

METHODS OF USE

Throughout this book various spiritual practices are described, with suggested methods of use. The following chart is intended as a general guide to the volume of essential oil appropriate for each method. See also *Safety and Precautions* on page 71.

Any objects used in the process of making a spiritual connection – such as diffusers, bottles, bowls and candles – should be reserved for that purpose only and set apart from those used in physical healing or environmental fragrancing. The objects should be aesthetically pleasing and treasured.

METHOD	AMOUNT OF ESSENTIAL OIL	PROCESS
Anointing	1–2 drops in ½ teaspoon of vegetable oil	Dilute the essential oil in an organic vegetable oil. Virgin, cold-pressed olive oil could be used although you may find the aroma of the olive oil overpowers the aroma of the essential oils. Almond is a good carrier oil to use for anointing.
Baths	1–6 drops	Run the bath, then add the essential oil and swish it around. The door should be shut to ensure the aroma remains in the room. Essential oils can be used in their concentrated form. For those with sensitive skins, the essential oil can be diluted in a vegetable oil – using 1 drop of essential to 1 drop of vegetable oil. For salt baths, add 2 drops

of essential oil to a teaspoon
of salt, mix well, then add to
the bath water.
**Some essential oils can
cause skin irritation.
These include basil, cin-
namon, clove, grapefruit,
eucalyptus piperata,
lemon, lime, peppermint,
and thyme. When used
singly, the above should
be used with caution.
When used in blends, they
can sometimes be used in
baths – depending on the
particular formulation.**

Body oils	10–20 drops in 30ml (1 fluid ounce) of vegetable oil	If using 1 essential oil, add it to the carrier oil already in the bottle.
		If using a blend of essential oils, put them into the empty bottle first, roll the bottle between your hands, then add the carrier oil, and blend again by rolling the bottle between the hands. For the uses in this book, it is better to make up small amounts, use them, and remake the body oil as required.
		Label bottles with their ingredients and purpose, adding the date of preparation.

METHOD	AMOUNT OF ESSENTIAL OIL	PROCESS
Diffusers	6–12 drops, but more if you wish	*Diffusers used for spiritual practice should be devoted to this purpose, and not used in any other context.* Diffusers or 'burners' have two sections: one for the heat source and one for the water/essential oil. The bowl portion in which the water and oil are put should be non-porous, and thoroughly cleaned between each occasion of use. Put in enough water to allow for evaporation; use already heated water. Put the essential oil on the water, with the heat source already in place.
Candles	1–4 drops per candle	Light the candle and allow some wax to melt around the wick. Then blow out the candle and add the essential oil to the melted wax. Essential oils are flammable, so ensure none gets on the wick. As the wax starts to solidify, light the candle carefully, preferably using a match rather than a lighter. Aromatic candles can be pre-prepared for later use.

METHOD	AMOUNT OF ESSENTIAL OIL	PROCESS
Hands	1 drop (between both hands) neat or diluted	Put 1 drop of essential oil on the palm of one hand, rub both palms together, Alternatively, first dilute the drop of essential oil in a small amount of vegetable oil. Holding the hands around your nose and mouth, breathe deeply. If praying, hold the hands in the classic position, palms together and near the face.
Water bowl	3–10 drops	This is a diffusion method. Place a small bowl in the room, away from small children and animals. Put boiling water in it, then add the essential oil. The steam carries the aroma around the room.
Washing feet	2–4 drops	This is often carried out as a symbolic gesture. Fill a large bowl with warm water. Take a teaspoon of salt, add the essential oil to it, then sprinkle on the water. Gently wipe the feet with a linen or cotton cloth.

METHOD	AMOUNT OF ESSENTIAL OIL	PROCESS
Washing hands	1 drop	Put a teaspoon of salt in the palm of one hand, add 1 drop of essential oil to it, then rub the hands together, and rub the forearms, up to the elbow. Rinse off with running water.
Showers	1–2 drops	Wash as usual. Put the essential oil on a separate washcloth, wipe over yourself – avoiding delicate areas – while standing under the running water and breathing deeply through the nose.
Clothing	1–2 drops	Only use this method on clothing that is not valuable to you. Put the neat essential oil on cuffs – where it can be raised to the nose when desired – or on a collar or scarf around the neck, from where the aroma will gently rise to the nose. Viscous and coloured essential oils leave a stain, so avoid oils such as myrrh, benzoin, rose maroc and chamomile (blue).
Tissue or handkerchief	1–2 drops	Put the essential oil on a tissue or cotton handkerchief, put it in a pocket, and take out and inhale when needed.

METHOD	AMOUNT OF ESSENTIAL OIL	PROCESS
Room sprays	6–10 drops, more if you wish	Use a new plant-mister. Put in half a pint (250 ml) of warm water, with ¼ teaspoon of salt, and the essential oils, and shake well. Spray high into the air, avoiding polished wood surfaces and materials that could be damaged by either water or essential oil.
Fires	1 drop per log or piece of wood	Prepare wood for the fire by putting the essential oil on each log or piece of wood. Leave for at least one hour before putting on the fire. Take care as essential oils are flammable.
Incense	3–5 drops	Essential oils can be added to fragrant twigs, incense cones, incense sticks or to the granule-type of incense that is placed on charcoal. Leave to dry before use, as essential oils are flammable.
Vision pillows	1–2 drops	Use essential oils on pillows to encourage sweet dreams or visions. Put the essential oil on a corner, where it will not come in contact with the eyes, or on a cotton wool ball which can be tucked inside the pillow case.

METHOD	AMOUNT OF ESSENTIAL OIL	PROCESS
Perfume	Dilute the essential oil with jojoba oil – 50% of each	Use a small amount, as you would a perfume. Avoid getting it on clothing.
Sweat lodges	5–10 drops	Mix the essential oil with the water that is to be placed on the hot stones.
Smudge sticks	1–4 drops, depending on the size of smudge stick	Smudge sticks are bunches of dried, aromatic plant material, usually associated with Native American culture. Essential oils can be added to the plant material. Alternatively, put the essential oil on a smelling strip.

CARRIER OILS

Most essential oils in their pure state are too highly concentrated to be used directly on the skin, so they are first diluted in a carrier oil. For example, 1 drop of essential oil may be all you need to use; that obviously will not spread very far, but diluted in a base oil it will cover quite a large area. Good carrier oils are: almond oil, apricot kernel oil, grapeseed oil and macadamia oil. Almond oil is easily obtained, has therapeutic qualities of its own, and can be used by almost everyone. Although olive oil has a venerable position in the Bible, it is too heavy for all-over body use.

There are a wide range of carrier oils available, and the words to look for on the bottle – which indicate quality – are 'organic', 'cold-pressed' and 'virgin'. 'Organic' denotes that the plant material was grown without using biocides: that is pesticides, herbicides and fungicides made from synthetic chemicals or petrochemicals. 'Cold-pressed' indicates that the oil has not been through a heating process to extract the oil from the seed or other source material. 'Virgin' signifies that the oil came from the first pressing of the oil material.

BLENDING ESSENTIAL OILS WITH CARRIER/BASE OILS FOR THE BODY
QUANTITIES TO USE

Number of drops of essential oil to use:			Blend the number of essential oil drops on the left into the volume of base oil on the right – which is either in ml or spoonfuls.			
Essential Oils				Vegetable Oil		
MIN	to	MAX drops	Per ml	Teaspoons	Dessert spoons	Table spoons
½	to	1	1	1	–	–
1	–	5	5	1	1	1
2	–	10	10	2	1	1
3	–	15	15	3	1	1
4	–	20	20	4	2	1
5	–	25	25	5	2	1
6	–	30	30	6	3	2

Pregnant or Lactating Women

Women who are pregnant or breastfeeding need to be aware that there are certain essential oils which should not be applied to the body at this time, and these are listed below. In all other methods, these women should use the minimum quantity of essential oil recommended in any particular section. (The oils listed here are in addition to those which should not be used by anyone which are listed under *Safety and Precautions* on the opposite page.)

Aniseed	Clary Sage	Marjoram	Rosemary
Basil	Clove	Myrrh	Sage
Bay	Cumin	Nutmeg	Spikenard
Birch	Fennel	Oregano	Tarragon
Black Pepper	Hops	Parsley Seed	Thyme
Cedarwood	Hyssop	Peppermint	Valerian
Cinnamon	Juniper	Pimento	
Cistus	Mace	Berry	

People on Medication

Use half the recommended dosages. For example, if it states 'use 4–10 drops', use between 2 and 5 drops.

People using Homeopathy

It's thought by some homeopaths that essential oils and other strong smells negate the effects of homeopathic treatments.

Tranquillizer Addiction

Use half the recommended dosage. For example, if it states 'use 4–10 drops', use between 2 and 5 drops.

Substance Addiction

Use half the recommended dosage. For example, if it

states 'use 4–10 drops', use between 2 and 5 drops.

Alcohol Addiction

Use half the recommended dosage. For example, if it states 'use 4–10 drops', use between 2 and 5 drops.

Safety and Precautions

Not all natural plants or plant products are beneficial to health. Deadly Nightshade can be poisonous and stinging nettles sting. The following essential oils should NOT be used under any circumstances:

Bitter Almond	Rue
Boldo leaf	Sassafras
Calamus	Savin
Yellow Camphor	Southernwood
Horseradish	Tansy
Jaborandi leaf	Thuja
Mugwort	Wintergreen
Mustard	Wormseed
Pennyroyal	Wormwood

(List as recommended by the International Federation of Aromatherapists code of practice.)

Essential oils are highly concentrated plant essences and should not be taken orally unless under medical supervision.

People with sensitive skin or allergic reactions to aromatic materials should always do a skin test twenty-four hours before use.

Some essential oils have been documented as being photo-sensitive and should not be applied to the skin before exposure to the sun. Of those mentioned in this book, those that may fall into this category are among the citrus oils – especially bergamot, and also angelica.

Chapter Three

PRAYER AND MEDITATION

Human beings have always yearned to contact infinite consciousness; they reach out – and find. The two universal ways this can be done are through prayer and meditation. Prayer is very proactive, in that we have something specific on our minds, and go for it. We ask for healing, help in finding love or a job. We entreat, with emotion. We ask for blessing, and give thanks. Meditation, on the other hand, is passive. We empty our minds, stop thinking about health, love and the job, and go deep within. We try to go beyond the cluttered mind: past the senses, the intellect, the creative impulse, and past even the spiritual layer of ourselves, to completely merge with cosmic consciousness.

It has been said that prayer is our way of contacting God, and meditation is the means by which we get the reply. But prayer also gives the reply – it is a two-way channel of communication. Meditation certainly offers a reply, in that answers to unposed questions might come to a person, but it is also a way of reaching the light and wisdom of God. Both are about communication with the divinity, although prayer reaches out, and meditation in. Prayer reaches out in supplication and humility; recognizing our connection with the divine, our familial relationship; saying 'Our Father, who art in heaven ...' Meditation also recognizes a familial relationship: between the original creative force that gave rise to the vibrations of the universe, now manifest in countless physical forms including us. The connectedness of things beyond our immediate life is at the root of both prayer and meditation, and is that which we yearn for. The warmth of connection enfolds us like a mother's arms, giving reassurance, comfort and the strength to go on.

Fragrance has accompanied many prayers to heaven, and provided the heavenly scent that can act as the focus for meditation. It acts as an avenue, a pathway, a slide, a conduit or rocket to the stars. Fragrance opens the consciousness, relaxes the mind and body, and puts us in another space – one where we are open and receptive to spiritual exploration.

PRAYER

> Seek, and you shall find; knock, and the door will be opened to you.
>
> St Matthew 7:7

A woman who did not believe in God went into labour. A couple of hours later she was oblivious to everything in the delivery room, unaware of how many people were there or what was going on. She was in another, very deep place, and started repeating the words, 'Oh God, Oh Jesus.' She prayed for help when it was most needed. Many people turn to prayer in times of great need, almost unwittingly. Other people have faith every day – they consciously believe in something or some One; and when they pray they have a direction in which to focus their thoughts. Faith is like love – it's either in you or not, to a varying degree, and sometimes it is hidden deep within.

Someone might ask, 'How can you believe in a God – who has ever seen Him?' Yet this same person might believe there are 'wormholes' in space, because scientists have calculated so – although nobody has ever seen one. Some people acquired faith in childhood, because it was all around them and they felt it too. Other people find faith suddenly, it hits them like a thunderbolt; while others feel a shimmer of faith within them and seek to expand the light.

Prayer is a way of contacting and tapping into higher spiritual knowledge, a connection to higher realms, the means by which we connect to the heavens and God. It's an interface between us and the universe, a way in which the small voice may be heard. We give thanks, or ask for miracles. People reach for the intergalactic telephone every time grace is said at dinner, either alone on the private line or with the family making a conference call. Jesus said we should ask for our daily bread, ask for forgiveness for our trespasses, and that we be delivered from evil. This many people still do: asking for a rise at work, forgiveness for doing what is known to be wrong, and protection from the hard world outside. Throughout the millennia, all over the world, people have sought help, and some have had their prayers answered. In 1997, the American magazine *Newsweek* published the results of their prayer survey: 87 per cent said God answered their prayers.

In scientific experiments involving humans, sceptics can always say that psychosomatic influences are involved: the human mind imagines things. This can't be said with plants. It is, then, interesting to know that when plants are prayed for – to grow healthy and lush – they respond positively. Author of the book *The Power of Prayer on Plants*, Revd Loehr, carried out 100,000 measurements on 27,000 seedlings, resulting from 700 experiments involving 150 praying people. He concluded that plants that had been prayed for, in relation to the control groups, germinated earlier, grew faster and with more vigour, had a better chance of survival, and had more resistance to insects.

Since the 1960s there have been around 300 scientific trials exploring the possibility that the human mind can affect living matter at a distance. In 1990 Daniel Benor reviewed 131 trial reports in a paper entitled *Survey of Spiritual Healing Research*. The subjects influenced during the trials included humans, mice, plants, red blood cells, fungi/yeast enzymes and bacteria. The positive results of the trials were found in fifty-six cases to have less than one chance in a hundred of being due to chance, and in an additional twenty-one studies the chance was between two and five chances in a hundred. In scientific terms these are significant results, and show that the mind can influence living matter.

How this may come about is, of course, the big question. In prayer, we invoke change by using thought, sometimes accompanied by the sound of our voice. Both thought and thought/sound go out into the ether, carrying their vibrational patterns, and causing change. The emotion behind the thought gives an additional charge to the vibrational pattern. Perhaps all this can be picked up or received by higher beings, who operate outside our usual visual range and physical realm. These celestial messengers may be angels or guardian spirits, who transmit – by ever finer vibrations – to the next realm and beyond, until our thought makes contact with the universal whole or God. Perhaps God hears our tiny voice in the ether, with no messengers in between. These things remain a mystery.

Science is equally mysterious though. After years of experiments exploring notions around John Stewart Bell's theorem – which states that reality is non-local – physicists now claim that subatomic particles that were once in contact always remain in contact, even if on opposite sides of the universe or planet. This can be measured because a change in one such particle elicits the same change in the other, whatever the distance, and instantaneously. If we all came from the same atomic source, even a *very* long time ago, we are all related, and related to the ultimate source – which some call God. Some subatomic molecules are now more related to others, but ultimately, we all came from the same place. Is it not then possible to conceive that – to varying degrees – all molecules of the universe have this bizarre (but natural) ability to communicate instantaneously with each other, and act upon each other? We've heard it in theology and poetry – 'that we are all brothers and sisters under the skin' – but now science is working towards proving it true.

The word 'pray' derives from the late Latin word, *precare*, to entreat. This word carries a humble, supplicatory connotation, and in times of great need we may appeal to God in some desperation. More usually though, prayer is like talking to a good friend on the telephone, a reassuring, happy time. The difference is that, unlike any human friend, the friend at the end of the universal telephone line knows everything about us anyway, so there's no point in trying to hide anything and we can be totally frank and honest.

Prayers are not always answered. Earthquakes, tidal waves, tornadoes and hurricanes sweep the planet and cause loss of life and destruction, despite prayers. People become ill and die, although they lead exemplary lives and are needed here on earth. These facts have deeply disturbed people, and given rise to much spiritual despair. Like many others, I have explored these questions through various spiritual traditions: some of which explain it by karmic law and reincarnation; others by divine retribution and 'the sins of the fathers'; others believe God does not intercede in the lives of individual people; while some think in terms of 'life's lessons', or 'their purpose being served'. The natural events are fairly easy to understand, as the planet – upon which we all depend – must be allowed to move and breathe at its own pace. It takes precedence over us. As for unwell people, that is the mystery – not surprisingly as we can't see the whole picture. If we knew *everything*, perhaps even their suffering would make sense. Plus a good deal of suffering is brought upon oneself or is the result of other human beings acting on us – 'it's all people's fault', and God punishes us collectively. All this is very difficult, but, if nothing else, it makes us question things, including what we do to ourselves, to other people, and the planet. This dynamic may work like this: if there is a cluster of child leukaemia cases in a particular location, society questions the cause and a nearby nuclear plant is thought to be the source of contamination and its closure is recommended. In the short term, the children suffer; in the long term, the planet may benefit. Although the children and their parents might think they are suffering alone, we are thinking of them and they are providing the fuel of determination which drives many an anti-pollution campaign. This is just an example of cause and effect, the parameters of which are difficult for individual sufferers to see. There are many other such examples, and examples of suffering which seem totally needless. But there may be factors in the equation we cannot guess at, even perhaps that which we tell our children when someone dies: 'The angels needed them.'

Given that not all questions or prayers can be answered, prayer still offers many benefits. It gives people peace and spiritual upliftment; offers hope for good health and help in all forms; a chance to express thanks for our blessings; the space to question ourselves or our situation; and the courage to change. In prayer, we arrive at a quiet place, a place of spirit. This place is in our hearts, there when we need it, and it has been a sanctuary for many people on this earth who have suffered greatly – as hostages or when under torture, for example – who say that being able to escape to that place of prayer was the thing that pulled them through.

It's easier to contact the higher vibrational beings when we have the atmosphere, the peace and relaxation, when no everyday thoughts crowd our minds and we can be still; for it is in the stillness that God's love and peace can be felt. And, perhaps, in that stillness we can hear the voice.

'Dear God . . .'

What are the thoughts and entreaties that fill the space between God and us? In the *Newsweek* survey, 73 per cent thought prayers asking for help in finding a job were answered. 'Give us day by day our daily bread,' they prayed, as Jesus said we should do in

Luke 11:3. With the emphasis placed today on monetary success, it's hard to believe that the space between us and the deity isn't clogged with millions of prayers asking to win the lottery, but 36 per cent of the respondents said they never pray for financial success. Probably they realize those thoughts have little importance in the spiritual world, whereas 'show me a way to transcend my present situation' has.

We can commune with the universe, ask questions, tell of our sorrows, our joys, the good things, the funny things. What we truly wish to pray for often emerges in the process of prayer itself. We might give thanks, say 'please', ask for guidance to be shown a better way of doing things, a better way of understanding, a way to feel more forgiving, or to be able to feel more love, compassion and empathy. And in making the request, we have already taken the first steps towards feeling these things.

Taking the Pathway to Heaven

In the Christian tradition, prayer often takes place on the knees, with hands together. Native Americans, on the other hand, stand looking up, with their hands outstretched and facing the sky, while Muslims put their heads to the ground. Beyond this – the basic physical position adopted – few are taught in any detail how to pray. We may even be given the wrong information. I was taught, for example, to pray only for others, not myself. It took me years, and a certain amount of guilt, to get beyond this notion and accept that it was OK.

In the process of praying for oneself, we often learn what it is we truly want, which may be very different to what we *think* we want, or tell other people we

80

want. So, imagine this: people praying for other people without being in a position to know what they really want! Indeed, we may not be getting what we need because someone else is praying for the opposite!

I often hear accounts of people who are so distressed at the thought of losing a partner, they sit at the deathbed, sometimes for days, willing the partner to live. The partner may themselves be praying to die in peace, without having to worry about the partner taking it so badly. Any such cross purpose of wills can take many forms, including praying for people who don't actually want to get better. This may seem an unkind thing to say, but doctors and healers of all kinds are very familiar with this syndrome, when someone puts up an often subconscious barrier to healing. In these cases, it may be better to pray that the person is led to understand why they do not really want to get better.

Prayers are often tainted with ulterior motives. I've heard people say they want a loved one to live for ever, or at least until they themselves die, and they pray for that, although the loved one may be in great pain and would prefer to die now. I recall one woman saying to me that she didn't want her husband to get well enough to come out of hospital until she'd had a chance to decorate the bedroom; and another who wanted her partner to get better extra quickly so he'd be home in time for her birthday. Better perhaps to pray that the person being prayed for gets their own prayers answered!

Many people find it easier to communicate with a messenger of God, an angel perhaps, because the infinite consciousness is so awesome. Fair enough, but just make sure you don't pray *to* the angel and make an idol out of it. Give the message to the messenger *as* a message.

Many people find it awkward or embarrassing to pray and for them written prayers may be an answer. The same sacred place in the mind, as used in thought or spoken prayer, can be used when writing down what it is you want to say – in a relaxed way, aware of the divinity that permeates all existence. Some put their written prayer in a special place; or create a prayer box; or burn the prayer and watch the smoke ascend to heaven. In the Shinto religion, prayers are written on little blocks of fragrant cypress wood which are kept at the temple for that purpose, and then thrown in the fire. Essential oils can be used in a similar way: fragrancing the paper kept in a box or elsewhere and being an olfactory reminder of the prayer in that place; or put on the paper-prayer before it's burnt. In ancient times fragrant materials were routinely burnt at the time of prayer and, indeed, the origin of the word 'perfume' is the Latin, *per fumum*, which means 'by smoke'. Alternatively, prayers can be written on a banner, as in Tibet, and hung outside to blow in the wind. These writing methods may also appeal to people who express themselves better on paper than they do verbally.

Some people speak their prayers out loud, others say them silently in their minds; but why not sing your prayer? There is a whole science to sound, the spiritual use of which includes chanting and the repetition of mantras, as well as song. Sound sets up frequencies in your whole being, as well as in the space that connects you to the divine. Singing is a very open activity – it opens the heart, allows and even demands a flow – which tends to make things spontaneous and honest. Openness and flow help the prayer reach its destination.

Prayer can take place anywhere – on the top of a

mountain, or at the supermarket checkout. You see those people on the street? Some of them are walking along praying. People pray on the bus, train or plane, or while walking through a forest. Often, when out and about, the desire to pray comes upon us, and when a prayer is spontaneous it comes from a place deep inside. It is heartfelt, and well received. Feel how the prayer rises from the depths of your being and escapes, riding on your emotion, into that space where it can be heard.

Prayer is quite often presented as a bargain: if this prayer is answered I'll pray every day, go to church or temple every week, or help out at the hospital, be a better person, and so forth. Such bargains are seldom kept. They may work for a while but then things drift back to normal. The cosmic consciousness that can see our past, present and future, knows that.

It's fairly easy to understand that bribery in prayer will not work. Suppose someone wants something and says, 'Dear God, if you give me that, I'll give a hundred pounds to the local hospice.' That's a bribe. If it were that easy people could have all they wanted – including love, health and peace – which is just not the case. This isn't to say you shouldn't give the hospice money – but do it because you feel empathy, compassion and love.

Suffering has played a part in certain branches of the Hindu, Muslim and Christian traditions, with people wearing hairshirts and beating themselves with whips. On a less dramatic scale, many people say to themselves, If I *really* suffer, surely God will answer my prayers. God may not want you to suffer. Try to reach for the light with faith that things will get better, secure in the knowledge that God will help you if you help yourself.

There's no point in praying for world peace if you constantly row at home or at work. Better to pray for peace in your own environment, and understanding as to why disagreements arise.

People who have never prayed, or have not prayed for a long time, may find themselves uncertain as to whether they're supposed to kneel, sit or stand, turn on the lamp or light a candle, put on some music or not. Regular prayer eventually irons out these questions, and a personal routine is found: one you have evolved naturally and feel comfortable with. The prayer can start out extremely simply, and then just be repeated, until you feel you want to add another, different element. As time goes on the whole process will become more refined.

In my practice, I've often heard people say they're worried they won't be able to kneel in church because of their arthritic knees. I say, 'Really, I'm sure God won't mind,' but they worry still, so indoctrinated are they in the 'right' way of doing things. It's sad we should think there is so little understanding in heaven, and God is surely too flexible to worry about a knee that is not. All our prayers will be heard, if they are genuinely said.

As we ask to be forgiven, so too can we forgive; and accept and contribute to universal forgiveness. We must be honest though, to ourselves as well as to God. This may be hard to start with, but, from shy and hesitant beginnings, eventually the whole truth will come out and we'll feel better for it.

Prayer should not be a duty, but something truly meant. We could read from a standard religious text, or turn to a beautiful poem or a passage from a book that strikes a spiritual resonance in us. It's important to be relaxed in prayer, and that is easier when we're genuine and follow our needs. Prayer has always been a wonderful aspect of human experience, and there seems to be a space reserved in our minds and hearts for it. From this innermost space we travel along a pathway of light, free from mental clutter and genetic memory, past the anguish and the fear, to that place of infinite peace that awaits us like a shelter in a storm or, on a good day, the most brilliant sun. What gets us there most surely is love: the most powerful voice or force in the universe. If the message is to get through, it needs love behind it. God is love, and love is what God hears.

BLOCKS IN THE FLOW

There are many people who would like to pray, and even think they ought to pray, but somehow feel they can't. There are others who dare not, or simply do not ask for what they seek because they have mental and emotional problems which block the flow between them and the deity; causing eddies of distortion in the vibrationary pattern their prayers would otherwise create. There are many issues in prayer, and it may take some time to sort them out. In the meantime, simply ask that a highway of communication between you and the divinity can be established, and that you will have the strength to remove some of the blocks that may stand in your way.

Fear

We live in a fear-based society, where everything hangs on threats and the fear of them being carried out. We're in fear of losing our jobs, of not being able to pay the bills, of getting ill. Even the idea of prayer can raise its own form of fear – the fear we won't do it 'correctly'. There's also the fear of being hurt in love *again*. So although we may pray for true love, there may be an emotional blockage to giving or receiving love. In this case, pray to help remove the fear of being hurt.

> ### ESSENTIAL OILS TO HELP DISSIPATE FEAR
> *Frankincense, Cypress, Rose Maroc, Cedarwood, Chamomile Roman, Sandalwood, Basil, Coriander, Ginger, Bergamot, Cinnamon*

Guilt

Guilt is one of the most widely used weapons of manipulation. It is applied most often in religious, family or personal relationship areas of human life. Some carry guilt because they feel they don't pray enough, or because their religious organization makes them feel they should attend *every* service or festival, happily and joyfully. These days there is a lot of guilt surrounding issues of health: we're made to feel we caused our own illness by eating the wrong food, or having the wrong attitude of mind. Whatever the root causes of guilt, when we do pray that guilt may accompany our thoughts.

The other side of guilt is forgiveness, and this is one of the main things people ask for in prayer . . . 'forgive us our trespasses'. We are also told to ask for help in forgiving people who have hurt us, but what about forgiving *ourselves*? If we can forgive ourselves and dissipate the guilt, it clears and purifies the paths of connection to the higher realms.

> ### ESSENTIAL OILS TO HELP DISSIPATE GUILT
> *Linden Blossom, Jasmine, Pine, Rose Otto, Juniper, Clary Sage, Benzoin, Clove*

Unworthiness

If we're told enough times that we are unworthy we may end up believing it. This causes many problems, but in terms of prayer, we may find ourselves praying for an improvement in circumstances at the same time as believing we don't deserve it. If the unworthiness is indoctrinated into a person during childhood, it is quite often the case that they gravitate towards the circumstances and people that reinforce that idea. However, many people, later in life, realize what they have been subjected to and shake off the shackles of unworthiness.

Wherever you may be in terms of unworthiness, remember, nobody is so unworthy they cannot pray and accept what is given. If you feel unworthy, pray that help may be given to you as you try to find a sense of worth.

> **ESSENTIAL OILS TO HELP DISSIPATE FEELINGS OF UNWORTHINESS**
>
> *Frankincense, Sandalwood, Neroli, Geranium, Rose Maroc, Ylang Ylang, Clove, Cedarwood, Cardamom, Mandarin*

Receiving and Accepting

Another block in the flow of prayer is being unable or unwilling to receive. Some find it difficult to receive or accept compliments, gifts or good wishes without immediately feeling the need to give the same in return. Or they may find it difficult to accept advice or wise comments. But in prayer, we must be receptive; open to receive the blessings and answers from above. Often these heavenly messages come fleetingly, softly and gently. They glide into the subconscious and then into the conscious so subtly and lightly that if we are not open to receive we might not recognize that they have come to us, or we may even ignore them.

Giving and Letting Go

Whatever you give in prayer – be it words, secrets, supplication, adoration, praise or gifts – do not expect something in return. You may be blessed, you may not. But giving in expectation is bribery and bargain, which has no place in the spiritual realm. Give generously, because you want to.

True prayer also involves letting go of that part of ourselves which ties us to the cruder vibrations and prevents us contacting our higher self or spirit, the voice of which is more easily heard in Heaven. It is better to give up preconceived ideas, because spirituality is an adventure into vast unexplored territory, and individual to each person. There is no need to give up your conscious *self*, only to offer your whole and higher self.

CREATING YOUR SPIRITUAL HAVEN

In ancient Egypt, amongst the wealthy at least, the preparation for prayer was very thorough. Apparently, they had a separate room which was sprayed with scent – not incense, but a scent very much like almond blossom – presumably from the older varieties. Before prayers, they bathed and put on white raiments. All over the ancient world, people put a special place aside for that which dominated their lives – the spiritual. So there is nothing new in creating a spiritual haven and, indeed, all over the world today people still do it. Even the poorest Indian home has a space where images of Shiva or Krishna, or one of the other many faces of the deity, watch over the whole household; in front of which there's a small shrine for burning incense and saying prayers. And few Catholic homes are complete without a picture of Jesus or the Virgin Mary; in front of which eyes will be closed, hands put together, and prayers said; while all over Asia, countless images of Buddha adorn quiet, and fragrant, prayer corners. At any moment in time, literally millions of people all over the world will be in the midst of deep prayer in their own homes.

We create a spiritual haven to have a special place to focus on the spiritual, and to contact the higher realms. It's a place we will come back to time and time again, perhaps for different reasons. We may go there to seek peace, focus our minds, clear our thoughts, or just be. And it is there we can open our hearts to the love in the universe that waits to receive us. Aim to create a peaceful, restful place where the mind, body and soul can concentrate on themselves for once, and be whole. It will be a place where you can draw the angelic beings close, and make your connection to the universe and God.

Most of us do not have the luxury of having a whole room to spare, but we can usually find a corner somewhere. That may be in the living room, bedroom, study, even the hall. *Where* is less important than what's in it, especially love. It is love in a house or place that makes it a sublime space to be in. The most exquisitely decorated palace is not beautiful if no love is generated there. The vibration of love, clear of negativity, carries prayer to its destination. It is the atmosphere of love that makes the haven spiritual.

If you have never created a prayer space before, start by cleaning the area – and whole room – thoroughly. If it is in a family room, do it when nobody is around. Clean everything, even inside wardrobes and cupboards, and have every ornament sparkle. While you do this, focus your mind on the divine, and imagine beautiful coloured lights, all the colours in white light, streaming into the room. If you like, play your favourite uplifting music. Not something that is 'beautiful' but just happens to be about unrequited love, and fills your eyes with tears and makes you sad. Play something that lifts up your spirits and fills you with optimism and joy.

If you wish, the cleansing can be done with salt which has long been used as a spiritual purifier. First, open the windows and say a small prayer. Then put the salt around the room before you vacuum, using a little in all the corners, including those in wall cupboards, starting away from the window and moving towards it. This dispels any uncomfortable 'feelings' that may have adhered to the fabric of the room.

When your sacred haven area is clean, think of what you will put in it. Start with a small table; if you don't have one use a solid box. Cover it perhaps with a beautiful clean cloth, then arrange on it some favourite or precious things. What these objects are is an entirely personal matter. They might include a gift from a friend, or a drawing by a child which makes love rise in your heart. Many people put a sacred or beautiful picture at the back, standing up on the table or attached to the wall. A plant brings life to the scene and will respond to the love you give in your prayers. Flowers are gifts which brighten our lives, and are a joy to focus on as we contemplate the beauty of creation. Put them in your best vase, and change the water regularly to keep them happy. Everyone has their own favourite flower: for some it's the tall white lily, for others the tiny white daisy that dots our lawns. In each bloom we can see the spirit of the flower, helping to create the atmosphere of peace.

Add anything else that means something spiritually to you. That may be a crystal, a stone, or a bunch of herbs. It may be a few small treasures gathered over the years. Candles are often lit in spiritual places, perhaps because they represent the spirit within us and signify change and transformation. We can focus on that light, and see the aura glow. Many cultures speak of a purple flame, the flame within. Finally, put your diffuser on the table, adding a tiny amount of salt to the water in the bowl.

Now sit back for a moment and feel the peace *you* have created. Light the candle – representing fire and spirit – which will symbolically burn your words and send them up to Heaven; and light the candle under the diffuser – representing light and soul – which will release the fragrance molecules and send them to their source. Then drop between 3–10 drops of essential oil into the bowl of the diffuser. Sit quietly just looking and sensing the peace and restfulness, then ask for blessings on your spiritual haven.

The most important thing about 'maintenance' is to keep negative energies away. Try to avoid having arguments in this area, or keeping the phone near by. As every person you have contact with influences you to some extent, and leaves something of their spiritual frequency in your subconscious mind, so a place is subtly changed by the people who come into contact with it, especially you.

HEAVEN SCENT

People have always, as far as we can tell, used fragrance to contact the spiritual realms. This is because fragrance performs many roles. It helps the mind to focus and concentrate. It also relaxes the mind and body, and opens the heart so it can receive. More than this though, it creates a link between the conscious and subconscious mind, allowing a chain of events to come forth. It expands the space between thoughts; that space leading to the oneness of the universe.

Which essential oils you use for spiritual purposes is very much up to you. This is a personal journey, and a matter of personal choice. Each fragrance suggested is only that, a suggestion. For each person a fragrance will resonate at a different tone and rate. Find which oils or blends resonate with you and keep those fragrances close to your heart.

In our day-to-day life we have favourite perfumes or fragrances, but they are not the ones to use now. For spiritual purposes choose something new and different, something that can lift you from your ordinary existence into the realm of the spiritual. The fragrance we use now is ultimately chosen to assist in prayer.

The following are some of the fragrances that have been used in spiritual practice and ceremony by various cultures around the world:

TREES
Pine, Silver Fir, Cedarwood, Ho-wood, Cypress, Rosewood, Sandalwood, Spruce, Juniper

RESINS
Frankincense, Myrrh, Benzoin, Styrax Balsam, Balsam de Peru, Galbanum

FRUITS
Lemon, Yuzu, Orange, Juniper Berry

SPICES
Cinnamon, Clove, Nutmeg, Black Pepper

ROOTS
Spikenard, Vetiver, Ginger

HERBS
Hyssop, Basil, Cistus, Sage, Marjoram, Myrtle, Rosemary

FLOWERS
Rose, Jasmine, Neroli, Hyacinth, Chamomile, Tuberose, Carnation, Narcissus

For those who like to walk through woods, the essential oils extracted from trees are very helpful. Throughout the whole world there are many species of pine, cedarwood and cypress, and these three are universally used in spiritual practice. If you are Japanese you may feel a particular resonance with Hinoki pine, which is indigenous to Japan, while if you are North American the indigenous Virginia pine may strike a particular note with you. People from Europe may prefer the fragrance of Scotch pine, and those from India sandalwood.

Resins have long been used in the making of incense all over the world. The material lends itself to the purpose particularly well, but there has also been a symbolic association in that resins seep from wounds in trees, as blood saps from us. In ancient Egypt, nuggets of resin were known as 'the sweat of the gods', and collected in reverence.

Resins including 'balsam' feature strongly in biblical fragrance. Frankincense and myrrh are still burnt regularly in many churches, and are particularly evocative of the Christian tradition. Benzoin, on the other hand, is more commonly used in spiritual practice in Asia; for example, in India, Malaysia and Java. In general, the fragrances of the resins are not as familiar as, say, the aromas of the herbs. To discern, then, whether they appeal to your higher self, they will need to be explored aromatically. The resins and root essential oils can be very pungent, and are usually used in small quantities.

The fragrances of flowers are particularly effective when connecting with the angelic realms. And don't forget the fruits – which have wonderful focusing and concentrating properties, individually or in blends.

When using essential oils for spiritual use, especially in diffusers, we have a great deal of choice. If we have no heavy thoughts, the lighter essential oils are in general more appropriate than the weighty types. In cases where a person is down and heavy of heart, although you might think a light essential oil better for the job of upliftment, the headier oils seem to match the job better, at least to start with.

The essential oils can be used in diffusers, baths and body oils. A drop or two on a vision-dream pillow, somewhere away from the eyes, may allow the answer you seek to come to you while you sleep. Dreams have always played a big part in mankind's spiritual quest. When praying, if you place the palms of your hands together, you may like to try putting one drop of your chosen essential oil on one palm, rubbing the hands together, and gently inhaling the fragrance. Some spiritual traditions do this, using powdered incense, and I wonder how many other cultures in the course of time have done this too. Holding a fragrance in front of the nose certainly helps the mind to focus and concentrate. Perhaps it was this aroma-holding position that led to the tradition of holding the hands together near the face when praying.

With time and experience a person may create for themselves many different spiritual blends of essential oils, for use during particular occasions, times of day or mood. More important though, in a sense, is to have just one fragrance blend that facilitates you making the spiritual connection. This one fragrance can be returned to in your spiritual haven at any time, reinforcing its spiritual connotation and meaning. The aroma then becomes synonymous with the place, and to re-experience it, even when out and about, at work, or when travelling, all we have to do is pull out a tissue with the blend on it, close our eyes and sniff deeply. Instantly, we return to that spiritual place which we experience actually within ourselves. This same action, of taking our favourite fragrance about with us, on a handkerchief or tissue or in a bottle, can of course be done with a single essential oil, if you have one that is particularly effective for you in making the spiritual connection. Whether from a blend or single essential oil, the fragrance of our choice opens the door instantly to another place.

Experiment with blends – varying the proportions, as well as the essential oils. It's amazing what a drop or two, less or more, will do to a blend. If it doesn't resonate with you, discard it and start again, until you get it right. By 'right', I mean what *you* know is right.

It is not easy to blend such a special oil, so be prepared to put some time into it. Perhaps we need a prayer. As Jesus said, 'Ask and you shall receive.' Eventually, some fragrance will strike a chord in you, so just be patient and keep looking.

When blending, try to clear all thoughts out of your mind, and all ego, and instead radiate love, empathy and compassion. I say 'try' because this is not always easy to do. There is help on hand, however, and sometimes in quiet moments of love and compassion I feel the presence of angels, who help me blend together spiritual fragrances. They are out there and they can be asked to help.

Angels have their own aromas, and they can be very difficult to replicate with earth-bound fragrance. The fragrance of a particular guardian who helps me has eluded me for years. I've smelt aromas that seemed similar but never exactly the same. The closest smell to it that I have found came from a bunch of magnolia blossoms given to me in a class. The aroma was rich and highly perfumed, and it gave me an immediate emotional impact. No-one else present had the same reaction, because for them it did not have the same connotations. Plus, we all perceive aroma differently on a spiritual level – just as responses to taste, sound, light and colour vary. Everything is vibration, interacting in a complex way; so choose what harmonizes with you.

The aromas we create reach out and meet those from the fragrant heavens, like the fingers of two hands mingling, making that connection we all seek. There are many types of spiritual fragrance, as individual as ourselves. I have my own special fragrance blend, which informs my mind it is time to be still and quiet and focus on the important things: the joy of being alive and at peace.

MEDITATION

In a talk at the Holy Names College, Oakland, California, USA, Sogyal Rinpoche, a master of Dzogchen Buddhism, told a story about a man, a top diplomat and maharaja, who sought the answer to the question, 'How do I meditate?' He asked the question of Sogyal Rinpoche's master many times, as is the practice, to elicit many perspectives on the subject. At a spiritual dance in Sikkim, the diplomat asked the master the question again. The master was enjoying himself and replied impatiently, 'Look, when one thought has ceased and died, before another thought has yet risen, isn't there a gap?' 'Yes,' the diplomat said. 'Prolong it. Prolong that gap. That is meditation,' the master explained.

A great number of books have been written on meditation, and I have written about it myself in *The Fragrant Mind*. Basically, it's very simple: it's trying to create stillness and peace in the mind, beyond the chatter and clutter that usually fills it. This is not to say meditation is about *nothing*. On the contrary, it is about *everything*.

In meditation, we come into contact with a vast reservoir of energy, passing through ever deeper layers of ourselves, as is explained by a Tantric nun: 'The human mind is on a continuum. There's the mind, the senses – our attraction or aversion to someone or something; then there is the intellect – the everyday computer, with memory; then the creative layer – where we go deep into the mind; and there is a flow – rather than the black and white; and a deeper than bookish knowledge. The next layer is intuition, expanded awareness, where you can really distinguish between what is right or wrong and, going deep, make good decisions. The next level is the spiritual level – the sense of oneness. The last layer is samadhi, which is complete merger in cosmic consciousness, total reabsorption. Human beings can complete the cycle: from infinite consciousness, to manifestation, to infinite consciousness.'

In meditation, fragrance provides something spiritual to focus on – and with eyes closed, which many people find additionally helpful. It's important though that the aroma evokes no memory for you which will just flood your mind and defeat the purpose of the exercise. For this reason, I suggest using blends in which no one ingredient dominates, and a new and unique aroma is created. This is accomplished by balancing out the ingredients, so that even if you do not use equal drops, as some essential oils are stronger than others, there is balance between them all.

Amongst the floral essential oils, linden blossom, jasmine and rose maroc make particularly good meditation oils, either individually or in blends. Some people might find these aromas too heavy, particularly as they progress with meditation when the lighter, softer florals, such as rose otto, neroli or diluted jasmine may feel more appropriate. Any essential oil can be lightened with dilution.

Which essential oils are chosen is entirely a matter of personal preference. Some people are drawn to the resins, such as frankincense, myrrh, benzoin, styrax or copal, or one of the many other balsams found throughout the world. A nice addition to any of these are the citrus types – eucalyptus citriodora and litsea cubeba. These two generally work as well in meditation blends as do the more usual citrus fruit oils.

Blends are excellent for meditation, and there are many essential oils you can choose from to create your own. For example:

INVIGORATING WOODS	CONTEMPLATIVE WOODS
Pine, Spruce, Cypress, Fir	*Sandalwood, Amyris, Ho-wood, Guaiacwood*

CENTRING FRUITS	AWAKENING FRUITS
Tangerine, Lemon, Cardamom, Vanilla	*Grapefruit, Orange, Mandarin, Lime*

Change your meditation blend as often as you wish. Each one will be special in its own way. Using essential oils with meditation helps to bring more vivid colours, more clarity and focus, to the event. Aroma during meditation can bring forth cellular or genetic memory – scenes and pictures from our past – or from times and places that are unrelated to our present life.

Many people are discouraged from meditation for the simple reason they cannot find a sitting position that is both comfortable and conforms to the positions usually adopted in pictures of people meditating – with legs crossed or with the posterior resting on the heels. It sometimes seems that one has to be uncomfortable to do it properly! This is not so. You can meditate in any comfortable sitting position, trying to keep your back straight – as this helps the flow through the energy centres along the spine. If no sitting position is comfortable – and this applies to many people – just lie on the floor. The most important thing is to be relaxed.

Some people tell me that when they meditate, they fall asleep. Does it really matter? In the sleeping state we often receive information, answers to questions, as well as information about the past, present and future.

Meditation could be said to be conscious sleeping. We are, though, more sensitive to noise at this time, and the slightest sound can have the same shocking effect as a cannon going off near by. So do take the phone off the hook and do whatever else is required to ensure you get a certain amount of peaceful time. In the profound quiet of meditation we can listen to our bodies. We may find the energetic source of any ache or pain, as well as the source of our spiritual selves.

There are now countless studies that show meditation definitely acts upon the body in, for example, slowing the pulse rate and calming physiological and neurological processes. Less easy to demonstrate than changes in clinical conditions, but well documented in people's reports of their experiences, is that meditation opens us up to receiving information. Answers to nagging questions or just plain unsolicited wisdom comes either from the higher self, the superconscious or universal knowledge. Meditation, then, is not about taking a rest, but about going on an adventure.

Chapter Four

ON PERFUMED ANGELS' WINGS

For he shall give his angels charge over
thee, to keep thee in all thy ways.
They shall bear thee up in their hands, lest
thou dash thy foot against a stone.

PSALMS 91:11–12

When you're sitting around with friends and have time
for a long conversation, ask if they believe in angels.
You'll be amazed by what you hear. On one such
evening, I heard an account of a meeting with an
angel, a rather handsome one it seems, in a bar in
Montreal, Canada, on a cold, snowy night. The lady,
Anne, was sitting at a table, quite near the stage,
watching the band with her back facing the main area.
Suddenly she was overcome with the sensation of
deep, unconditional love, and she could feel it emanating at first from the door, then passing the length of
the bar at the rear of the room until it stopped. She
said she smiled to herself because it was so absurd.
She knew, without having *seen* anyone, exactly where
this person stood. It was like love-radar. And she was

certain of her feelings. 'I knew I loved whoever was in that space, and it didn't matter whether it was a man, woman or gorilla. That's why it was so funny – in a split second, my whole outlook on life had changed.'

After a while she turned around, knowing exactly where to look of course, and saw a tall handsome man standing there. She turned back, and had another laugh to herself – this was too good to be true! When the band finished, she got up and went back to her friends at the bar in the next room. Before she knew it, the man was standing behind her; she turned around and was amazed to see gold rays coming from around his head. The man had a halo! Nobody else seemed to notice. It was turning into a very unusual evening.

'I think he was an angel,' Anne told us. 'I've never felt so relaxed with anyone. It was a level of relaxation that is far and away more absolute than with a lover, or family, or friends, or while on my own. It was another *level* of relaxation, like I'd just come extra alive.' Of course, we all wanted to know what happened to him. Apparently, they talked for hours at the bar, and he walked her back to where she was staying. The next day, she would be getting on a plane to London while he planned to be in Los Angeles: they were going in opposite directions. 'The strange thing is,' she continued, 'I knew we had no future, and didn't ask for, or give, an address. I knew I'd see him in Heaven, and that was enough.' Very appropriately, the bar was called 'The Rainbow', which made him the gold at the end of the rainbow!

Some people believe in angels because they have 'seen' them, even in some cases before their eyes beheld them. Other people believe in angels because they have heard their voices, or smelt their sweet fragrances and known they were near. When these things happen, there is no turning back . . . you *believe* in angels. Accounts of meetings are often quite extraordinary – which is, when you think about it, what we might expect. Experiences are also very personal and varied, and full of love, poetry and drama.

I met an angel twenty years ago, and so have no doubt they exist. The light and peace that angels emanate is so profoundly different from anything on earth, it's impossible to confuse it with everyday reality. The light I saw was an overwhelming luminescence, shining in rays from every pore of the figure, who was beautiful in the extreme. The sense of peace that settled upon me was amazing, and it was alive in every molecule of my being.

Meetings with angels are a joyful gift, and a source of inspiration. I have no idea why the illuminated one visited me in my home at that time. I had not asked to see one, and was not aware that I needed comfort. Perhaps that first angel came just so I could know angels exist. Certainly, the memory has been there for me to draw strength from – particularly when there have been obstacles to overcome – and it will be there for me in the future. As well as the deeper certainty they bring, angels also look out for our immediate physical safety. I know I've been helped many times by angelic beings, like when driving along, one whispered 'pull over' in my ear – which allowed me to avoid a collision, and turned out to be excellent advice.

One experience I'm particularly grateful for happened on holiday some years ago. A group of us were sitting with a high sand-dune barrier between us and the beach which was some distance away. The red flag was up, and we'd been advised the sea was dangerous that day. With my three-year-old playing with friends and their parents nearby, I lay on my front, put my head on my arms and, without realizing it, drifted off to sleep. I was awakened by a voice that said just one word, 'Sea.' It was not a loud voice, nor a particularly insistent one, but it had me on my feet in an instant and flying like the wind to the seashore. I reached the water just as an enormous wave poised itself over my little girl, who stood there watching the watery crest above her, oblivious to the danger. I grabbed her in my arms, pulled her away, and thanked the voice from the bottom of my heart.

I'm inclined to believe an angel whispered in my ear, rather than it being intuition, because I have seen a shining being standing in my own living room and *that* wasn't intuition! Angels are very physical when they want to be, and very etheric when they want to be. They straddle the two universes. This experiencing of them accords with the current theological position which, according to Canon Emeritus of Ely Cathedral, describes angels as 'spiritual beings intermediate between God and mankind'. He adds that it's thought angels were created before mankind, and that they were somehow implicated in 'the Creation's Fall from perfection', hence there are 'fallen angels'. In *New Catholic Encyclopedia*, angels are described as 'celestial spirits who serve God in various capacities'. Pope John Paul II has stated that angels do exist and that they 'have a fundamental role to play in the unfolding of human events'.

Religious literature abounds with accounts of angels. They feature strongly in the Bible, and the Koran, and they're known as devas or 'shining ones' in Hinduism. The sacred mountain of Kanchenjunga, on the border of Nepal and Sikkim, is known as 'the five thrones of the Shining Ones'. There are also Native American accounts of being advised by 'shining beings' during vision-quests, rather than by the usual totem animals, and stories about 'the feathered people' and 'the winged ones'. In European art, angels grace the corners of innumerable religious paintings, put there by Renaissance and other artists who believed implicitly in their existence. In countless towns and villages in Europe, angels carved in stone have been built into the fabric of medieval and later churches to protect the congregation within.

> *But verily over you*
> *(Are appointed angels)*
> *To protect you, –*
> *Kind and Honourable, –*
> *Writing down (your deeds)*
> *They know (and understand)*
> *All that ye do.*

Koran, Sura 82:10–12

Angels have a fragrance which, in my experience at least, precedes their 'appearance', or remains after they 'disappear'. Perhaps the fragrance was also there when I actually saw the angel, but was 'cut out' as my senses focused intently on the vision in front of me. I tried really hard to remember each visual detail, and was mesmerized by what appeared to be wings. Each 'feather' seemed to be a centre or vortex of energy made up of light – the spine in particular being a source of great light – yet also a route to the infinite, while each delicate strand coming off it was a chain made up of many sparkling lights. Each sparkle on each strand had its own energy field, and together they made the form of each superluminous 'feather', which was less a material feather than an arrangement of light in a feather shape. The overall effect was extremely powerful and awe-inspiring.

I've found the fragrance of angels elusive in the sense that it seems to have no source. It just suddenly appears and suffuses the whole body and mind. I can recall two aromas quite distinctly, neither of which I have encountered before. One was fairly similar to a heavy, deep, exotic rose maroc. The other was a light fragrance that was sweet and floralish, but not just floral, also a resin – imagine frankincense as a flower but without the same aroma. Sometimes I will smell an angel without seeing one, and I know it's the fragrance of angels because it's so pervading and fills my nose even to the point that I feel I can't inhale any longer.

After such powerful aromatic experiences I always have a good look and sniff around to see if there was any other possible source for the phenomenon. I check my clothes for perfume; my essential oil store for any open bottles or spills; I sniff all the plants and flowers; and run through my mind who has been in the house, possibly wearing scent; but no source for the strange fragrances has ever been found. Others in the house have smelt it too – and the mystery remains long after the fragrance has gone.

People who report fragrance associated with angel visitations invariably say it was like jasmine, rose, lily, hyacinth or violets. Personally, I expect people use these descriptions because the actual smell is impossible to describe – as we have nothing to compare it to on earth – and the fragrance of these particular flowers is as close as we can get. I've also smelt something *like* the aroma of freesias, but not quite. We should not expect the fragrance of the angels to reflect what is here on earth, as the angels are of

Heaven, not earth. Indeed, as H. C. Moolenburgh MD has commented in *A Handbook of Angels* (1988), 'I think at times we take in the perfume of the angel hierarchies themselves.'

Fragrance is one of the sacred codes of the celestial heavens. We can in some sense consume the aroma of angels like angel food, an etheric manna from heaven, which is also angelic illumination. At the same time, fragrance invites the angels towards us, a celestial go-between. As light is contained within fragrance, it is a means by which we can communicate, a form of light transference which carries our message to the illuminated realms. Sometimes the fragrance of angels is overpowering, at other times it is barely perceptible, like a breath exuding a heavenly fragrance that only briefly touches the skin, a lightness etherical but tangible. Perhaps to smell an angel is to be kissed by the divine.

If angels are a link between the minds of man and God, fragrance is one language we speak. Fragrance stimulates and releases truth, opening our higher self, making us receptive to angels as we vibrate more spiritually, aligning our energy more closely with the angelic realm. The energy of angels is very powerful, so powerful that in most instances our feeble human bodies could not withstand the force of their presence. Angels vibrate at such a high rate that their frequency could easily fragment or immobilize us. The individual guardian angels that have been assigned to us may have the means to tap into our mortal frequency, with a little help from us in the form of prayer, right-thinking, love and, perhaps, certain fragrances which put us in a state of spiritual grace. Perhaps when we are vibrating at a low emotional level – with anger, fear, hostility and guilt – they cannot come into touch with us for reasons to do with our own safety – or predestination – and can only stand by or help from a distance, invisible to us.

Today, all over the world, people are speaking openly about their experiences with angels, who assist people with warnings or rescues and offer consolation when things are tough. Some people are realizing that angels are our co-workers in positivity, although for others, angels remain the stuff of legends and fairy tales. Our perceptions are coloured not only by culture but by experience. This may come as a waking vision, or in a dream state, it may be the whiff of a celestial aroma, a sound, or merely a feeling of presence.

Acknowledgement is important. If we tell ourselves angels are not real, then they will not be. If we consciously dismiss angels as something from a bygone era, they may not show themselves to us. With their unconditional love, they may not wish to disturb our chosen life-view. This isn't to say they're not going to help – they do the work anyway. But if we consciously, or even subconsciously, exclude them that makes it less easy for them to cross over to the physical plane and help us. To give their help, they need our willingness to receive it.

> *Behold, two (guardian angels)*
> *Appointed to learn (his doings)*
> *Learn (and note them),*
> *One sitting on the right*
> *And one on the left.*
> *Not a word does he*
> *Utter but there is*
> *A sentinel by him*
> *Ready (to note it)*

Koran, Sura 50:17–18

Once you start connecting with angels they're everywhere. It's like anything – your focus point shifts. From being 'blind' to angels, you suddenly notice them on cards or architecture and even in real life. Angels do not have to prove their existence to us. Angels are the thoughts of God manifest. When we can all connect through the spark of love in our heart, then the angels will be visible. In holding love, no matter how small, no shadows can enter. When we all hold this divine spark of unconditional love, then the earth will glow and the work of the angels will be done.

We may well smell, or see angels, looking as we expect them to – as designed by our cultural beliefs. In the Christian tradition they usually appear as sparkling white with wings, or they come in golden splendour, with halos. This may be an aspect of what Native Americans call 'shift changing' or 'shape changing' – the ability to change etheric shape, and change kinetic energy into dynamic energy. The same angel-energy may come to different people in different forms, as our intellect will accept. It may be seen in human form and shining white or gold light. It may have two wings, or four, or six, or none, or big enfolding wings like a dove. Some people may see colourful robes – of deep blue or turquoise, or silver and gold. Some may see an intense diffuse light and no form as such. Some smell a fragrance, many do not. Some people simply sense a presence and call it, if not 'an angel', 'my guardian angel', or 'my guardian spirit', 'spirit guide' or 'spiritual keeper', a 'messenger' or 'traveller'. These words may describe a whole world of etheric beings that exist between humans and the deity, or they may all be manifestations of the same thing. One thing is sure: there's *something* out there, and it's looking after us.

Angels, speaking or not, manifesting or not, act as guides, teachers and protectors. They are consoling like a trusted parent, counsellors in life and in death. They bring spiritual upliftment and balance. The word 'angel' means messenger, and whatever form they take, this is their constant role: being the link, the channel, carrying the messages between us and Heaven.

The roots of many religions can be found in angel visitations. *The Book of Mormon* is based on 'the gospel of a new revelation': laws written on gold tablets which lay buried in the ground of a hill near Manchester – a village near Lake Ontario, New York State, USA – until their whereabouts were revealed by the angel Moroni to Joseph Smith in 1823. He described Moroni thus:

Not only was his robe exceedingly white, but his whole person was glorious beyond description, and his countenance truly like lightning. The room was exceedingly light, but not so very bright as immediately around his person.

Moroni can be seen atop many contemporary Church of Jesus Christ of Latter-day Saints 'temples', with trumpet in hand. The New Jerusalem Church follows the teachings of the eighteenth-century Swedish mystic and theologian, Emanuel Swedenborg, who wrote of angels he had seen in human form 'a thousand times': 'I have conversed with them as man to man, sometimes with one alone, sometimes with many in company.' Mary Baker Eddy, who founded the Christian Scientists, wrote: 'They are celestial visitants, flying on spiritual, not material, pinions. Angels are pure thoughts of God, winged with truth and love, no matter what their individualism may be.'

In an introduction to one edition of the Koran, N. J. Dawood writes: 'For Muslims it is the infallible word of God, a transcript of a tablet preserved in heaven, revealed to the Prophet Mohammed by the Angel Gabriel.' Their first encounter took place as Mohammed either slept or was in trance, while in a cave on a mountain in spiritual retreat, and the Koran was transmitted over a period of time. So important was Gabriel to Islam, that the five pillars of belief include angels: 'But it is righteousness – To believe in God, And the last day, And the angels, And the Book, And the messengers.' (Koran, Sura 2:177)

One well-known prayer speaks of angels: 'May Michael be at my right hand and Gabriel at my left, before me Uriel and Raphael, and above my head the divine presence of God.' Kabbalah, the mystical tradition of Judaism, teaches that angels are God's messengers and can turn themselves into different 'shapes' – forms and manifestations.

Throughout the Bible, accounts of angels abound. In the Old Testament, Jacob has a dream in which he sees a ladder between earth and Heaven, with 'the angels of God ascending and descending on it'; and an angel even leads people into battle: 'Behold, I send an Angel before thee, to keep thee in the way, and to bring thee into the place which I have prepared.'

In the New Testament, Joseph, on learning that his fiancée Mary was pregnant, and 'not willing to make her a publick example, was minded to put her away privily'. The story continues: 'But while he thought on these things, behold, the angel of the Lord appeared unto him in a dream, saying, Joseph, thou son of David, fear not to take unto thee Mary thy wife; for that which is conceived in her is of the Holy Ghost.

And she shall bring forth a son, and thou shalt call his name Jesus . . .' In St Luke, the angel Gabriel had told Mary the same thing. News of Jesus' birth was spread by the shepherds, who'd been told Jesus was 'a Saviour' by an angel.

There was great sadness, however, when Jesus was crucified and put in the sepulchre. At dawn the next day, the two Marys went there: '. . . the angel of the Lord descended from Heaven, and came and rolled back the stone from the door and sat upon it. His countenance was like lightning, and his raiment white as snow.' And he said, '. . . go quickly, and tell his disciples that he is risen from the dead . . .' In the Epistles of Paul the Apostle, we hear the following:

There are also celestial bodies, and bodies terrestrial: but the glory of the celestial is one, and the glory of the terrestrial is another.

1 Corinthians 15:40

Let brotherly love continue. Be not forgetful to entertain strangers: for thereby some have entertained angels unawares.

Hebrews 13:1–2

The appearance of angels can be dramatic, with 'a great earthquake' as at the sepulchre, or as St Paul states above, we may be unaware of who they are. Angels weave in and out of human existence, their missions to perform in countless different ways. Any dictionary of angels has so many entries, with so many names and events, it seems there have been many human–angel interactions over the years. Angels have been ascribed to nations, fire, water, earth, air, wind, hurricanes, tornadoes, earthquakes, lightning, comets, as well as to strength and beauty, to plants, herbs, fruits, trees and animals. In many spiritual traditions, including Judaism, Christianity and Islam, angels have been most prevalent, particularly within the mystical traditions. Indeed, over the years angels have proliferated and caused major confusion amongst academics. Gustav Davidson, in the introduction to his *A Dictionary of Angels: Including the Fallen Angels*, says he became overwhelmed by the sheer number of angels that appeared in the literature, which '. . . yielded a boundless profusion of angels (and demons), and I soon had more of the fluttering creatures than I knew what to do with'. No doubt some of the fallen angels, or 'dark angels' (those without light) as they are sometimes called, can be accounted for as excuses for things people did wrong; 'the fallen angel made me do it' syndrome. But there is another dimension to this subject, which the Anglican priest and author, Dr Martin Israel, interpreted thus for the TV programme *Network First*:

> *I doubt whether anything defies the divine fiat. I think God created dark angels like the light angels. The dark angels are here to make us grow on through our own experience in life. We have to undergo darkness as well as light to grow as people.*

There are two main sources of information about angels: books and people's experiences, and the two are often very similar. You could say that someone is influenced to believe something they read in a book, and have a 'vision' which materializes the thought. In other words, they imagined it. It's hard to believe this is the case with some of the many very down-to-earth people I've spoken to about angels.

Although angels are so closely associated with Judaeo-Christian and Muslim traditions, they exist in other parts of the world too. In southern Australia, the Great Spirit of Aboriginal myth goes by the name of Nepelle, and he has a messenger, Nurunderi. In western Ireland, the late Irish poet, George W. Russell, described meeting beautiful 'Shining Beings' and 'Opalescent Beings'. He believed this latter group were what the pre-Christian Irish people called 'gods':

> *... there was at first a dazzle of light ... this came from the heart of a tall figure with a body apparently shaped out of half-transparent or opalescent air, and throughout the body ran a radiant electrical fire, to which the heart seemed the centre. Around the head ... there appeared flaming wing-like auras. From the being itself light seemed to stream outward in every direction; and the effect left on me after the vision was one of extraordinary lightness, joyousness, or ecstasy.*

This feeling when meeting angels is so 'out of this world', it is not confused with any other day-to-day mind-event, or dreaming experience. I asked Anne, who met her angel in the bar in Montreal, 'Did you imagine it?' She said, 'Look, out of all the things that have ever happened to me in my life, that was the *most* real. What happened that day was very deep, and very wise – more wise than I could dream up!' This aspect of the experience, receiving knowledge, sometimes with no words being exchanged, is too extraordinary to attribute to imagination. There are only two alternatives: either there is an angel within, that emerges and floods us with visions, profound wisdom and infinite peace; or there are angels without. Or, maybe, there are both.

ANGELIC AROMAS

The Angelic Vibrations; the Attractants of Fragrances

Angels are able to utilize the vibrational effects of fragrance, as this is perhaps the nearest the physical world can offer to their own. It may be the frequency they recognize and are drawn to, rather than the smell itself. By utilizing the fragrances of nature – which each have an individual frequency – with clear intent and purpose, it is possible to use essential oils to bring angels closer. In such a time as we are living, we need to be able to contact the messengers so they can assist us with our spiritual growth and send our prayers and messages of love out into the universe.

We need to let ourselves and others understand that the majority of people on the planet want peace, love and compassion, and that we are not all driven by greed, ego and bitterness. If the angels or shining ones are willing to help us, should we not take the thread of light offered to us, grasp it within our hearts and give praise and thanks for such help?

Contacting angels is not as simple as using a fragrance. Think of it like this: the angel is the driver of a bus, travelling to different realms. Fragrance is the route the bus travels, it puts us in the right place, but we need to signal as well. At a bus stop this is done by putting out our arm, when using fragrance the signal is a mental one, and so when using angelic vibrations, we need to use prayer, meditation, and good intent and purpose.

Angels are not the destination, but the route to it. Nor do they travel our journey for us, only assist us on our way. They are not there to do everything for us –

so don't ask 'please will you clear away my doubts and fears' but, rather, 'please be close while I deal with my doubts and fears.'

A particular angel has been assigned to you, and to be able to get on their wavelength, as far as is humanly possible, we need to find our angel's or guardian's vibrational fragrance. If we have already smelt it, that makes it somewhat easier, but we can *never* make a copy of that fragrance by using substances that are of this earth. Let that be understood. We can only get as close as we can to it.

If there were a flower or plant that produced an essential oil with a vibration that always attracted angels, we'd all be growing it. But the heavenly vibrations are different to those on earth, and to find them, the most likely route is through making blends, which have a vibration different to those generated by the plant world as they grow on this planet individually. Once you have an idea or picture of your particular needs, and wish to send it to a messenger, experiment with making your own blends, until you hit upon the right note.

What follows is a list of individual fragrances – essential oils which can then be blended. Your own soul fragrance is the one at which you vibrate, and the angel assigned to you will be able to lower their vibration to this, and connect with you through it. When you find it, it's an indescribable feeling of completeness, as if you dissolve into the perfume. I've seen this happen a few times while teaching. The look on the person's face is of ecstasy, peacefulness and youthfulness – as years of hardship just seem to melt away. It's an unbelievable sight, like all transformations.

The Angelic Fragrances: 62 Profiles

The following list is based on my own, and other people's, experiences of angels and their fragrance, and on the experiences of my Aroma-Genera students which have been full of insight as their own life tales have unfolded. There are many other fragrances which have not been listed here, but as I have no personal experience of them in terms of the angelic realms, nor am I aware of other people's first-hand experience of them, they have been omitted. The information below is from real-life experience, as opposed to that of legend and mythology, and although one cannot say how it works, it certainly seems to work for many people.

Angels are messengers, fellow servants of universal good and, with the right intent, we can ask them for support. Angels join with us on both spiritual and earthly matters. Although we may feel the need of them most strongly when tragedy strikes or sorrow envelopes us, angels are there also to share in our times of happiness, positivity and joy.

ANGELICA SEED

is named after angels, many of whom are associated with the plant in legend. Its aroma can be used by those who feel uncertain, or spiritually neglected, and in this respect need to call upon their personal angel. It seems to have more effect when blended with other fragrances.

BASIL

assists in awakening, awareness and understanding. It allows the clearance of a muddled mind that puts up a barrier to contact with angels.

BAY

brings the angels of our future closer. It can assist us in
looking forward, particularly if we tend to dwell on what
has been, rather than look forward to what is to come. It
can create a positive note which enables assistance to be
given. To see ahead and plan for that rainy day.

BENZOIN

enables the spirit to receive blessings. It enables us to
learn the joy in receiving as well as in giving, and to learn
of the interchange of spiritual energy that takes place.

BERGAMOT

has an aroma that can clear away the fogginess that often
muddles us, so allowing the higher spiritual self to become
attuned to our helpers. This has no specifics attached,
except it is a receiver.

BIRCH

assists in struggles of a spiritual kind, clearing away the
physical barriers that impede us by keeping the veil down.

BLACKCURRANT

assists in fearful situations, perhaps recognizing elements
of ourselves we would rather not face. For learning to forgive, and to be less judgemental.

BLACK PEPPER

is a protective fragrance which, used with the right intent
and purpose, allows our guardian angels to bring protective elements into our lives. It can also help us when we
are fearful of reuniting ourselves with spiritual aspects of
life after long-term neglect.

118

BROOM

assists in harmonizing our mind, body and higher self, and in receiving insight.

CARAWAY SEED

is a seed oil which has protective properties, and it enables our angels to assist us in viewing our life in a spiritual light rather than a physical one.

CARDAMOM

allows the spiritual to become interwoven with the physical. In some cases, it clears the mind sufficiently for our guardian to give us insights into how we can improve our spiritual welfare.

CARNATION

has a scent of the angelic realms . . . some report it as being close to their angel's fragrance. It should be used sparingly, to open us up to receive spiritual insight, clarity and compassion.

CARROT SEED/TOPS

is used for visions, and the realms that assist in vision-quests.

CEDARWOOD

brings the angels of wisdom closer. For purification. For the angels that watch over, helping and assisting us when in need, and for their vibration to come closer when the wisdom of the ages is required.

119

CHAMOMILE ROMAN

touches the inner child, the delicate spirit that needs to be reconnected with the divine angels – of the highest order. To bring inner peace and joyfulness.

CINNAMON

is joyful. The unknown exploration when we step with uncertainty and need assurance that help is at hand if we need it.

CISTUS

can be used when a person is experiencing disconnection from the spiritual self, bringing fear. It can connect to the spiritual realms with ease and bring the whole being into balance. Sometimes associated with the visitation of angels as a strong, overpowering aroma.

CLARY SAGE

gently awakens the angelic realm of the subconscious, bringing harmony and purpose. For the times when we pray for assistance from the angels, to reveal our purpose, or at least understand a little of why we tread such a path.

CLOVE

for when we are afraid and in need of angelic assistance, or need to believe they are close by. To send with joy our thanks to these realms in celebration.

CORIANDER

is a signal of new life. Useful when praying for guidance and assistance while you tackle a new job or try to change an area of your life.

CYPRESS

is for when we are grieving. During bereavement this fragrance brings the angels to console us, and assist in the transition and release from the earthly love which can sometimes attach us too strongly to the departed.

DILL

brings together all the current aspects of life – for the breath of life. To look at areas of painful emotion. Can be used in vision-quests to bring inner understanding.

FENNEL

assists in physical matters, keeping the mind stable and functional, yet uplifted. To remain grounded, and to help understand the lessons to be given in this lifetime.

FRANKINCENSE

aligns with the spiritual; a 'calling' perfume. To call upon the divine orders, and to send love and prayers. Also for protective elements. To assist in keeping the heart pure and full of understanding.

GERANIUM

will allow us to be centred enough to bring the angelic realms closer for comfort and reassurance. It contains an aroma which assists in understanding both the opportunities and disappointments that may come our way.

GINGER

is a fragrance that brings stimulation and protection. Its courage and fearless fragrance can be used when we need to stimulate ourselves into action but lack the courage to do it, and so it brings into our aura a strengthening energy which is transmitted by our guardians.

GRAPEFRUIT

to rejoice for the upliftment of the angelic realms, in joyful appreciation. Clears the pathways to direct connection with a messenger, energizing the subconscious connections.

HELICHRYSUM (ITALIAN EVERLASTING)

for persistence, endurance and courage, enabling the path ahead to be clearer. Full of awareness of perhaps the dangers and pitfalls of life.

HYACINTH

is another flower of the angelic realms that is reminiscent of many descriptions of angelic odours. It can be used when we find it difficult to express ourselves, and need consolation and assurance that we are not alone and help is always near by, if it is the will of God.

HYSSOP

for the removal of emotional uncleanliness and assistance in the expansion of the protective beings, but very much on the physical plane, assisting in the removal of the heritage of guilt and fear miasms of a psychological nature. Purifying for those who believe they have sins which must be forgiven.

JASMINE

is a favourite of the angelic realms. Often a similar, but not the same, fragrance heralds their arrival and departure. A fragrance of the shining light-beings. For assistance in love, compassion and purpose.

JUNIPER

for assistance during purification, perhaps after nightmares or such like. It can be used during meditation to help bring the beings of light into the setting, and to understand why negative experiences may be troubling you.

LAVENDER

awakens harmony. It's a vibration that brings the angels of compassion closer when we are in need of comfort, companionship and recognition that help is always available to us, and that we are never alone.

LEMON

is vitalizing and purifying to the mind, body and soul. It allows directness and clarity in prayer. Angels often use this vibration to send feelings of happiness and calmness to us, to remind us to use the fertility and richness of the planet correctly.

LEMONGRASS

is cleansing for the physical which impedes the spiritual. For times when the emotions are embedded in misery and unable to escape from it, and in need of help to overcome it.

LINDEN BLOSSOM

for when sadness blocks the heart from feeling love, and when in need of inner peace and happiness. An angelic aroma which brings the peace and contentment that can only come from the angelic realms.

MANDARIN

is for the inner child. To reconnect with the angelic keepers of our childhood, bringing back briefly the innocence of childhood prayers.

MARJORAM

can be used to help assist us when we become obsessive, or when we can find no release from persistent mental anguish. It may bring assistance on an angelic level to release those holds over us.

MELISSA

is for past-life lessons, and assistance in moving forward and gaining wisdom from lessons learnt. Letting the angels that have accompanied you through lifetimes give you understanding and support.

MIMOSA

comes within the angelic realms of dream states. For the angels who watch over us during the night when our soul is for a short time free of the mortal body.

MYRRH

brings understanding and compassion, assisting the wounded healers who are unable to forgive themselves. For expanding the spiritual, and to help those who are in need of energetic rescue.

MYRTLE

is for forgiveness. When we wish to be forgiven and cleared of guilt and need help – when no other avenue is left open to us.

NARCISSUS

is said to help at times of transition, and to enable the angelic realms to come closer, bringing the fragrance of passing to the heavens. Often experienced by those who see angels.

NEROLI

has the sweetness of angels' breath, the gentleness of peacefulness. It reaches the higher self and the spiritual part of our being.

NUTMEG

brings the dreams of angelic realms into conscious thought. For assistance in physical neglect, and to slowly help in clearing away debris we no longer need.

OAKMOSS

helps us to connect with the earth plane, and to realize that we are on earth for a reason.

ORANGE

brings the joy of our assigned angels into our hearts, to be touched with the happiness that remains within us always – if we can only acknowledge it.

PALMA ROSA

assists when we are feeling neglected or misunderstood
and would like the comfort of the angelic realms.

PATCHOULI

assists in our connection with the planet and the past
vibrational patterns which we may encounter upon our
journey.

PEPPERMINT

is strong and clearing, and can be used to clear a pathway
when barriers have been erected and all help has been
refused.

PETITGRAIN

gives gentle awakening. It allows us to gently awaken our
consciousness and connect, if only briefly, with the subconscious and higher self, attuning with spiritual growth.

PINE

allows the angels of nature to enter the atmosphere. For
assistance during vision-quests, dream states, balancing,
and for holders of the star energy. Their fragrance lives on
after they have left, with only their ethereal shapes and
auras left behind. This connecting ability remains in the
fragrance. The angel to assist in creativity which stems
from the heart.

ROSE

is a fragrance of angels which comes in various scents — some are headier, some are lighter. Rose can be used to bring your consciousness closer to your angel, and to the angelic self which dwells within you. To inhale rose is to inhale the love and kisses of angels.

ROSEMARY

brings protection when unwell. It's used to bring the healing elements of angelic beings forward – although all elements of these beings can be healing if God wishes it. It helps us recognize that we have a conscious mind, a subconscious mind and a superconscious mind, and that we are always spiritual beings.

SAGE

is for when it's difficult to understand man's doings, and to bring the spiritual energy of the light beings close. To purify environments, to truly connect into the spirit of our home (every home does have a heart). To bring the wisdom of the ages into our hearts.

SANDALWOOD

assists in the joining of the physical and spiritual realms, the reaching beyond ourselves into the universal whole. For those who cannot visualize the connection between the conception of the universe and the conception of mankind.

SPIKENARD

contacts the angels of potentiality. It expands or contracts, revealing the secrets of the soul and the light of the universe.

THYME

is strengthening and gives courage when courage and strength are needed to overcome fear and disillusionment. For when we need to call upon the deity for physical assistance. During visions and dream states messengers bring insights of our physical obstacles and of how to overcome them.

TUBEROSE

is a fragrance associated with a particular type of angelic being – seemingly one who brings messages very clearly and with much love. The fragrance assists us in understanding our life's purpose, and perhaps in how better to give the love which we have been given in abundance from the angelic realms and God.

VERBENA

assists us in attuning to the higher spiritual self, in attempting to complete the harmonization between mind and spirit.

YARROW

is a fragrance for when in search of spiritual understanding, stimulation and clarity. Some report that yarrow can bring answers into the mind following prayer.

YLANG YLANG

is calming and soothing for those with troubled minds, and those who find it difficult to like and forgive themselves but who need to forgive, and to find a place in their hearts to love themselves. To look at this wonderful world we have been given with love and the understanding that we are all beautiful and part of it.

Chapter Five

FRAGRANT TRANSITION

> And there came also Nicodemus, which at
> the first came to Jesus by night, and
> brought a mixture of myrrh and aloes, about
> an hundred pound weight. Then took they
> the body of Jesus, and wound it in linen
> clothes with the spices, as the manner of the
> Jews is to bury.

ST JOHN 19:39—40

One of the most interesting questions in life is what
happens after death? This question is relevant not
only to us, the living, but to people we have loved and
who are no longer with us – we live in hope that they
or their spirit live on. Each spiritual tradition has its
answer to 'the big question', and it's very confusing
that they differ so much in their beliefs. Our ancestors
didn't have this problem as they usually grew up and
lived within one spiritual tradition and adhered to
that. Today, people can travel the world, watch TV programmes about other cultures and beliefs, and read
innumerable books, with different answers, on the

subject. No wonder so many people are in spiritual 'crisis', unsure of where to turn, and even more uncertain about what the inevitable future will bring.

One source of information comes from near-death experiences, which are remarkably similar: the spirit first floats above the dead body, watching doctors or other people trying to revive it, hearing all that goes on, then they see a bright white light, or a tunnel, appearing before them. At the end of this tunnel, or on the other side of a river, there is someone to greet them, variously described as a lone figure shining brilliantly, an angel, Jesus, a spiritual guide, or loved family members and friends, even pets. Whatever the differences in these accounts, one thing is constant: the profound sense of peace. This so envelopes a person, they often don't want to return to this life, but are told their time has not yet come. These near-death experiences are often associated with fabulous fragrances, which are described as 'heavenly', 'delicious', 'unbelievable' and 'indescribable'.

Fragrance plays a unique part in the interfaces between the living and their earlier life, between the living and the dead, and between present and past lives. Indeed, aroma is a language that traverses many layers of existence, an avenue not only of exploration but of explanation.

The most common of these aromatic revelations occurs between people who have died and people they loved who have been left behind. The following story was told to me by a client: 'I used to live with this fellow, and loved him very much, but he left me and I never heard from him again. That had been a long time ago. Then, one evening I drove past a road that led to where he lived, and had a very strong urge to drive past his house. I fought the feeling, but it was so difficult and I felt torn apart. I hadn't thought about him for ages but now, all of a sudden, he flooded my mind. I was at traffic lights, telling myself to be strong and not to even think about driving past the house. The lights changed and I drove home. All the way, I had a deep emotional sensation, remembering how good we had been together, and I felt the hurt all over again. Suddenly, the emotion changed, and I felt flooded with love. The next day I had almost forgotten about the incident, and was getting on with my work, when I smelled his aftershave. It was an unusual one he'd had sent over from Italy. It was in my nose, and everywhere I went I could smell it. Suddenly, I knew he'd died and passed on, and this was his way of saying goodbye and that he had really loved me. I cried for a while but the smell kept hitting me, again and again, and the love filled me. I must have fallen asleep in the chair, and when I woke up there was no smell. All the pain and hurt I'd felt for years had gone. I knew then I could find someone else because before that I'd always been alone, afraid to be hurt again. His passing and sending me love made me realize I'm loveable and deserve to find another person, and that my life could start again.'

Stories of aromas particularly associated with a person who has passed on are not uncommon. It is sometimes the smell of flowers that the loved one liked, or that they used to give to the person left behind. Other smells associated with people also occur, such as perfume, tobacco smoke and aromas associated with their work – coal with coal miners, for example – or of foods they particularly liked, such as garlic. The more general aromas of people are also found lingering in the air, and these aromas may be quite imperceptible to others. But, more commonly, the aroma is simply a powerful floral fragrance with no particular connotation to either the recipient or the person who has passed on.

These fragrances which occur at times of bereavement bring with them memories and comfort. Perhaps they are brought by angels, so we know that person is at one with the heavens and is sending this message of love. Perhaps the spirit of the dead person has come to say goodbye, to let us know they are there in the ether and are moving on. Some would say it is just the mind playing tricks, but it is not just the aroma that comes. Associated with it is information which is often as clear as a bell, and comes not from within, but from without. The fragrance is reassuring because it is a link, but it is also transformational in that it can jolt us out of a behavioural mould, allowing us to move on, in some sense ourselves released.

This experience of 'scenting' happened to a Mrs Case of Exeter, England, who then went on to research the subject. In the private publication which resulted, she wrote:

> *People who have lost their sense of smell can smell it. Sometimes two people can smell it, and a third cannot. Sometimes many people share it; and often, as in a service in church, only one person smells it and the others notice nothing. Sometimes the scent is diffused, and at others localized.*

One of her informants, a widow, wrote: 'I felt dreadful all that day and eventually prayed for the phenomena of scentings and warmth to return and next day it was back again and remained with me another week or two, gradually lessening as my burden of grief became more bearable.' Mrs Case notes that 'the sanctity derives from the agent, not the recipient', meaning that these kind of extrasensory olfactory experiences relate to ordinary human beings who have passed on to that place which produces 'the odour of sanctity'. This phenomenon is different to that whereby people living here on earth produce an 'odour of sanctity', signifying their special holiness.

Christian saints often emitted sweet-smelling fragrances, both when dead and alive. The sweet aroma of St Patrick apparently filled the room in which his body lay. The English St Milburga, a daughter of Merewald, Prince of Mercia, founded a monastery for virgins in Wenlock and died in the year 700. Her body lay in a vault in her church for 400 years and was almost forgotten, until a sweet-smelling perfume emitting from her tomb led to its rediscovery. The seventeenth-century St Theresa of Avila spent twenty years as a contemplative sister of the Carmelite order, then became a reformer, before dying at the age of sixty-eight. Some years later, a sweet fragrance began to come from her grave, and the body was exhumed and found to be fresh and whole. In the twelfth century, St Isiodore's body was disinterred forty years after his death, and again 400 years later, and both times was found not to have decayed and to be emitting a fabulous odour. And in the early seventeenth century, the coffin of the Russian St Juliana, when opened so one of her sons could be buried with her, was found to have a beautiful fragrance coming from it.

The Greek Orthodox St Demetrius left relics which exuded a sweet-smelling oily substance. This phenomenon, which also occurs with icons, is known as 'myrrh gushing', and the substance was said to have healing properties. A basilica was built on the site of St

Demetrius' death and pilgrims used to collect the fragrant oil from a basin in the crypt which can be seen to this day in Thessaloniki. The relics themselves stopped producing the oil when they were stolen by Italian crusaders in the thirteenth century, and although returned to Greece in 1980 have not exuded it since, although a strong fragrance is often smelt around them. A 'myrrh'-exuding icon can be seen today at the monastery of Malevi near Tripoli in the Peloponnese.

A great number of saints were said to be fragrant during their lives. St Francis of Assisi is said to have smelled of lemon; St Rose of rose; St Catherine of violets; and St Cajetan of orange blossom. St Lydwyne's aroma had several components, including cinnamon, ginger, clove, rose and violet; while the breath of thirteenth-century Blessed Herman of Steinfeld was like a garden of fragrant flowers.

This 'odour of sanctity', as it is called, denotes the person had been elevated to some higher level of existence, one closer to the divine. It puts people in a category other than that of the base, material life. The aromas have an unreal and powerful effect, seeming to break the aromatic rules, such as having no apparent source. The historical records show people were concerned to highlight this, and explained these aromatic happenings occurred despite there being no incense, spices or fragrant ointments or balms around. Fragrance is supposed to be of the air, but in the case of the seventeenth-century Venerable Benedicta of Notre Dame du Laus, she was said to be so divinely fragrant, everything she touched became perfumed. Aroma is supposed to travel downwind, but an Indian saying goes, 'The fragrance of a flower travels with the wind, but the odour of sanctity travels against the wind.'

Experiences of smell phenomena are happening today, all around the world. If they only involved one person the unusual aromas could be dismissed as the figment of an overactive imagination. But often hundreds of people are 'witness' to the same aromatic event, and we can suppose that something less explicable is going on.

THE FRAGRANCE OF THE SPIRIT

Your spiritual fragrance transforms the atmosphere of the world like an incense stick transforms the atmosphere in a room. The incense stick spreads its fragrance regardless of the conditions and people in the room.

Brahma Kumaris

Everyone has their own spiritual fragrance which carries the vibrational frequencies of the spirit, and is in harmonic resonance with their inner self. This fragrance is completely different to that produced by angels or any other heavenly beings. These personal spirit fragrances seem to comprise various smells – such as deep, rich resins, fully flavoured fruits, fully open flowers, verdant grass, meadows, trees or woods – although they are unlike any fragrance on earth and, like angel fragrances, are difficult to describe. Each fragrance has a complexity of highs and lows that weave in and out of each other, reflecting the journey of our soul. It reflects all the places we have been, all the people we have been in contact with, all the emotions we have experienced, and all the personalities we have passed through – including those from other realms and, perhaps, other lifetimes. And it is the combination of all these things that comprises our spiritual perfume. We carry the smells associated with past times, just as we carry those of this lifetime, and they are all woven inextricably together, as pieces of the same aromatic cloth. Our personal spirit-fragrance is the one we are most at ease with but, at the same time, it has the capacity to affect us emotionally on the very deepest levels, stirring and moving us in ways which can be exciting, provocative, illuminating and liberating. Ultimately, our spiritual fragrance will connect with the glorious soul fragrance, an aspect of the universal whole.

MAKING THE TRANSITION

We make plans throughout our lives and even plan our funeral, but seldom do we plan our own death. This is not the case with Tibetan lamas, who place great store on the abandonment of grasping, yearning and attachment. They give everything away before death, if possible of course, so there will be no argument over the distribution of the physical possessions, which could negatively influence the next incarnation. Some, at what they consider the right time, simply close their eyes and release their spirit. In other cultures, especially nomadic ones, old people choose to be left behind if they have difficulty keeping up, and starve to death. However, most of us do not embrace or accept death in this way; we fight it tooth and nail and think that by planning for it we're giving in.

The more usual scenario is that we experience someone else dying, and find ourselves making plans for the funeral, if not the death itself. Flowers are an essential part of most funeral practices, perhaps because their fragrance brings a special atmosphere to the event. When Mother Theresa died in 1997, flowers that looked like tuberose surrounded the coffin, and I wondered if this was her favourite flower, and whether they had been in the room as she made the transition. Certainly, this very aromatic flower would have filled the room with its heady perfume; as essential oil of tuberose equally would have done.

Aromas are so personal, it's impossible to suggest essential oils to use at this most important time. This is the time to use fragrances we have loved, that induce in us peace and joy. If we are too weak to organize it ourselves, friends and family can be asked to get the essential oils and diffuser, so that the enveloping etheric clouds of fragrance can accompany us on the journey 'home'.

Make sure you use pure, natural essential oils, rather than the man-made synthetics which, to the untrained eye and inexperienced nose, can be disguised to look like the real thing. If ever there was a time we returned to nature, it is this – our true nature. We all have an image perhaps of what the afterlife will be like, but one thing is almost certain, there are no man-made chemicals in Heaven.

People who have died and been resuscitated, and had near-death experiences, notice delightful aromas: we will breathe in the fragrant heavens as we pass over. But when we are lying there, waiting for this to happen, what do we smell? Let us hope it is not the urine of a patient in the next hospital bed, or a nurse with body odour. Even in the comfort of our own home, we may not appreciate the smell of frying coming from the kitchen. Unpleasant odours will make it harder to find any beauty there may be in death. This is the one time in life to embrace the beautiful; thinking of the wonderful things we have done in our life, and of the special people we have known; and, hopefully, being in the company of people who shower us with their unconditional love. Sweet-smelling aromas, well-chosen and sensitively used, contribute the beauty of nature to the dying experience. And in a hospital ward, it attracts people to the area, making it less lonely.

Sogyal Rinpoche, author of *Tibetan Book of Living and Dying*, has said:

> *What counts at the moment of death is whatever we have done in our lives. Help the dying person not to face death empty-handed, help him or her to find meaning in his or her life, even if he or she has many regrets now he can make the end of his life meaningful. Our state of mind at the moment, a change of heart at the time of death, can influence our future and powerfully transform our karma. Our last thoughts and emotions before death have a powerful and determining effect on our immediate future. The quality of the atmosphere when we die is important. When someone is dying we should do all we can to inspire positive emotions, sacred feelings like love and compassion . . .*

If the love and emotions can be expressed, the tears allowed to fall, before the actual moment of death, the spirit can be released undistracted.

This brings us to a very important point. If preparing essential oils for someone who is dying, don't think of it as a potion to draw them back to the living. No earthly fragrance can bring them back. Think of it as simply providing a pleasant atmosphere in which they can pass over, or as a cloud of delicious fragrance to waft them on their inevitable way; our last parting gift.

USING ESSENTIAL OILS FOR MAKING THE TRANSITION

Which essential oils you use is entirely a matter of personal choice. The essential oils are profiled in Chapter 11, and you may find that or other sections of the book useful. If you like flowers, pick from the flower essences, and if they are not right for you there are also herbs, fruits, seeds, woods and resins to choose from. When you are happy with a fragrance or blend, you may find your perception of the aroma changes, as you are on the journey of your own soul-fragrance evolution.

Blends have a delight all of their own, and a richness which is perhaps appropriate at this time, although many people have a single favourite fragrance which can be found in essential oil form and may prefer that. Here is just one suggestion:

Rose Maroc	2 drops
Jasmine	2 drops
Hyacinth	1 drop

This is quite a heavy fragrance but if only a small amount is used the aroma is sweeter and lighter: the strength depends on the dilutions you use. The effect will be very different if you use 2 or, say, 8 drops in a diffuser. It is always better to use smaller amounts to begin with, then see if the person making the transition would like more.

Spritzers

One way fragrances can be used is in a spritzer which mixes water and essential oils together. Boil some water with the essential oils added, keeping the lid shut very tightly. The ideal thing for this is a stainless steel pot used for making herbal infusions or for cooking. Allow it to cool, without opening the lid, and place in a fridge for twenty-four hours. When you take it out there may still be some oil floating on top, which can be spooned off and used in a diffuser. The water that remains will have a delicate light fragrance, ideal for spraying around the room or on the body. For those who like to use frankincense in a blend, use only a small amount as it can overpower the rest of the fragrances when used in this way.

Hydrolats

Another way of using natural, water-based fragrance is to blend hydrolats, which are the floral waters left after distillation. Rose and orange flower (neroli) are just two of the fragrances that could be used, and are ideal for spraying rooms, bedclothes and around people, as they have antiseptic properties as well as a delicious fragrance. However, because only the water-soluble components of the plant remain in the water, the hydrolat will not smell exactly the same as the flower. Lavender hydrolat smells not at all like the lavender we know so well, and rosemary hydrolat can be quite camphorous.

FRAGRANCE AND TRANSITION –
THE LONG TRADITION

In the ancient world, fragrance was an essential element in the funerary rites. In Genesis 49:33, Jacob 'yielded up the ghost', and in 50:2, '... Joseph commanded his servants the physicians to embalm his father'. In 2 Chronicles 16:13–14, King Asa 'slept with his fathers', and was laid 'in the bed which was filled with sweet odours and divers kinds of spices prepared by the perfumer's art'. Some versions of the Bible say 'apothecaries' art'. An account of the death of the Persian King Yezdijird, in AD 652, says he was embalmed with spices and perfumes; while the ancient Egyptians, as we know, used a great deal of fragrant material in mummification.

Fragrance had deep symbolic meaning to our ancestors who considered it a gift of the gods. It was, indeed, seen as both an expression of the divine, and as something that conferred divinity or immortality. The fragrant sap of trees – the resins of many ancient incenses – was seen as the sweat or tears of the gods; while the unaccountable loveliness of scents from flowers and herbs were seen as tools of divine inspiration. The ancient Taoists, with their eyes ever on transformation, noted that a solid incense stick becomes, with fire, a fragrance which disappears in the air, while the ancient Roman writer Lucretius was struck by the idea that the soul is part of the body, as fragrance is part of a piece of frankincense resin. He wrote of death, 'the breath of life is driven without ... scattering abroad like smoke.'

So important to the ancient Greeks was the custom of anointing the limbs of the departed with perfumed oil that they felt obliged to do this also to their greatest enemies if there was nobody else around to do it. After a cremation, at which incense would be thrown on the fire, the bones and ashes were washed with wine, mixed with precious ointments, and placed in a funeral urn. At one point in Homer's *Odyssey*, the practice is described: 'But when the flames your body had consumed, With oils and odours we your bones perfumed . . .' According to Eugene Rimmel, 'Perfumes were thought such an essential part of funeral ceremonies that scent-bottles were painted on the coffins of the poorer class of people as a sort of empty consolation for the absence of the genuine article.' Fragrances were daubed on the tombs, and scented flowers strewn around.

All this was too much for the writer Anacreon, who thought the precious fragrances should be enjoyed in life:

> *Why do we shed the rose's bloom*
> *Upon the cold insensate tomb?*
> *Can flowery breeze or odour's breath*
> *Affect the slumbering chill of death?*
> *No, no; I ask no balm to steep*
> *With fragrant tears my bed of sleep;*
> *But now while every pulse is glowing,*
> *Now let me breathe the balm flowing;*
> *Now let the rose, with blush of fire,*
> *Upon my brow its scent expire.*

Ode 32

The most extravagant user of aromatics in ancient Rome – in death as in life – was the Emperor Nero. At his wife, Poppaea's, funeral, it's said that more incense was consumed than could be produced in 'Arabia' in a year. The Romans put ashes and bones in urns with

142

perfumes, like the Greeks, and the more perfume that was used, the more wealthy the departed were or the more loved they were said to be.

For thousands of years in India, the funeral pile has contained scented woods, such as sandalwood, spices, fragrant gums and resins. The main centre for these fragrant materials is the town of Ghazipur, conveniently located for their biggest market, the Hindu spiritual centre of India, Benares, just a little down-river, on the Ganges.

Muslims in Pakistan associate fragrance very closely with Heaven and say that 500 angels gather near a person who has died and, just before the body is sprinkled with scent by the attendants, the angels sprinkle perfume brought from heaven. When the soul leaves the body, it is smeared with the fragrance of paradise and transported to Heaven.

In Japan, the youngest child sets fire to a pile of fragrant wood, and fragrant materials are also thrown upon it; while in China, at least until a hundred years ago, the body was perfumed, much incense was burnt, and those in the funeral procession carried burning fragrant material.

The reasons for using fragrance when making the transition are many, including the idea that the rising of the smoke literally carries the spirit of a person to higher realms. Because sweet-smelling fragrance was so strongly associated with the heavenly realms, a person was expected to be aromatically acceptable when they arrived there. It was through aroma that the dead and the eternal met.

Muslims of the Indian subcontinent have traditionally burnt incense, which might include benzoin, sandalwood or patchouli, in an *oodsoz*, or censer, and this is lit at the moment of death, and placed by the feet of the body. In the United Arab Emirates, perfuming the body is done partly so the deceased should be sweet-smelling when meeting God, but also because fragrance is said to attract angels and banish evil spirits. This idea has been, and continues to be, very widespread, right across the world.

Not everyone can bear the idea of dying. The Chinese in particular have a long tradition of seeking 'the herb of immortality' or 'the fungus of immortality', and many great tales have been written around characters who made the heroic attempt to locate them. Describing one such 'Gold Medicine', in AD 400, is Ko Hung (Pao Pu Tse):

The medicine should be prepared on a famous mountain ... The compounder ... should perfect the purification and ointment of the body with the five perfumes ... when the medicine is made, not only will the successful manipulator be immortal, but all the rest of his family will become immortal as well.

Chapter Six

REMEMBRANCE OF FRAGRANCE
PAST

The details of burial, the herb that was
used to ward off sickness, and the statues
of gods are all typical of classical
regression.

DR BRIAN WEISS, *Through Time into Healing*

Memories are in our cells, or in the spaces between
them, or in their electromagnetic field or aura.
Cellular memory has long been reported by body-
workers, such as aromatherapists, reflexologists,
rolfers, and shiatsu, kinesiology, acupressure and
connective tissue massage (CTM) therapists, amongst
others. During body-work, when certain parts of
the body are being manipulated, earlier events in this
life, and in past lives, are sometimes released and
recalled.

A different perspective has been put on this subject
by heart and lung transplant patient Claire Sylvia, co-
author of *A Change of Heart*. At the age of forty-eight,
after the transplant, she developed a new liking for
chicken and beer, and experienced the sensation that

another person was within her. In a dream, she met 'Tim L.' who, after some research, she discovered was in fact the young man whose organs had been donated to her following a fatal motorcycle accident.

These two dimensions to the subject of memory are interesting enough, but there are more. Richard is a lighting engineer for an American ballet company, and was on tour with them in Germany. The coach stopped for a break in a layby near a hamlet, and Richard came out to stretch his legs. He felt drawn to walk down a path between two houses until he came to a pond. At this point he can't remember what happened, but the others told him later. Apparently, he'd started shouting and yelling and waving his arms about, obviously very distressed. Some residents came out of their houses and figured out he must have something to do with the coach, and they brought his companions to the scene. Richard was speaking German, a language he had never studied, and explained to the coach driver that he was a German soldier drowning in the pond, having fallen through the ice. There are tens of thousands of recorded cases of people experiencing other lives, many of them including xenoglossy which is the ability to speak fluently in a foreign language without having learnt it in this lifetime.

These feelings, of having died in another place and time, happen to children too. I can think of one little girl living in rural Ireland, who remembered being hit by a truck on a road in America – a place she'd never been – and described the red and white logo on the side of it. The parents were intrigued by this as they lived a very simple life without TV or Coca-Cola, and the girl was not familiar with American culture, let alone place names. Subsequently, they took their daughter to the USA and confirmed the details.

Another little girl, who was three at the time, told me she'd left a family behind and didn't 'belong' in her current family. Suddenly, like a window into another world, she stopped being three, and spoke with the vocabulary of an adult. She told me she'd been a man, married with children – giving the wife's name – and had died falling off a fun-fair carousel. Then she noticed a flower, and, enraptured by it, ran off and was three again.

Many books have been written about past-life experiences, usually those that have emerged during hypnosis. We have, then, several ways of recall: hypnosis; always knowing, as in the case of children; suddenly realizing, as in the case of Richard; and through body-work. There is another route into the past – through aroma which can bring back memories not only of earlier events in this life, but in lives experienced before.

Many contemporary religions believe in past lives, while others have in the past adhered to this doctrine but no longer do. Hinduism and Buddhism teach reincarnation believing that the soul must pass through many lifetimes, each one teaching valuable lessons, until the spirit reaches perfection and can ascend to a higher place. Rebirth was a concept long accepted in the Jewish tradition until the nineteenth century. Today it remains part of the teachings of the Hasidic sect, and has continued through the mystical Judaic tradition of Kabbalah. Amongst Christians, it was accepted until Emperor Constantine, in AD 325, decided to edit references to it out of the texts.

Where are the past-life memories coming from? Some would say they are not about spirit transference, reincarnation of one spirit into the body of a person at a later time. Rather, that our DNA, or the etheric energy that enfolds it, carries memories of activities/ emotions experienced by our direct ancestors. Depending on whether a gene is active or recessive, we inherit hair and eye colour, body shape and other physical characteristics. But we also carry things for which no genes have been found, such as generosity, meanness, the love or fear of certain things, temperament, emotional aspects and general approach to life. If such intangible things can somehow be replicated, perhaps there are other, energetic, 'genes' that carry memories, and the emotions that are associated with them.

But how do we explain the visitation of 'Tim L.' to Claire Sylvia in the dream? Can the cell, including its associated energy field, hold the memory and behaviour not only of the person up to and until the moment of death, but also hold to itself the individualized 'spirit' of the person?

Many questions are raised by these issues. Organ transplants give a modern twist to other-life existences, but basically this is an ancient subject which has played an important part in the spiritual development of people around the world – many of whom have their own body-work systems, ways to go into a hypnotic state, spontaneous experiences and aromatic ceremonies.

Aroma and memory are, of course, inextricably linked. Olfactory nerves are actually part of the brain, extending from it into the nasal cavity, where they meet aroma molecules, via receptors. Nothing gets closer to the brain than aroma! The brain, we now know thanks to research in psycho-neuro-immuno-endocrinology, is an ongoing system, producing neurochemicals which have receptors on cells in all parts of the body – a continuum with undefined borders. Aroma induces the release of brain chemicals, and thus can affect the whole body.

In addition, from pictures of the auric field of aromas – in the form of essential oils – we can see they have a colourful dynamism that interacts with the auric field of a person. Aromas, then, are unique in being the one physical/etherical thing which appears to reach all parts of our body and, perhaps, all parts of our spirit.

Is it any wonder that smell has such a profound effect on us, or that extended memory can be triggered by certain aromas? Aroma is one of the means by which memory is laid down by its as yet mysterious recording mechanism. Aromas that have no particular association for us in this lifetime can act as a trigger, releasing the memory association that may have been laid down in a former life. The mechanism for this may be essentially physical, with the aroma molecules acting on the cells indirectly by stimulating neuro-secretory hormones to act upon the cell-receptors. Looking at it from an energetic viewpoint, there may be a parallel universe in which aroma is itself the key which unlocks the memory-receptors. And as the etheric energy is eternal, rather than physically mortal like the flesh, the memories can relate not only to this lifetime, but to other times held in the etheric field.

During Aroma-Genera – a system I have developed for the release of emotions that are attached to experiences of past events, both in this lifetime and beyond – a fragrance associated with a particular personality sometimes brings to the front of the mind a time and story that belongs to another epoch. Nine particular blends are used, and, by inhaling them with eyes closed, other space-times are reached.

149

Some of the present-life memories that are recalled can seem very trivial, and they show how sensitive human beings really are. A child can be deeply hurt by a casual offhand comment, or made to feel inadequate by being unable to tie a shoelace. Even newborn babies can get traumatized, as, for example, in the case of a woman who remembered, as a newborn baby, being separated from her mother in the delivery room, and put behind a curtained screen. It's frightening to think how many babies have had to undergo similar distress because adults don't understand the emotions even newborns can experience. So many hurts are being carried forward in time, unbeknownst to us. Memories arise from adulthood too, and reveal emotions we may have hidden even from ourselves, such as loss and fear.

Past-life memories can, unlike present-life recall, involve death. This is sometimes traumatic, and sometimes not obviously so, although there is always an emotion attached. For example, one woman recalled being hung for stealing an apple. She asked, bewildered, 'An apple? An apple? They'd hang me for an apple?' and it was the emotion of unfairness that clung tenaciously to her present. In another case, a man recalled a lifetime in which he was so fat that when he died his family had difficulty in getting him out of his bed and down the stairs. He was very embarrassed that his dead body had continued to release horrible, smelly odours. Not coincidentally, in this lifetime he has an obsession with cleanliness or, rather, had an obsession before it was dissipated by the Aroma-Genera session.

As we know, there are often several traumatic moments in a person's life. One Native American woman with a fear of enclosed underground spaces had it explained during Aroma-Genera. She was a young girl of three or four and waiting for a tornado to pass with her family in the root cellar of their house. Suddenly she got the sensation they were not safe where they were and told her family who disagreed. But she was so insistent everyone eventually left the cellar, only seconds before the whole building collapsed into it. It was the meeting of the past aroma – of the cellar and roots – and the present aroma – one of the nine Aroma-Genera blends – that brought this memory out of the lifetime's memory vault. The girl and her family did not die and were not harmed by the experience but she was still holding the fear, until it was released by Aroma-Genera.

I've heard hundreds of similar stories during Aroma-Genera sessions, and am led to believe that it is the *emotions* around a particular situation that get trapped within the electromagnetic field, or etheric field, or bio-plasmic field, or orgone or other variously termed field of a person. It is not so much the dying, or the people or circumstances of a particular memory, its magnitude or triviality, but the emotion – the core feeling – that carries forward and interferes with the flow of life.

What is so clear from past-life or earlier present-life recall is that events in the past can rest in the energy, causing it to flow in the wrong direction. The past emotion sits like a rock in the river of life, sending us off course. These rocks of distortion send us into directions that relate to the past, not to the future we should enjoy unencumbered by the past. We become, as the saying goes, 'bent out of shape'. We are hindered by emotions such as anger, anxiety and shame that bear no relation to the life we are living right now.

151

The Aroma-Genera experience is very gentle and releasing. No hypnotic techniques are involved. At all times the person is fully aware of the present, and also of the sensation they are involved in, enabling them to discuss each step of their experience as a detached observer. Indeed, the aroma seems to allow us to straddle two time-place existences. Take for example the case of Martin, who recalled being an innkeeper at a place some distance from London during the great fire of 1666. He described standing with his wife watching the dramatic scene on the horizon as London burned, sending the aroma of burning wood far and wide. At one point his voice lowered and he appeared to be talking to someone – he was giving highly detailed instructions to his wife to prepare more beds and food, as they would surely be busy tonight. He was having two conversations, in two times, as we might have two conversations with two people in our one time. The present-day Martin, objectively viewing his old self, was amused that he had been more interested in the monetary fortune to be gained from London burning than in the fate of the people directly involved in the fire. Interestingly, in this lifetime, Martin works as a healer with people suffering post-traumatic stress, and he hypothesized that he was now making up for his past selfish behaviour, and perhaps assuaging the subsequent guilt he may have felt.

Aroma-Genera is not a regression therapy. It involves working with personality types which may be imposed on us, or adopted by us, to get us through the present-day life. However, through Aroma-Genera, personalities from somewhere else do emerge. There is always a key moment, a pivotal point which keeps coming up until its message is understood and resolved.

This is not a process that can be undergone alone, and the blends cannot be put together in an arbitrary way. Using aroma as a regression tool is a precise science. There is absolutely no need for standard regression techniques – where a person is led back in time – the aroma does that instead. Nor is there any need of hypnotism. The state induced by aroma is *not* like being regressed, or hypnotized, and neither is it like dreaming, or day-dreaming. Aroma takes us down another route entirely.

Aroma-Genera is a system that uses aroma like a searchlight, seeking within that which waits to be found. But there is another approach when a particular aroma haunts a person, either in a positive or negative way. For example, a person might find a particular aroma abhorrent for no apparent reason and this may be indicative of a hidden story that could be released by that aroma. In these cases a sample of the aroma could be taken to a psychotherapist, counsellor, Aroma-Genera practitioner, or someone else professionally trained to understand the psychological process that goes on in memory recall. They can support the individual on the journey and, when the relevant memory-source is reached, help him or her understand the connection between that past experience and their present life and behaviour patterns. Also, there may be a particular aroma that draws a person enigmatically to it, and there may be a story in that.

I remember going to the Max Factor Museum in Los Angeles and being struck by an aroma I did not know. When I say 'struck', I mean that inhaling it caused a profound reaction in my solar plexus. This aroma and I have a history which I have yet to discover. It conjured up images of which I have no conscious memory, of a time before my birth. One day I'll return to that museum with my essential-oil kit and attempt to replicate the aroma. Then, with the help of someone to guide me through, I'll hopefully understand what significance it has for me.

If you have found while undergoing body-work that you have memories, or any other experience which is different to normal, and there is an aroma attached to it which corresponds with an essential oil, take a sample of that next time you go. Inhale the aroma before the session begins and ask the therapist to work on the same place that caused the memory or other reaction last time. Be very open with the therapist about this – you should not keep anything to yourself. It is important to verbalize and discuss any such experiences. Aside from the fact that you need to bring them into the open so they can be released, if any event involved physical hurt, the energetic emotional reaction can be stored in the body tissue and organs and your therapist will want to know about it.

If there is no aroma-memory – and if there is – write down the details of any unusual happening during body-work sessions. Questions you might ask yourself are, 'Which part of the body was the therapist working on at the time?' and 'What was the emotion I felt?' Try to be conscious of what is occurring as there may be important life-lessons in it.

Reactions to particular aromas are highly individualistic. One person may have no reaction at all, while another may find a far-memory is revealed. Aromas are like pigments that colour our experiences of life, and each painting is unique.

There have now been so many books, articles and TV programmes about past-life experiences, they can hardly be denied. The question is, 'What are they?' In some cases, they are undoubtedly an illusion – someone has read something, overheard something, or seen something which they later adopt as their own experience. In most cases, these are innocent mistakes, caused by being half asleep, in a daydream, or some mental state in which reality and fantasy become mixed up. Children may be particularly prone to this. If everything we ever see, smell and hear is retained in our vast memory vault, who can say that a baby didn't watch a TV programme in, say, 1960, and recalled it as a 'past life' in 2000? Some 'past lives' might be pure hallucination, caused by mysterious events in the brain biochemistry. Perhaps too, past lives are 'simply' genetic memory, an invisible inheritance we carry deep within. However, in many cases, there is absolutely no possibility of this because the ancestors and the date and location of the recalled event don't match up. This is especially so in recalls relating to the last thirty years or so, when the whereabouts of ancestors can be easily confirmed.

Those who work in this field are familiar with the options, and are also familiar with the profound release that can come from experiencing key moments in past or far-lives – and in the present life – and see that major changes in behaviour and life-direction can result. When a person is freed from encumbering emotions of past lives or of other lives encountered along the spirit's journey – they soar like a bird into a happier future. This release can be physical, and chronic pains and ailments are sometimes said to lessen; it can be behavioural, and old ways of relating change for the better; and it can be spiritual, as people find their own true selves. In a sense it doesn't matter whether the techniques used access the personal subconscious, the superconscious or the universal consciousness. What is clear is that we find that which we seek consciously or unconsciously, and need to evolve. In this, aroma can play a transformational role.

Chapter Seven

FRAGRANT CLOUDS OF PURITY AND PROTECTION

Human beings are far more sensitive than can be accounted for by sight, hearing, touch, taste and smell. We react in different ways to people and places, 'feeling' them to be beneficial to us or not, although such differences cannot be accounted for by the way they look. A person might walk into the room and appear perfectly normal, in that they are dressed like everyone else and behave in much the same way, but we might feel suddenly, unaccountably distressed. Or we might walk into a room and feel uncomfortable in it, although it's clean and well-furnished. It may even be our own home that feels, at times, uncomfortable in a way we cannot explain.

Unseen energies are a part of life and, although invisible, affect us deeply and even change the course of our actions. People say, 'I just want to get out of here,' and, although we may not have the same feeling, we understand that some unpleasant energy phenomenon has taken place and reply, 'OK, let's go.' You often hear people say of a person, 'They sap my energy,' and although there's no energy to *see*, we know exactly what they mean and sympathize. You even hear people occasionally say, 'I felt a presence in the room,' and, although we don't know exactly what this 'presence' is, we've known similar experiences at some point in our lives and accept what they say. Even though we may have a limited vocabulary to describe these invisible energy experiences, they are there nonetheless. If invisibility meant non-existence, there would be no such thing as portable radios, TVs and mobile telephones because these are the receiving hardware that interpret bits of invisible information floating through the air. Our bodies are the receivers of other, natural, unseen energies, some of which are not welcome in our lives.

Judging by the number of talismans, ceremonies and rituals used by people around the world, from earliest times, dealing with these unseen forces has been a very widespread human activity. They have been variously perceived as 'bad luck', 'the evil eye', 'spirits' and in more modern times as 'negative thought forms', 'distressed emotional frequencies' and so forth. Some Christians wear a St Christopher's medal as a pendant to protect them while travelling, or the cross of the Crucifixion; while a feng shui expert might rearrange the furniture in a building to redirect the 'wind and water' forces, to bring good energies and fortune.

In dealing with the invisible forces, and despite differences in belief, geographical location and time, people have often used fragrance as a protective shield between them and the perceived negativity. This manipulation of fragrance for spiritual ends binds people very distant from each other in belief, space and time, and often they use the same widely dispersed species of plant to facilitate more or less the same thing. Cedarwood, pine and juniper are among those plants that have been widely adopted in this way.

Native Americans living along the Thompson River burnt juniper to keep 'ghosts' away, and in Tibet juniper is offered daily to good spirits. In several Native American cultures, the aroma of burning sweetgrass or sage purifies the energies and attracts the 'supernaturals'. In some Arab homes, on Thursdays, frankincense is burnt in a censer and carried through the living rooms and bedrooms – to expel evil spirits and invite the angels in. In the souk in Cairo, Egypt, and elsewhere, people make a living going from shop to shop, censing each in turn with frankincense burnt in a censer or even on a small piece of charcoal in a rusty tin can, to dispel any negative energy customers may have left behind, making the environment more inviting to potential customers.

Such practices have been going on for millennia. The ancient Mesopotamians, Egyptians, Greeks and Romans all used fragrance not only to attract beneficial energy, but to keep inauspicious energies 'at bay'. The Greeks fumigated homes with bay leaves, while in the early days of Rome verbena or other fragrant plants were hung above doorways to deter *il malòcchio*, the evil eye. Censers were kept burning by front doors in classical times, even by the poorer households. In medieval Europe, 'witches' were the feared bad spirit, and rituals were carried out at pivotal points in the year with the object of dispelling them from the vicinity. These often involved walking through the village or town waving bunches of smouldering fragrant herbs or woods to send the aroma into every nook and cranny. Juniper and rosemary were amongst those widely used. In the feng shui spirit-placating rite, *tun fu*, incense is used.

Many of the incense ingredients used throughout history and today are healing agents – myrrh, frankincense, cinnamon, clove, hyssop, sage, cedarwood, juniper, cypress and pine, amongst others. No wonder then that incense, and fragranced ointments and salves which may well have conferred health, should be seen as 'protective' – a beneficent agent of the deity – and this was especially the case when it was thought that physical health was inextricably linked to spiritual health.

The unfortunate Europeans who suffered during the plagues of the fourteenth to seventeenth centuries must have been sure they had in some way transgressed when they read this in the Old Testament: 'If thou wilt diligently hearken to the voice of the Lord thy God, and wilt do that which is right in his sight, and wilt give ear to his commandments, and keep all his statutes, I will put none of these diseases upon thee, which I have brought upon the Egyptians: for I am the Lord that healeth thee.' The agents for healing at this time, these people's saving grace, came in the form of fragrance and perfumers. Fragrant materials became highly sought after, especially rosemary, cloves, garlic, rue, melissa, rose, lavender and juniper, and were vital protection when gathering with other people, in church for example. Around 1700, Daniel Defoe described one such scene in London: 'the whole church was like a smelling bottle; in one corner it was all perfumes; in another aromatics, balsamics, and a variety of drugs and herbs; in another salts and spirits.' In 1646 France, Arnaud Baric gave a full description of the role played by perfumers who, under the lead of 'the health captain', went through houses fumigating them with perfume burnt on coal fires. At the end of the long day, the perfumers were themselves cleansed by standing in the 'steaming room' – a cloth tent with perfume material boiling away in a pot.

It is a curious thing that so many fragrant plants should be protective to the health. It is almost as if we are invited by the creative force of the universe to examine them, taste them, put them in our food, enjoy their aroma, and in other ways make use of them. The healing properties of many fragrant plants were of course well known in ancient times, which may account for the widespread practice of aromatically cleansing strangers or guests before allowing them into the village or house.

A hundred years ago in central Borneo, the Blu-u Kayans burnt bundles of fragrant *plehiding* bark when strangers arrived, to drive away any accompanying 'evil spirits'. In Turkey, Afghanistan and Persia visiting guests were first cleansed by burning branches of fragrant plants or incense, while aboriginal Australians saved their hosts the trouble and came with their own lighted bark or fragrant burning sticks. As well as fragrance, fire and loud noise have been widely employed, as J. G. Frazer put it in *The Golden Bough*, 'for the purpose of disarming the strangers of their magical powers, of counteracting the baneful influence which is believed to emanate from them, or of disinfecting, so to speak, the tainted atmosphere by which they are supposed to be surrounded'. In the contemporary world, the practice of aromatic cleansing is still ubiquitous in the Middle East, where it is perceived as a hospitable kindness to guests. In tents in the desert, a few small pieces of aromatic resin may be put on the brazier, while in towns you are more likely to be greeted with rose water sprinkled from a long-stemmed *gulabdan*. Guests in Turkish households have lemon-scented cologne sprinkled on the hands, so it can be wiped on the arms and neck. This fragrant nicety is also offered by the conductor to passengers on long-distance buses.

Fragrance is also widely used to cleanse buildings, especially those used for spiritual practices. When Saladin retook the Mosque of Omar in Jerusalem from the Christians in 1187, he had it purified with rose water; and when Mohamet II captured the Church of Sancta Sophia in Constantinople in 1453 and made it a mosque, it was likewise first treated with rose. Sage is the most sacred herb of the Yuwipe Native American Nation, and it is this which covers the floor of the medicine man's house as he goes about the purification process.

Fragrance and spirituality have always been inextricably linked. In Mesopotamia 4,000 years ago, incense was used both to attract the goddesses and gods, and to repel malevolent spirits. In Muslim terminology, jinn are said to be an order of spirits which can assume human and animal form and exercise negative influence over people, and *pirs* are people brought in to deal with them – often incorporating the inhalation of jasmine oil as part of the proceedings.

THE BENEFICENT HOME

Our home should be an oasis of peace, or at least a place where we feel 'at home' with ourselves: centred and complete, healthy, creative and joyful. Most of the time this may be the case, but if we've been burgled, the house just feels 'dirty' – even, as one person told me, when a cat-burglar silently went through the place wearing thick gloves and disturbing nothing but the safe. The initial reaction after such a violation is often, 'It doesn't feel like it's my place any more; I want to move *now,*' but this is seldom a practical possibility. If we move home, to a place previously occupied by other people, again, the energies can feel uncomfortable.

It is not only the energy of those who are present that we have to think about, but the energy of those who have passed through that particular space before. Walls, so it is said, hold the energy of people who occupied that room in former times. The love and joy – or fear, anger and pain – somehow get imprinted in the very fabric of the building. Whether this is the case or not, it is certainly true that walls hold ancient aromas, as has been discovered by workers for commercial dehumidifier firms who have smelt the aroma of incense burnt long ago emanating from the walls of churches during treatment. Aroma is tangible compared to love, fear and thought, but all have a vibration and an energy that can linger.

Healers who work within the auric fields of people – the energy field around the body of a person – feel that field, in some cases, as sticky. This same, grey, etheric quagmire quality can suffuse a home, or a room in it, and can be felt by sensitive people and animals. It's variously described as 'thick', 'heavy' and 'dim'.

After a burglary, or when moving into a new place, it's very appropriate to perform a spiritual cleansing, but even invited visitors to our home can often leave their vibrational imprint behind. If they are full of sadness or misery, or the kind of people who radiate negativity or soak up positivity, that can be a real burden on the energy of the premises (as well as on us!). They leave feeling replenished, but you and the house feel depleted – and it may be time to work on the energy of both you and the place.

When a building holds energies which are having a

detrimental effect, they can be expressed as, perhaps, the feeling that the place is never really clean (despite the fact that, to look at and touch, it is clean), and wanting to clean it over and over again; or, conversely, as the feeling that you don't want to clean, touch or disturb anything; a general feeling of discomfiture; always wanting to rearrange furniture; or simply, being depressed as soon as you open the front door. The energies in a home can also account for physical sensations: feeling tired all the time; getting headaches; or feeling pressure on the head. Clearly, these things could also be symptoms of some physical disorder, and before considering the energetic quality of a home as the cause, put on your coat and get down to the doctor for a check-up. Obviously too, arguments in a home may account for an atmosphere of disquiet; and electromagnetic fields generated by electrical pylons, for example, have been said to account for the symptoms listed above.

CLEARING THE ATMOSPHERE

Rooms can have a different atmosphere which cannot always be attributed to such things as decor, light, ceiling height, or even good or bad feng shui – the flow of *ch'i* energy around a home depending on its location and the placement of doors, windows, furniture, mirrors and plants, among other things. Rooms also have an aroma which reflects all that is contained, and goes on, in them, including activities such as cooking; the aroma of things such as furnishings; and the presence of living beings such as people, animals and plants. Humidity can change an atmosphere, and the aroma of mildew can these days be treated with various commercial products and appliances, while the dryness of central heating can be counterbalanced with humidifiers. All these are things we should bear in mind when considering the atmosphere of a room or home.

Another factor is cleanliness. If a place doesn't feel conducive to good energy flow it may simply need a good clean. We're not talking about untidiness here, but uncleanliness, the solution to which is obvious. When thinking about cleaning in terms of energy, however, add salt to the water, along with some essential oils – whichever aroma you enjoy.

As you go around your home, take a box and throw in all those items of clutter which you know you will no longer use, or you don't really like. According to the philosophy of feng shui, they clutter your mind as well as your home, and could be given to a charity shop which may benefit from them more than you. Washing windows is especially good for energy flow. It gives a different look to the outside of a home, and a different feel to the inside. Add essential oils to either the water or to the cloth – the citrus oils are particularly good for this job.

Spiritual cleansing is different to the usual cleaning routine and involves much more thought and a little more preparation. Here is a traditional method of transforming the subtle energies of a room. Before you start, focus your mind on the job at hand, and invoke that which is the source of your spiritual strength. Pray that the cleansing will bring light and peace. Mix a tablespoon of salt with two drops of frankincense essential oil and leave it to dry. Open a window or a door leading to the outside, which allows circulation of air, then sprinkle a tiny amount of the mixture around the room, including the corners, gradually moving towards the open window or door.

Another method involves using salt water in a bowl, wetting the fingers and flicking the water in all directions, being careful not to damage certain fabrics and furniture. Essential oils can be added to this water-salt mix. A very ancient method is to dip a small bundle of fresh herbs into salt water, shake off the excess, and use this to flick the water around the room. Some cultures use a small branch of a tree, or you could use a single flower.

The spiritual house-cleansing process can be done while diffusing your favourite essential oils. Some people pray while cleansing; others use loud noise which has often been used to scare negative elements away. This can be done in the traditional way, with drums, bells, rattles, gongs, clapping or chanting, although I know people who prefer loud music, as they feel this is very effective in getting the energy up and moving. When the atmosphere feels lightened, use one of the following cleansing blends of essential oils – or an essential oil or blend of your choice – in a diffuser, plant mister, or simply in a bowl or mug of steaming water. Put on some tranquil music, light a candle, then have a cleansing bath – suggestions for which are in a later section. Finally, put some new life and happiness in the room or rooms in the form of plants or flowers.

CLEANSING BLENDS
for Diffusers, Herb Bundles, Misters and Water Bowls

Frankincense	7 drops	Pine	5 drops	Lemon	3 drops
Benzoin	2 drops	Fir	3 drops	Orange	3 drops
Myrrh	1 drop	Cypress	2 drops	Grapefruit	4 drops
Sage	2 drops	Sage	2 drops	Clove	3 drops
Cedar	6 drops	Myrtle	6 drops	Black pepper	3 drops
Juniper	2 drops	Hyssop	2 drops	Cinnamon	4 drops
Coriander	5 drops	Rose	6 drops	Spikenard	3 drops
Fennel	2 drops	Jasmine	2 drops	Ginger	4 drops
Dill	2 drops	Linden		Vetiver	3 drops
		Blossom	2 drops		

Misters and Sprayers

One effective method of distributing the essential oil molecules around a space is by using a plant mister or sprayer. Using a new one, put in half a pint of warm water, then add 6–10 drops of essential oil – or more if you wish – screw the cap back on and shake well each time before spraying. Spray high into the air, making sure the water-essential oil molecules will not fall on any furniture or furnishings that may be damaged. The space around people can also be sprayed with these aura-cleansing sprays, but the eyes must be kept closed.

Water Bowls

Hot water releases the aroma molecules in essential oils and sends them rising into the air. Any glass or china heat-proof bowl or container can be used. Put 3–10 drops of essential oils on the water, and place the bowl(s) in the corner(s) of the room.

Essential Oil Cleansing Bundles

Make a collection of smelling strips by cutting up a piece of white absorbent paper into long strips. Put your chosen essential oils on these. They can be gathered together like a bunch of flowers and tied with bows, or plaited and in other ways made decorative. Use them to spread cleansing and energy-enhancing fragrance around a room.

Salt

There are many ways to use salt as part of spiritual cleansing. It can be used on its own, or mixed with essential oils. It can be put in water and used to purify rooms, spaces, objects and people. It can be added to baths.

Essential oils can be added to salt and crushed minerals or gems – such as crystals – and used to purify rooms and objects, or put in baths. Which particular essential oils, gems or salt you use will depend on what you are setting out to achieve.

As the seas are so polluted these days, sea-salt may carry those vibrations, but it also carries the energy of the sea. Rock salt gives the energy of the mountains and the earth.

ENERGY-CLEANSING BATHS

Every time we walk into an enclosed space – whether it is at work, on the bus, in a shop, cinema or theatre – we are putting ourselves in contact with other people's electromagnetic fields. Our auras mingle, for example, when standing shoulder to shoulder with other commuters in an underground train during rush hour. Some of these people may be disturbed, distressed or depressed and in other ways energetically needy. The interaction of energies between people involves giving and taking. There is good giving, when we feel enriched energetically, and there is the kind of giving that comes from a hyper person that leaves everyone feeling exhausted. With taking, the issue is willingness to donate that energy. We don't mind giving energy to our children, for example, and we freely allow the people we love to take energy from us, even though it may leave us feeling depleted. But there are also times when people draw the energy out of you – a kind of energetic violation, although most energy vampires may not consciously be aware of what they're doing. I've found that many of these people have been energetically abused at some time in the past and have an unstable personal boundary.

This is not just a physical-presence phenomenon, because we can find ourselves giving and taking in relation to another person, even over the phone. In fact, we don't even need that equipment because we can hear the phone ringing on the other side of the room and know from the change in our energy that on the end of the line is a specific someone we don't want to talk to. When they say their name, they just confirm what we had already sensed in some inexplicable way.

The effect of all this can be disturbing to our own vibrational pattern, and there may be times when we feel the need of a spiritually cleansing bath. The purpose of this is to 'wash off' the unwanted thought-forms or energies we may have picked up. Spiritual cleansing is about preserving the integrity of our spiritual core. It is of great importance particularly when we've had the unfortunate experience of being in

169

touch, perhaps not literally, with a person whose vibration is altogether more nefarious.

Energy-cleansing baths are not about removing everyday grime and pollution which should be done first by having a shower or bath and washing with soap. First, clear and enhance the atmosphere by using one of the methods in the Clearing the Atmosphere or Holy Smoke – for Purification sections in this chapter. Open the window or door to oxygenate the room. Some of the old traditions would use sound at this point – with clapping, chanting, drumbeat, singing, praying, laughing, shaking rattles or shouting – and if your inclination is to use sound you could use one of those methods, or check through your music collection for something that seems appropriate!

For people who want to bring in the four elements of water, earth, fire, and air, these are already there. The 'water' flows into the bath; the 'earth' comes from the salt or crystal(s) you place in the water; the 'fire' comes from the candles you place around the bath; and the 'air' comes from the fresh air you have just allowed in the room and the aroma of the essential oils you will use.

Essential oils on their own are unique amongst the gifts of life in that they incorporate in some sense all four elements – they are liquid and thus water-like; they are products of plants of the 'earth'; they are flammable and burn like fire; and they release a fragrance which is part of the air.

Bathing or being submerged in water is a sacred symbolic ritual in many traditions, often signifying full entry into a particular practice or way of worship. It also symbolizes rebirth and change, whether this is a change in the direction of life or in its purpose. Cleaning invisible energies with water is an everyday occurrence at nuclear power stations around the world, as workers finish their shift with a shower to assist in removing any radiation. Bathing is about being 'clean' in many senses.

Focus on what you wish to achieve from your bath and look at Chapter 11, the essential oil spiritual profiles, to choose those which seem particularly useful at this time. Essential oils carry the energy of the original flower or plant, yet have undergone transformation through fire and water in the distillation process. Again, we can see the four elements: the earth of the plant material; the fire that lights the still; the water that extracts the essential oil molecules; which are released into the air. The essential oils help cleanse the energetic field of the water, whether you use single essential oils, make your own blends, or try one of those suggested below.

Energy-Cleansing Bath Blends

Add up to two tablespoons of salt to the flowing water. When the bath has been run, add the essential oils, swishing them around a bit, with a prayer in your heart.

Neroli	3 drops	Myrtle	3 drops	Rosemary	2 drops
Orange	1 drop	Clary Sage	1 drop	Eucalyptus	1 drop
Petitgrain	2 drops	Lemon	1 drop	Lavender	3 drops

| Chamomile | 3 drops | Frankincense | 4 drops | Rose | 3 drops |
| Mandarin | 3 drops | Lemon | 2 drops | Neroli | 3 drops |

These blends can also be used in diffusers, herb bundles, misters, water bowls, or essential-oil cleansing bundles.

The Elements

When carrying out purification, you may want to incorporate all the elements, or those you consider essential. Some traditions, for example, include wood or metal amongst the core elements and others do not. What you use is a matter of personal choice, as you devise what suits you at any particular time.

When cleansing a room or person with essential oils or herb bundles, focus on the four directions in turn – north, south, east and west – and carry the fragrant material in those directions before making a complete circle. In some cultures, before doing the circle, the fragrant material would be lowered to the earth and raised to the sky.

The following chart shows some of the ways people bring the elements into purification and cleansing practices:

Fire	Air	Earth	Water	Sound	Metal	Wood	Light
Candles	Aroma	Salt	Bowls	Prayer	Gold	Sticks	Candles
Diffusers	Open windows	Stones	Misters/ sprays	Chanting	Silver	Wooden objects	Mirrors
Incense	Open doors	Crystals	Fountains	Singing	Copper	Incense	
Open curtains to let the sun in	Wind chimes	Flowers		Music			Open curtains to let the sun in
Fireplace	Plants	Plants Herbs Fruit Peel		Mantras			

HOLY SMOKE – FOR PURIFICATION

Smoke comes from fire which has always been considered one of the main elements in purification, along with prayer. In Buddhist temples in Japan and China, the smoke from burning material is used not only to send prayers upwards, but to smoke the body for spiritual cleansing, purification and healing of the auric field. People can be seen using their cupped hands to direct the smoke over their heads and shoulders before entering the temple. Incense is often used, and, as I have discovered on occasion, some rather less aromatically pleasing materials. I have found myself in thick, pungent clouds of smoke, which filled my lungs and clung to my clothes all day.

The small lumps of resinous incense burnt in censers in Christian churches – particularly of the Orthodox and Coptic traditions – can produce large amounts of smoke, which pervades not only the building, but engulfs the congregation within. Native Americans use smudge sticks made of fragrant herbs, grasses and trees; directing the smoke around people as well as places with a feather.

All these, and other, traditions use the smoke of natural, fragrant plant materials. The purpose of these ceremonies may be specific in that they mark a rite of passage – such as birth, menarche, manhood, marriage, menopause, retirement and death – or aim to improve ill-health. Or they may be more general in that they aim to cleanse the auric field and alter the energy residing within a space or emanating from a person. Smoking is thought to clear negative influences, restore balance, induce spiritual purification, increase spiritual awareness, or prepare the body-mind-spirit for sacred ceremony. Smoke is also used to cleanse environments, whether at home or work, and in exorcism.

Essential oils incorporate the two elements that constitute the smoke ceremonies – fire and fragrant plant material. They do not of themselves produce smoke – unless burnt on charcoal – but many people find this an advantage. In burning fragrant plant material, the aroma is released by the heat, but so too is a great deal of smoke. Essential oils are also readily available, whereas some of the plant materials traditionally used are not. Essential oils can be used on their own – in diffusers or simply on smelling strips – and directed, as in smoke ceremonies, around the head and body of a person or around a room.

Whatever material is used, and whatever the purpose, the other crucial element is spiritual thought. As you go about the business of using holy smoke, or essential oils on their own, invoke your spiritual source and put your whole mind into asking for assistance in achieving your goal.

Essential oils are flammable, and care should be taken with them when using fire of any kind. The only time I recommend using essential oils in conjunction with fire is in candles, by the method described in Chapter 2. Shop-bought 'aromatherapy' candles may contain synthetic fragrances, which have nothing to do with aromatherapy or cleansing and purification. You can make your own essential oil candles using candle-making kits and pure, natural essential oils.

Natural resins have, of course, been placed on braziers or censers for millennia, but few of us own the equipment to replicate this system of use. If you do, the incenses traditionally used – depending on the culture – include frankincense, myrrh, copal, benzoin and gum arabic in resin form. In Asia, especially

Japan, fragrant woods such as *jinko*, *kara-mokkoh* and *kyara* are highly prized, and come in delicate strips which are placed on charcoal or in small incense burners. They are generally used to raise the spiritual energetic level of a person, rather than for purification and protection.

If you have a fireproof incense dish, usually made of pottery or metal, essential oils can be used in conjunction with small round pieces of charcoal that are sold specifically for use with incense. But, be warned, the effect is dramatic as the essential oil smoke shoots high into the air, and before trying this method do a test-run outside, and stand well back. The charcoal does not always look as if it's alight when it actually is, so care must be taken. Patience is required: the charcoal will light in one place, and tiny sparks can be seen running across the surface as the heat activates the entire piece, which can still at this point be black. In fact, it is red-hot, without the red! Wait until this process is complete before adding the essential oils, which should be used in moderation.

Smudge Sticks

In the Native American spiritual traditions, smudging plays a central role. Smudge sticks are long bundles of fragrant plant material, wound tightly, lit at one end until the material catches fire, then blown out so it continues to smoulder releasing the smoke.

The fragrant materials used by Native Americans are usually sage, wormwood, cedar or sweetgrass. Occasionally, depending on the location within the USA and Canada, the soft young stems of pine are used – these have pine needles attached and are very pliable. There is also a plant called prairie lavender

which is included in the smudge sticks of certain
Nations; although it is not of the same species of
lavender known throughout Europe it has somehow
acquired the name lavender from early European
settlers.

Sage

There are many types of sage, including *salvia apiana*
which can grow very tall and be over one hundred
years of age. Another variety often used is *salvia
columbarne*. Sage brush, *artemisia tridentata*, belongs
to the wormwood family, rather than to the sage.

Wormwood

Artemesias belong to the wormwood family although
they are sometimes called sage. They bear no resem-
blance to the sages we know in Europe. In Native
American culture, *artemisia spinescens* is sometimes
used in smudge sticks.

Cedar

Often, the trees that are called cedar are actually of
the juniper family, such as *juniperus virginiana*. All
types of cedar needles are also used, including *thuja
occidentalis*.

Sweetgrass

This is sometimes called vanilla grass, and is
hierochloe odorata, a tall green grass which becomes
yellowish when dried. On drying, its aroma
becomes more apparent. In some Nations it is put on
the hot stones of sweat lodges.

In all the above, it is the leaves and soft stalks that are
used. Smudge sticks are held in the hand, carrying the

smoke to where it's required, or the smoke is directed by the hands or with a feather. Other cultures use a small branch of a plant or tree to direct the smoke, often of the same species as that used in the smouldering fragrant material. You could also use big crystals to spread the smoke around, or other stones that you are attuned to – or amber, which is a resin from a plant.

Making Your Own Smudge Sticks or Herb Bundles

Before starting any activity as spiritually directed as making herb bundles, wash yourself, or at the very least wash your hands and forearms, letting the water run down them, to flush away any energy held.

All plants that are picked and dried should be honoured. Take only one stem or two, so the plant can continue to flourish. Have empathy, and show the plant respect. Ask permission of the plant, that you may take this branch to perform your spiritual practice. Your intuition will tell you whether it is right or wrong – when another plant should be chosen.

Pick stems that are long enough to be bound together. Look in your garden to see what has grown and matured. The herb garden is a good place to start; you could use sage, lavender, rosemary, thyme, oregano or clary sage. If you have access to cypress or pine, you could use a small, young branch. It is sometimes said that herbs or other materials that are indigenous to the region should be used, but my favourite, Californian white sage, comes from a place far away from my home.

Essential oils can be added to your bundle before tying. They are highly concentrated energy forms and will increase the energetic potential of the plant(s). Use them in moderation, remembering that they are

177

flammable. Try to use an essential oil or oils that are compatible with your bundle, that is, from the same kind of plant. However, if a particular herb, plant or tree – such as cypress, cedar or pine – is not available, by adding that essential oil we can bring the plant's energy into the smoke, in fragrance form.

Arrange a small handful of stems and leaves, not using so much that there will be difficulty in burning, or too much smoke produced. Put the stems in a rubber band to keep the pieces together while you tie the bundle, removing it when you've finished. Take a long piece of doubled cotton thread and place the top of the bundle on the middle of it. Using the two ends, bind the bundle together tightly, in a criss-cross fashion. Start at the top, criss-crossing the length of the bundle, and finish by winding the cotton around the bottom part of the stems. You'll now have a cone-shaped bundle. It needs to dry before it'll burn, so hang it upside down in a dry place; an airing cupboard would be ideal.

To use the herb bundle, ignite the end then put out the fire so it's just smouldering. Hold a small fireproof bowl under the bundle to catch any alight pieces that may drop as the bundle burns. Then walk around the room slowly, wafting the smoke into all the corners so it gradually clears away negative influences and ener- gizes the protective, cleansing frequencies. If smudging a person, walk around them; if smudging yourself, move the bundle around yourself, or move your body, so the smoke can enfold you. Start at the top moving down to the feet where the energy will dis- perse into the ground. The smoke can be directed with a cupped hand, a feather, a bunch of fresh herbs or leaves, a flower, or a crystal or stone – whatever feels right for you.

Do this with pure thought. Some people do it with prayer, chanting or singing but do what feels right for you. When you have finished, place the bundle down carefully with a fireproof dish underneath, as it might still contain burning material – the idea is to have a spiritual smoke 'wash', not set fire to your home! Then, open a window.

Decorative Bundles

If you do not plan to burn the bundle, a whole world of possibility opens up. Bundles can be bound incorporating colour, texture and meaning. Essential oils will add fragrance and energy. Try flowers like marigold or rose. Spices such as cinnamon sticks and clove, and fruits in the form of dried lemon or orange peel, are cleansing in their own right. Small pieces of fragrant wood can be added and, depending on how you plan to display the bundle, other objects wound into the arrangement – such as crystals and minerals, and the small light rocks that are the resins in their original form.

Herbal Smoke Bowls

Another method of using smoke involves putting a drop of an essential oil on a small amount of dried material on a big shell or a piece of fireproof pottery or glass, then setting light to the material and putting out the flame to release the smoke.

Chapter Eight

MULTIDIMENSIONAL BODIES

There will always be mysteries; the universe is too large to allow for anything other than that. I'm hoping, though, that in the not too distant future science will be able to explain one of the most intriguing aspects of life – multidimensional radiant bodies. Apart from the physical body, we have an 'aura': a light which surrounds the body and is often depicted as a halo in paintings of saints and holy people. We also have energy centres in the body, known as chakras, and, according to some, an etheric body, an astral body and a mental body – all usually invisible energy fields which connect us to the universe. These names have arisen from the European esoteric tradition of the early twentieth century, which has its roots in ancient Indian and other Asian ideas. More recently, people talk in terms of 'the light body' and 'the emotional body', and 'auric field', which are all aspects of the same phenomenon.

Very few people can see auras or chakras, let alone the etheric, astral or mental bodies. This is not to say they don't exist. Anyone with the right kind of sensitivity, opportunity and practice could, if doing regular therapeutic work with people, feel the auric field and chakras. Many of us might have an idea of the way the various energy fields might be operating, but in this area of study there is a great deal of speculation and little scientific proof.

One person who has done valuable work in this area is scientist Dr Valerie Hunt, working both with the most technologically advanced equipment and specialist research environments, and with people with visionary powers that are probably as ancient as the human race itself. Some call what she studies the aura, although Dr Hunt, author of *The Infinite Mind: the Science of Human Vibrations*, prefers the term 'energy field'. At the same time as machinery recorded electromagnetic energy in people subjected to various research procedures, clairvoyants and healers recorded what they saw. The correlation between these, taken together with the concurrent recorded experiences of the research participants, including herself, led Dr Hunt to hypothesize that 'the energy field is the highest level of the mind of man, and that it is through this level that we interrelate with the cosmosphere.'

It's well known that there's an alternating electrical system that can be measured with electrodes placed on the surface of the body, and this alternating current of the nervous system affects a great deal, including the brain, muscles, glands and our touch sensation. The on-off quality of this energy is reflected in the beat of a heart, the contract-relax double action of a muscle, and the peaks and dips of a brain wave. Many of us have had this energy monitored through, for example, an electrocardiogram (ECG) machine, which measures electrical heart function, or an electroencephalography (EEG) machine, which measures the electrical activity from different parts of the brain and determines whether we are dead or alive.

Dr Hunt was interested in another form of electro-magnetic energy in the body, which is thought to derive from the fact that each subatomic particle and cell in the body has an electrical element. Dr Hunt has discovered that this second energy is continuous, not alternating. From her recordings, Dr Hunt could remove the data relating to brain, heart and muscle frequencies (0–250 cycles per second), and identify data coming from this second electromagnetic system (which oscillates at 500–20,000 cycles per second, and maybe more as the machinery couldn't record any higher). This energy field is smaller in amplitude and higher in frequency than the brain-heart-muscle system, and eight to ten times faster. The millivoltage is between a half to a third as strong as that of a resting muscle. Changes in readings from this energy field, caused by sound or light, occurred before those in the body. Dr Hunt believes 'a person's primary response in this world takes place first in the auric field, not in the sensory nerves nor in the brain'. The field apparently increases when a person walks barefoot on grass, or takes a swim, or cold shower, 'probably because of the increased negative ions,' says Hunt.

At the physics department of the University of California in Los Angeles, Dr Hunt's research continued in the Mu room – a seven-foot square environment in which the electromagnetic energy of the air can be manipulated. It's large enough to accommodate more than one person, adding an extra dimension to the experiments. There she discovered that if the electrical level was reduced, the 'aura' or 'energy field' became disorganized, and the subjects lost the sense of where their bodies were located in the space. When the electromagnetism was depleted, there was more inter-action between the fields of the people as each would

182

try to compensate by drawing on the energy of another in the room. The result was everyone's field became even more depleted.

All of this is fascinating enough, but there were more interesting effects to discover. If the electrical field in the room was increased, the auric fields returned to their usual state, and the people reported an expansion of consciousness and clarity of thought. When the electrical level in the room was normal, but the magnetism decreased, the people found simple co-ordination tests, such as putting a finger to the nose, difficult. With the electricity the same, but the magnetism *increased*, the subjects had vastly increased motor ability, being able to lean over at an extraordinary angle, and to balance on the toes of one foot.

Working concurrently with clairvoyants, Hunt discovered that when the auric field was depleted in the Mu room, a fishnet effect of energy could be seen flowing through the whole body. The pattern of the flow did not correspond with the meridian lines of classical Chinese medicine, for example, but seemed more to follow the path of connective tissue.

Dr Hunt also carried out research involving rolfers: therapists who deeply manipulate the connective tissue of a body. Such manipulation can cause a person to feel emotions, see pictures in their mind, and remember incidences in the past. It was found that if a subject experienced imagery – spontaneous pictures – there was a back-and-forth energy shift between the throat and brow chakras. Memory appears to be related to chakra, or energy-centre, activity.

Many other eminent scientists have tried to measure the electromagnetic field, starting in 1845 with German inventor Karl von Reichenbach who called it an 'odic force'; Russian physicist Vladimir M. Inyushin who referred to 'bio-plasma'; Dr Harold Burr, Yale professor of neuro-anatomy, who in *Blueprint for Immortality* spoke of 'life fields'; and Robert Becker MD, co-author of *The Body Electric*, amongst others. There have also been those who have captured the energy in photographic form, notably Semyon and Valentina Kirlian. Many of the electromagnetic researchers worked in relative obscurity, but today on many a high street you can have your aura visually recorded by 'aura imaging' or Kirlian photography cameras.

THE SUBTLE BODIES

Theosophical literature states that there are three bodies aside from the physical. They are presented here not as fact, but as a sounding-board or framework we can use to think more deeply about the subject of multi-dimensional bodies.

THE ETHERIC BODY OR 'THE BODY OF LIGHT'

- It is the blueprint upon which the physical body is built; the densest of the subtle bodies.

- It is a field of energy that exists within the same space as the physical body, and interpenetrates it.

- The field is composed of many threads of energy, with light and force: the body of light.

- It vitalizes the physical body.

- As in a web, it connects us to all parts of the universe; it connects us to higher realms.

- It has a three-fold action: it receives energy; it assimilates energy; it transmits energy.

- The threads of energy criss-cross through our etheric body and energy centres or chakras occur where many lines cross. There are thought to be seven main ones – five along the line of the spine and two in the head – plus many minor chakras.

THE ASTRAL BODY OR 'EMOTIONAL BODY'

- There are seven subplanes of astral matter which, in different proportions and density, form a parallel world to the physical which it inter-penetrates; each type of physical matter attracts astral matter of the same density.

- It is composed of very fine substance, with colours, and is constantly moving.

- It is where the feelings, emotions and passions are expressed; and acts as a bridge between the physical brain and the mind.

- When a person dies, their consciousness withdraws into the astral body, and continues its journey on the astral plane. An alive person can 'leave their body' temporarily, and go 'astral travelling'.

- The aura is the manifestation of the astral body, and extends from the surface of the physical body to various degrees, from a few inches to feet, yards or further. The aura can be seen as colour, and felt.

THE MENTAL BODY

- It is an ovoid mist which encloses all the other bodies, and has very fine colours.

- It interacts strongly with astral matter.

- It is very much affected by everything in our environment.

- A person controls the fineness or the density of their mental body by the quality of their thoughts; spiritual thoughts produce higher vibrations.

Auras are an aspect of our natural selves, and of the natural world. There is nothing weird or magical about them. Some people can see and feel them and some can't; this has less to do with any special powers of perception than with our desire to experience them, and our application to that goal. Here then are some ways to expand your vision and sense of touch.

The first exercise involves trying to see a phenomenon Wilhelm Reich, Austrian psychoanalyst, called 'orgone dots', and theosophical literature calls 'vitality globules'. One of the best descriptions came from Jirij Moskvitin in *Essay on the Origin of Thought* where he talked about brilliant sparks of dancing light, describing them as having tiny 'tails'. These light particles dart through the atmosphere in all directions, and the easiest way to see them is in daylight against a light blue sky.

To see them, another way of looking is required, rather as with 'magic eye' pictures which appear at first like a disorganized but repetitive pattern of colour. To see these, the eyes are crossed, or made to focus differently, but to see the shimmering light particles, you need to get beyond normal vision, not by going cross-eyed, but instead by focusing in the distance, as if you were looking for a spaceship in the far blue yonder. The first thing you'll see is little grey or see-through wiggly bits, which are on the surface of the eye and are probably some kind of dust. Then, going beyond them, some people see a watery effect, as if watching water running downwards in a wave-pattern on a piece of glass. Going beyond that, you begin to see small dancing flashes of light that seem to flicker on and off, but which can be followed and seen to be individualized particles continuing in a vitalized course. These globules appear like gold or silver, which may be the light reflecting off them, and some have very light translucent colours. They can be seen even from an aircraft window, and at that altitude they appear to be larger and clearer. Once you have seen light globules it becomes much easier to understand that the atmosphere is full of energy and actually quite dense.

If you spray essential oils into the air, the light globules are attracted to the aroma molecules and combine with them. To try this yourself, don't use the usual spray/misting method which involves water, but use instead a small perfume sprayer and pure undiluted essential oils. Watching the attraction of aroma molecules and dancing light is an interesting experience and makes me wonder what relationship they have. There is certainly a great deal yet to learn. Intriguingly, the French National Centre for Scientific Research, in conjunction with the National Centre for Space Studies, have carried out research which shows, according to Annick Le Guerer in *Scent*, 'that aromatic molecules are one of the basic components of the interstellar space in which new stars are constantly being formed. This interstellar "atmosphere" or gas is also the almost-direct source of the atoms of which we ourselves, along with the earth and the other planets, are made.'

To Feel Your Own Aura

First, with both hands opposite each other, move the hands quickly in a repeated chopping movement, with one hand going down while the other goes up (body therapists know this movement as 'hacking'), about four inches apart, in the air in front of you. Then run a hand up your arm, about three inches away. It will be easier now to feel the electrical pull.

To See Your Own Aura

Carry out the chopping movement as above, then place a hand over a piece of white or light-coloured paper. In the right light, you may be able to see your aura as a thin layer of light. When we connect with things, as when picking them up, the aura of the body extends to enfold the object, so the white light will be seen not only around the fingers, but also the pen or whatever has been brought into the field.

You can play with this energy field, moving the object slowly and watching the auric field enlarge and soften as it drags behind. I've watched this interaction with the human energy field using leaves, flowers and, of course, essential oils. This phenomenon raises all kinds of questions, but it may explain why some people 'get along' with some machines and some don't: perhaps the electromagnetic energy field of people differs enough to have different effects on machines. Perhaps too, it goes some way towards explaining how psycho-metrists work. These are sensitives or clairvoyants who can hold a piece of jewellery or an object belonging to another person and 'read' it, by relating the emotions and experiences of the person it belongs to. They may be tapping into the energy field which still lingers from the owner – a field which, if it can store information, must be rather 'intelligent'.

Aura Fluffing

Agitating the aura makes it become clearer and lighter. This is a kind of auric maintenance, as if dusting it off. The movement is a fluffing or flapping of the hands, moving them vigorously in the area five or six inches above the surface of the body.

Aura fluffing may have been what some of the ancient traditions did when 'working' in this area; such as when Native Americans fan or wave a feather in the auric field, as part of the smoke rituals, including the use of smudge sticks; or when African shamans wave a bunch of herbs or a rattle near the body of a person.

One interesting aspect of aura fluffing is that it can reveal 'referred pain syndrome' – when pain appears in one part of the body although it has its source in another. If the aura is fluffed, for example, around an area of burning pain in the shoulder and neck, that pain may relocate (or appear to relocate) as a contraction in a muscle under the scapula, the shoulder blade. When the true original site of any problem can be located a more accurate treatment can be applied to it.

Aura fluffing dissipates the density of it briefly, allowing it to rebalance itself, cleansed and energized.

ESSENTIAL OILS AND THE HUMAN AURIC FIELD

Having worked with essential oils in therapeutic practice for so many years, and seen how they can affect the human aura, it was a great pleasure to watch their dynamic interactions through Polycontrast Interface Photograph (PIP), invented by Harry Oldfield, joint author of *The Dark Side of the Brain*. As well as taking images of the energy field of essential oils on the end of a smelling strip, a few of which are shown elsewhere in this book, we watched the essential oils interacting with the head, or hand and arm, or whole body. The energy of the essential oil radiates outward from the drop of that oil, touching upon the human aura and enlivening it.

The colour photographs reproduced in this book show the effect when a drop of essential oil is placed in the palm of the hand, and the auric field is seen to be far more vibrant, colourful and wider, than in the control situation when the subject is photographed with no essential oil.

Essential oils are a way of connecting cosmic energy to us. Plants take the energy of the sun and transform it, through photosynthesis, into the food-energy upon which all animals rely. Essential oils are the concentrated form of that sun-energy, and are, as can be seen from their auric pictures, highly energetic. Their vibrations can, by close association and harmonic vibration, transfer to us the ultimate source of that energy: cosmic power.

Using essential oils in the auric field brings into it a new energy. The colours of the aura become brighter and clearer, while a shift in the density of the aura, and the energy above the chakras, can be felt. If

190

the vibration of a person is low for any reason, such as a depressed mental state or ill-health, the essential oils can stir or agitate the auric field, stimulating it to reorganize itself into a state of harmony. The simple way to look at this is to say it 'lifts' the spirit, by raising the vibration. But it is not essential oil itself that causes the lift in spirits because the human organism does that for itself. What the essential oils do is, as it were, clear the auric quagmire in which we may have got stuck, allowing us freedom to shift our perspective, change our spiritual position, and move on to a higher state of being.

You know when sometimes a TV screen is out of sync, and the colours are not all in the right location, and there's a shadow around the images? By adjusting the aerial, we bring the images back into sync; locked together in the proper position so a coherent whole results. Essential oils seem to have the same effect on the human aura 'bodies', bringing them into sync, locked together in a harmonious whole. Harmonized in this way, we are more able to get in touch with our higher selves, our spiritual core, the source of our strength.

Choosing Essential Oils for Subtle Energy Work

There is a flow of energy, not only between essential oils and people, but between people and essential oils; it's a two-way street. When choosing essential oils at any time, then, we need to consider the source of those oils in terms not only of the plant species, location it was grown, growing and distillation conditions and so forth, but the human source of the mental energy that also affects these highly sensitive products of nature. In a way, one could suspect a crystalline action here, in that the essential oils seem not only to transfer energy, but to absorb and hold it, just as a crystal can hold and give out information. (Think of the first 'crystal radios', and the computer revolution in Silicon Valley, California; silicon is crystalline.) This phenomenon is well known to scientists who increasingly study crystals with great interest. There's a rumour circulating in some scientific circles that NASA currently has a programme in place where, in 'the black room', a huge crystal sits in a pool of purified water, from which information is transferred by the water-memory mechanism, and from which a computer picks up the informational 'bytes' and records them. Scientists watch as information seeps out of the crystal, in much the same way as archaeologists have watched clay tablets with cuneiform writing being dug out of the ground. There is a language, both on the clay tablets and in the crystal. Deciphering the information is, of course, another matter. Archaeologists have over the years successfully worked on many ancient languages and today scientists are working on the even more ancient code: the language of the universe that is hidden in crystals.

If we think of essential oils as liquid crystals, we should also ask ourselves what information has been absorbed by them in terms of energetic-transference – including other people's thought-forms. Essential oils have many qualities, only some of which we know well and appreciate. Their chemistry is best understood, and this is how essential oils are usually defined. At University College, London, Dr Luca Turin has been working on the vibration rate of aromatic materials, which is a feature of their chemistry. He believes it is the vibration of an aroma molecule that makes it 'smell' a certain way, rather than its molecular shape – which was until recently the usual explanation for the smell-mechanism (i.e. the shape of the aroma molecule 'locks' into an olfactory receptor which sends a message to the brain). Establishing the vibration rate of an aroma molecule involves electron-tunnelling spectroscopy, and building up a database of the frequencies of essential oils will take years, according to Turin.

When working with the aura and chakras, the vibration rate of essential oils may be more important than their chemistry, although they are of course related. Another aspect of their chemistry, or rather their molecular shape, is their ability to refract light – either to the left, to the right, or not at all.

The electrical frequency of essential oils can be measured in megahertz, although the reading changes dramatically depending on who has handled the oil. At present, it remains an inexact science, but one of great potential for working with auras and chakras, and the physical body; when these can also be routinely measured and compared to an optimum scale.

Some people lay great store on the colour of essential oils for subtle energy therapy. The colour of oils can vary quite considerably between different species; from clear to yellow, orange, red, brown, green and bright blue. These are one of the most obvious differences between essential oils, and colour has its own vibration, but this is actually a very complex subject, and is discussed in Chapter 10: Energetic Aromatherapy.

Another difference between essential oils is their viscosity, which leads to an area of difference – evaporation rate – which has an importance when working with the human energy fields. The aura is a part of ourselves that is more connected to the spiritual realms than is our physical body. When thinking in energetic terms, we talk about 'grounding' a person who might be too 'spaced out', almost as if they could float off into the sky; or about 'centring' a person whose energy is dissipated and all over the place; or about 'lightening up' a person who is too 'heavy' energetically.

There's little point in using a grounding oil on someone who is already grounded to the spot, or lightening up someone who is already so light they are practically floating through the ceiling. Few of us have this last problem, however, and indeed, are seeking to 'lighten up', in the sense of realizing spiritual potential. Really, we want to seek balance, and find the spiritual core that is at the heart of that balance.

The evaporation rate of essential oils tells us something about their quality in terms of energetic frequency. It's not the whole story, but a part of it which needs to be considered. In perfumery, the evaporation rate of essential oils is categorized in three ways: top note for quick evaporation; middle note for average rate of evaporation; and base note for slow evaporation, the aroma that most endures. When two or more essential oils are blended together the story becomes more complex, so in a particular perfume, for example, an essential oil might be classified as one of the components in the 'middle note', and in another perfume it may be a 'top note'. Everything is relative, and when blending essential oils for energetic work that is certainly true.

Each essential oil has its top note, middle note and base note. You can experience this yourself by putting a drop of any oil on your skin and sniffing it immediately, five minutes later, half an hour later and so on. Close your eyes and feel how deep each aroma can be.

To compare the evapor...
essential oils you will need...
These can be made out of any...
or even out of natural undyed m...
essential oil on three strips, choo...
the three different evaporation-rat...
keep coming back to the strips over a...
see how their aromas change. The quic...
ation rate, the quicker the aroma m... ...ave
released into the air – and the quicker th... ...an move
through and influence the auric field.

Evaporation Rates within the Auric Field

TOP NOTE	MIDDLE NOTE	BASE NOTE
Aniseed	Bay	Balsam de Peru
Artemisia	Black Pepper	Benzoin
Basil	Cardamom	Cistus
Bergamot	Cedarwood	Galbanum
Cajuput	Chamomile German	Myrrh
Caraway	Chamomile Maroc	Orris Root
Chamomile Roman	Cinnamon Leaf	Patchouli
Citronella	Clary Sage	Sandalwood
Coriander	Clove Bud	Styrax
Eucalyptus Globulus	Cypress	Valerian
Fennel (sweet)	Geranium	Vetiver
Fir	Ginger	
Frankincense	Helichrysum (Italian	
Juniper	Everlasting)	
Lavender	Hyssop	
Lemon	Jasmine	
Mandarin	Lemongrass	
Neroli	Marjoram (sweet)	
Niaouli	Melissa	
Orange	Nutmeg	

Peppermint
Petitgrain
Pine

Rose Otto
Spearmint

Oregano
Palma Rosa
Parsley Seed
Rose Maroc
Rosemary
Rosewood
Sage
Tagetes
Thyme
Turmeric
Violet Leaf
Yarrow
Ylang Ylang

Using Essential Oils in the Auric Field

Method 1

Put 1 drop of neat essential oil in the centre of the palm of one hand, rub the hands together, and smooth around the outside of the body. Start on the side of the body, from the feet, working to the top of the head. Then repeat the movement on the front of the body, feet to head; then on the back, feet to head.

Method 2

Use the essential oils in the spray/mister method, spraying around the body and over the top of the head. With this method, it is preferable to first combine your essential oils, making a synergistic blend, and leave them for seven days in a peaceful place, away from electromagnetic activity such as electrical equipment. On the eighth day, using a new perfume mister, put in one ounce of the purest water you can get, which should come in a glass, not a plastic, bottle. Add the essential oils and shake well.

ESSENTIAL OILS TO ENERGIZE	ENERGIZING AURA-CLEANSING SPRAY	
Lemon		
Pine	Pine	4 drops
Fir	Spruce	5 drops
Spruce	Fir Needle	5 drops
Eucalyptus	Basil	3 drops
Peppermint	Lemon	3 drops
Basil		
Coriander		

ESSENTIAL OILS TO HARMONIZE	HARMONIZING AURA-CLEANSING SPRAY	
Geranium		
Lavender		
Petitgrain	Geranium	4 drops
Mandarin	Juniper	2 drops
Clary Sage	Petitgrain	6 drops
Ginger	Orange	6 drops
Fennel	Fennel	1 drop
Cistus		
Juniper		
Orange		

ESSENTIAL OILS TO AWAKEN THE HIGHER SELF	SPIRITUAL CONNECTION AURIC-FIELD SPRAY	
Frankincense	Galbanum	1 drop
Neroli	Frankincense	4 drops
Rose	Rose	7 drops
Jasmine	Jasmine	2 drops
Linden Blossom	Neroli	7 drops

In the auric field, colours are often seen. They are said to reflect the physical, mental and spiritual aspects of a person. A great deal has been written about this, and a summary of that information is below:

Collective Data Regarding Auric Colours – ancient and recent texts

Generally, it is thought these colours indicate:

Red *Physicality*	**Pain; muscular problems; inflammation; strong emotional states.**
Orange *Creativity*	**Strong imagination; emotional; feelings; weeping.**
Yellow *Rationality*	**Strong-willed; frustration; intellectualism, logical; analytical.**
Green *Harmony*	**Harmony; rested; balanced; reconciliation with past hurts; letting go.**
Blue *Peace*	**Peace; strength; calm; at ease; recognizing true self.**
Violet/Purple *Mysticism*	**Connecting to higher consciousness; connecting to true self.**
White *Spirituality*	**Transformation and meeting with the spirit.**

Chapter Nine

VIBRATIONAL AROMATHERAPY

There is nothing less scientific than to deny something because it cannot be explained.

Saying, quoted by DR JEAN VALNET in
The Practice of Aromatherapy

Aromatherapy *is* vibrational, as it utilizes tools which each have an individual vibration – the aromatic essential oils – that affect living, vibrational people. When I trained in physical therapy and phytotherapy in mainland Europe, more years ago than I care to remember, we were taught vibrational theories, as Rudolph Steiner, spiritual scientist, had great influence there. Others talked about vibrational aromatherapy in their particular fields, such as Marguerite Maury in the field of rejuvenation. Looking back now at the teaching material supplied to students in the early days of aromatherapy, it's clear that vibrations were very much part of the language and concepts taught.

The roots of modern aromatherapy can be found in the intellectual life of Europe in the 1960s, which was very open-minded to the holistic view, not only of the person, but of nature and the universe in general. Wholeness was discussed in the broadest of terms. In those early days, it was a therapy generally reserved for the wealthy who could afford the luxury of visiting the private European clinics. Arnold Taylor brought Maury to England to teach, and under the influence of her style and practice, which included massage and body-work, aromatherapy developed.

As aromatherapy became more generally available, there was a need to validate it by focusing on the physically obvious medicinal qualities of essential oils – and there are hundreds of research papers quantifying the various properties of them. Science can now see how aromatherapy works; that there are established physiological mechanisms at work. Moreover, from other more recent work in the area of brain chemistry, science can even explain how aromatherapy can make a person feel good emotionally. All this is a long way from how things were at the outset, when the term 'aromatherapy' was equated with 'nice-smells-make-you-feel-good-airy-fairy-psychological-nonsense-and-not-only-that-it's-good-for-the-skin'!

Essential oils use is now understood to be something rather more scientifically interesting than 'perfume'. Aromatherapy has gone through this period of acceptance, consolidating the facts established by scientific research with actual practical results, leaving unsaid a whole aspect of our work that could broadly be put under the term vibrational aromatherapy. Energetics is what holds it all together.

Those of us who learnt aromatherapy when it was seen as a body, mind and spirit – whole person –

therapy have always discussed it in terms of vibration and frequency, and some of us have taught it in that way. People who came into the profession when it was going through its very pragmatic, scientific stage, may have by-passed these important aspects. The latest group joining the profession come to it knowing they have to learn the scientific-medical facts, but also the vocabulary of energetic aromatherapy – auras, chakras, subtle bodies, energy exchange; these terms are now in common usage. There is, however, nothing new about vibrational, frequency or energetic aromatherapy. It's been talked about for decades, and known about ever since people mixed fragrant plants and oils together and used them on their bodies, which was tens of centuries ago.

'Vibrational aromatherapy' is not something that can be practised alone because it *includes* 'physical aromatherapy' and 'emotional aromatherapy' – they are integral to each other, part of a single whole. To be a 'holistic aromatherapist' you have to know all about the physical, emotional and spiritual – in terms of both body and oil. It is not therefore an easy option, although I daresay there are those who will set up practice as 'energetic' or 'vibrational' aromatherapists on the basis of the idea that 'all illness starts in the etheric'. It doesn't matter where the illness starts, the point is that it is there – manifesting in the physical, mental, emotional or spiritual, or all four. To treat a person energetically, all aspects of a person must be understood. Energetic therapies cannot be short cuts by-passing the physical, because vibration *is* part of essential oils and the physical body. You can't ignore it. The subtle and physical bodies of a person work together like the printer's primary colours – one does not make sense without the other, and you need all the colours, or 'bodies', to see the whole. Vibrational or energetic aromatherapy *is* aromatherapy.

THE CHAKRAS

In the etheric body there are centres of energy, sometimes described as wheels or vortexes. There are seven main chakras and twenty-one minors. Healers often bring one of the minor – the spleen – chakras into the main group of seven because the spleen is so directly involved in the immune system and in healing the physical body. The main chakras are said to be related to the physical body in the following way:

Crown Centre	pineal gland (or some believe pituitary)
Brow Centre	pituitary gland (or some believe pineal), eyes and brain
Throat Centre	speech and hearing, nervous system, thyroid gland, lungs and bronchial tubes, digestive tract
Heart Centre	heart and lungs
Solar Plexus	stomach, digestive system
Sacral Centre	genital system
Base Centre	kidneys, excretion, adrenal glands

The 21 Minor Chakras

2 at the front of both ears, midway between the upper ear and the ear lobe
2 above each breast
1 where breast bone meets
2 in both palms of the hands
2 in both soles of the feet
2 at the outer corner of the eyes

2 at the gonad glands
1 close to the liver
1 by the stomach
2 by the spleen
2 back of both knees
1 connected with vegus gland, near the thymus gland
1 close to the solar plexus

BODY SCANNING

By scanning the body you can determine areas of the body that are misaligned or lacking in healthy energy flow. The hands are held a couple of inches above the skin and skimmed over the body to feel the general state of the aura, and to locate areas that are particularly hot, cold or even clammy. The chakras are most clearly felt as different, having above their location an energy which differs from person to person. There is no substitute for actual practice in scanning, by which comparisons can be made of the different feel of auras and chakras. The aura can be felt two inches above the surface of the body, and the chakras at around six to eight inches.

The body has an electromagnetic field that can be registered by mechanical equipment. The therapist can become a living form of that kind of equipment, with practice. One day all therapists may make scanning a preliminary procedure to hands-on therapy, in much the same way as neurologists nowadays routinely attach electrodes to the surface of bodies to help them make a diagnosis when once such equipment was totally unknown. If we, the therapists, were inert, we couldn't body scan; as it is, we are ourselves electrically sensitive and mechanically able to pick up energy, if we have been tuned into the practice.

Body scanning simply involves running the palms of both hands over the body of a person, looking for changes in the energy field. This obviously has to be done with great awareness, and I feel it helps to very slightly bounce the hands to feel what resistance is there. If, for example, you feel a hot spot over a shoulder, it could indicate pain or injury; perhaps an old injury that is still manifest in the auric field. Such injuries may not be bothering the person now, today, but when they are fatigued at some time in the future, or under physical, emotional or spiritual pressure, this old pain may return to the body, even if the injury or wound has healed physically. Old wounds can come back to haunt us if, in reality, they never went away – they were stored in the subtle body under 'unfinished business'. Working in the subtle body not only identifies such lingering problems, it is the route through which to transform them, by clearing and strengthening the energy field. Chronic physical pain that just will not go away often responds well to anti-inflammatory essential oils, such as chamomile, used in the energetic field, preliminary to physically working on the body.

When scanning a body, essential oils can be placed on the hand, which is moved in slow, small circles over the area, hovering just above it. Then, after working on such an area, wash your hands before continuing with the scan. Moving over the body and clearing as much as you possibly can within the subtle body can often release long-buried physical injuries, emotional crisis and trauma. Gradually, layer by layer, impediments holding the client back from complete wellness appear to dissipate, and the person's physical body will be better able to respond to any physical treatment subsequently applied.

All therapists work with the aura and chakras, even if they don't realize it. Every client comes to us with an energy profile. We may talk about it in generally accepted terms, such as 'He has a high energy level,' or 'He's hyper,' or 'Her energy level is very low – she needs a boost.' What we are talking about here is a frequency that can now be measured by sophisticated equipment. This energy is subtle, a quality of the energy field that is unseen by the naked eye, but tangible nonetheless. We might find ourselves saying of a person operating from one chakra area more than the others, 'His emotional pain is deep in the belly,' or 'Her heart is broken,' or 'His head rules his heart.' All these are imbalances. Ideally, a person needs all their chakras, all their body areas and energies, working in a vibrant, clear way, unfettered by emotional and physical pain. Through no fault of their own, only circumstances, people may have become imbalanced in terms of energy. Perhaps their parents were emotionally cold which disallowed the flowering of a warm and vibrant heart, and subsequently, a less active heart chakra developed. People can become imbalanced for countless reasons; our job is to provide the environment in which energy balance and healing can take place.

To begin with, simply look for the general energy level, and work to balance that. With experience, you'll come to know the energy of the various chakras, and be able to see which have an excess of energy or a depletion. You can look for heat, cold, lack of energy, excess of energy, and something very tangible, the *feel* of the aura, which can, in cases of impoverished mental and emotional habits or ill health, be felt as a clammy, gooey cloud.

Chakras relate to particular vertebrae, which in turn relate to particular nerves and organs. By feeling the chakra-energy, you can often cross-reference, and question the client about the health of relevant areas of the body. People do not mean to hold information back; they might not think it very important, having more pressing problems, or they might simply have forgotten. By scanning the aura above the surface of the body, you have another diagnostic tool at your disposal which, with good communication with a person, can often reveal problems hidden deep within the body.

Chakras and their Related Vertebrae and Physical Body Areas

CHAKRA	LOCATION	VERTEBRA	NERVES AFFECT:	PHYSICAL DISORDERS:
Crown Chakra	Situated at fontanelle Affects to 1C	1C	Blood supply to the head; scalp; bones of the face; brain; pituitary gland; inner and middle ear; sympathetic nervous system	Headaches; anxiety; insomnia; nervous breakdown; amnesia; chronic tiredness; dizziness/vertigo; high blood pressure; migraine
Brow Chakra	Situated at atlas Affects 1C to 3C	2C	Eyes and optic nerves; sinuses; mastoid bones; auditory nerve; forehead; tongue	Sinus problems; deafness; allergies; eye conditions; earache; feeling faint
		3C	Face bones; cheeks; teeth; trifacial nerve; outer ear	Neuralgia; neuritis; eczema; skin complaints
		4C	Lips; mouth; nose; eustachian tube	Sinus problems; adenoids; hay fever; anosmia; lip ulceration; nose polyps
Throat Chakra	Situated at 5C Affects 3C to 7C	5C	Neck glands; vocal cords; pharynx	Laryngitis; throat conditions; swollen glands; frequent loss of voice; inability to swallow; goitre
		6C	Tonsils; neck muscles; shoulders	Neck pains; upper-arm pains; frequent coughing; tickles in throat; stiffness in shoulders

CHAKRA	LOCATION	VERTEBRA	NERVES AFFECT:	PHYSICAL DISORDERS:
		7C	Thyroid glands; bursae in the shoulders; the elbows	Bursitis; hyper-thyroidism; hormonal problems
		1T	Oesophagus and trachea; fingers; hands; wrists; arms up to the elbow	Asthma; breathing difficulties; shortness of breath; frequent coughing; aches or pains in lower arms and hands; backache
Heart Chakra	Situated at 2T Affects 7C to 3T	2T	Heart; heart valves; coronary arteries; thymus gland	Heart conditions; chest pains; angina; circulation problems; high cholesterol; palpitations
		3T	Lungs; bronchial tubes; pleura; chest; breast	Respiratory problems; lung congestion; breathing difficulties; chest and breast pain; mastitis; breast cysts
		4T	Gall bladder; common duct	Gall bladder disorders, including stones; persistent viral infection; digestive problems; inability to absorb nutrients

CHAKRA	LOCATION	VERTEBRA	NERVES AFFECT:	PHYSICAL DISORDERS:
Solar Plexus Chakra	**Situated at 5T** **Affects 3T to 8T**	**5T**	Blood; liver; solar plexus	Liver conditions; low blood pressure; anaemia; circulatory conditions; auto immune diseases; rheumatism; persistent viral infections; blood disorders; emotional crises
		6T	Stomach	Digestive problems; frequent indigestion; heartburn; dyspepsia; lack of appetite; hiatus hernia; nausea
		7T	Pancreas; islets of Langerhans; duodenum	Ulceration; gastric conditions; diabetes; digestive problems; hormonal disorders; certain viral infections
Spleen Chakra	**Situated at 8T Affects 8T to 12T**	**8T**	Spleen; diaphragm	Lowered immunity; blood disorders; anaemia; emotional crises
		9T	Adrenal glands	Hormonal conditions; inflammatory conditions; immune system problems; stress; tension

CHAKRA	LOCATION	VERTEBRA	NERVES AFFECT:	PHYSICAL DISORDERS:
		10T	Kidneys	Kidney problems, including stones; chronic tiredness; nephritis; diabetes; drowsiness; nausea
		11T	Kidneys; ureters	Urinary problems; cystitis; prostate problems; hyper-tension; cysts
		12T	Lymphatic circulation; small intestines; fallopian tubes	Crohn's disease; parasitic infections; irritable bowel syndrome; abdominal cramps; vomiting; nausea; lowered immunity; circulatory problems; infertility (female); salpingitis
		1L	Large intestines (colon); inguinal rings	Diverticular disease; colitis; constipation; excessive gas; diar-rhoea; intestinal cramping; varicose veins
		2L	Abdomen; appendix; upper leg; caecum	Abdominal cramps; breathing difficulties; excessive acid; varicose veins

CHAKRA	LOCATION	VERTEBRA	NERVES AFFECT:	PHYSICAL DISORDERS:
		3L	Uterus; ovaries or testicles; sex organs; bladder; knee	Menstrual problems; endometriosis; menopausal problems; infertility; joint problems; impotence (male); haemorrhoids
		4L	Muscles of the lower back; sciatic nerve; prostate gland	Prostate problems, including difficulty in urinating (male); back pain; sciatic pain; lumbago; leg ache and pains
Sacral Chakra	Situated at 5L Affects 12T to sacrum	5L	Lower legs; ankles; feet; toes	Poor circulation in lower torso and legs; oedema in legs; weakness in legs; leg cramps; sciatic pain
		Sacrum	Buttocks; hip bones	Sciatic pain; sacroiliac mis-alignments; spinal curvature; skeletal conditions
Base Chakra	Situated at coccyx Affects from 9T to coccyx	Coccyx	Rectum; anus	anal itching (puritus); haemorrhoids; anal fissures; con-stipation; uterine prolapse; prostate problems

The chakras listed on the left relate to the conditions at the far right, or to their related conditions. Where there is deficiency or excess in the energy/function of one chakra, it will be compensated for by the opposite action in the adjacent chakras. The spleen chakra, usually considered a 'minor' chakra, has been included here because it actually has a major action on the physical-energetic body. It often over-links with the solar-plexus chakra, there being a close energy-compensation action between the two – which is why when the solar plexus is depressed by impoverished emotions, the spleen is given more work to do. In order for the upper chakras to resonate with clarity, the lower chakras need balancing first, providing a strong scaffolding for the clear reception and transmission to and from the upper chakras. The radiation of energy from any particular chakra blends with the energy of those adjacent to it, to a greater or lesser degree depending on the proximity of the adjacent chakra.

Essential Oils for the Chakras

Crown Chakra Frankincense, Neroli, Rose

Brow Chakra Angelica Seed, Hyacinth, Juniper, Lemon, Pine, Rosemary

Throat Chakra Basil, Chamomile, Cypress, Hyssop, Linden Blossom, Peppermint, Petitgrain, Rosemary, Rosewood

Heart Chakra Bergamot, Geranium, Jasmine, Lavender, Mandarin, Melissa, Rose Maroc, Tangerine, Ylang Ylang

Solar Plexus & Spleen Chakras Black Pepper, Cardamom, Cedarwood, Coriander, Hyssop, Juniper, Lime, Marjoram

| **Sacral Chakra** | Benzoin, Cardamom, Clary Sage, Elemi, Fennel, Sandalwood |
| **Base Chakra** | Balsam de Peru, Myrrh, Patchouli, Rosewood, Thyme, Vetiver |

USING VIBRATIONAL AROMATHERAPY IN TREATMENT

Whether the treatment is professional or non-professional, it takes thought and planning. For those professionals who are contemplating incorporating energetic or vibrational aromatherapy into their practice, setting the right environment helps create an atmosphere of a spiritual haven, even in your usual practice room.

Music

Some therapists enjoy using music and others do not. It really depends on how the therapist feels rather than the client – unless, of course, the client dislikes your chosen tape. It's surprising how opinions vary on which music is relaxing and which is not, so do choose most carefully.

Sounds

Some therapists like to include sound, such as singing or crystal bowls, gongs, or tapes that claim to synchronize, or attune, the human aura. Sounds 'clear' a room or change the energy of a room very quickly. This is most often done at the beginning or end of an individual treatment, or the working day. For those who work as clinical aromatherapists, using anything other than their usual medical skills not only takes up valuable time, but also might seem just a little too New Age. Being in this situation myself and not wanting to use anything superfluous, I was told by a sound expert that sound memories, as vibration or sound waves, can become embedded in the fabric of buildings – which made me think about it in another way. Now, to clear away the conversations of the day, the 'informational clutter', I might ring a bell, clang a gong, or even simply strike a glass. Apparently that does the trick.

Colour

Colour – including white – is applied on the walls, of course, but it is equally present in towels, the couch, massage-table coverings, and in pictures and plants. Try to create a haven of peace and tranquillity that feels fresh and enlivening at the same time. Pictures and accessories can provide a splash of colour while the rest of the furnishings can be chosen to produce a peaceful feel. There are many helpful books on this subject.

Aromas

Constantly using different aromas in a room presents a real conundrum for many therapists. A person may have been treated for a rheumatic condition with oils that are a completely different requirement and aroma to those needed for the following person who has, say, an anxiety crisis regarding the inability to feel any type of spirituality – a common occurrence these days.

What can you do – especially as many rooms do not have a window that can be opened? Extractor fans used for five to ten minutes between treatments seem to be the most effective solution. Those with air-conditioning systems may find the atmosphere is effectively dealt with. An ionizer is another way in which an atmosphere can be changed. Background radiation is another consideration, and there are now several companies selling machines which are said to stabilize the frequencies, deflect them or neutralize the 'field incoherence'.

Accessories

According to *feng shui*, large crystals placed in corners of the room, and mirrors that face doors, deflect energy. Lots of green, living plants and running water also help. Flowers and floating candles in a bowl would pretty up any area. The lighting should be arranged so that it does not shine directly on the client.

Treatment

So the room is ready, the energies are right, the sound waves have been cleared and all is harmony and peace. The consultation is complete, and the planned treatment is compatible with the medical history and psychological profile, and an aromatherapy treatment with the additional vibrational work is to take place.

To begin with, the client should be lying on their front, so work can begin on their back. Hand scanning is used, and if an area of either hot or cold is located the energy can be harmonized by moving the palms of both hands in very slow circular movements over the area. Then the hands are gently lowered through the energetic field onto the body, and that position is held for a while. This area can then be worked on

215

directly using the essential oil blend already prepared for the client, before continuing with the body scan – if that is not yet finished – or normal treatment practice.

At what you judge to be the appropriate time, the chakras are balanced; starting very gently at the solar plexus where the emotions are centred. Beyond this, if using the chakras in a treatment, much depends on the particular client and condition. Although many people suggest working up the chakra system, or down, I personally first work downwards from the solar plexus to the sacrum, until balance is achieved; then from the top crown chakra, I work downwards towards the solar plexus, where any emotional problems can again be soothed and calmed, before then finally checking that all chakras, from base to crown, are in balance.

Many people are neglectful of one half of their body, or the other, depending on their personality, life situation and health, and this system helps in the awakening and acknowledging process. During the scanning and balancing procedure, physical problems such as muscular armoury, pain or misalignment can be corrected as far as possible, using the usual physical treatment methods.

When the client is turned over, on their back, treatment continues with scanning once again, when any ailments or energy still not in balance can be harmonized. The treatment should finish with the head being gently cradled in the hands.

The position of the chakras in relation to the vertebrae and their associated organs, and the sympathetic and para-sympathetic nervous systems, should be taken into account. Please refer to the chart on pages 207–11. Another factor in treatment is the emotional muscular sites – the places where particular emotions are held in the musculature, as shown in *The Fragrant Mind* (page 223). The emotions held in the muscles may in fact alter the energetic field and could give a false reading if not taken into account.

Essential oils appropriate to the mind, body, spirit and character of the person should be chosen with care, taking into account the psycho-spiritual aspects and interactions of the individual oils.

> Students make up their oils according to the same formulation, using the same essential oils, vegetable oils and bottles under the same atmospheric conditions. Yet when the finished products are compared, each one is slightly different. It is impossible for two people to reproduce exactly the same thing because each person has different hands and a different electromagnetic field, both of which influence the finished product.

> MICHELINE ARCIER, *Aromatherapy, Health and Beauty Care with Massage and Essential Oils*

Miasms

The man who invented modern homeopathy, Samuel Hahnemann (1755–1843), was the first to identify miasms, which are basic vibrational patterns of disease. Miasms are said to have their origin in the subtle or auric fields, and set up patterns in an individual's body, mind and personality, causing preset physical or emotional reactions or behaviour. The manifestation of miasms are through the subatomic, atomic, molecular, electromagnetic, biochemical, physiological and psychological energetic pathways. Some people believe miasms can be inherited genetically, or even transferred from one person to another by resonance – by being close to a person who has one. A miasm can also be acquired from our parents, or in the womb, through the intelligence of the genetic code, in cellular memory, through emotional trauma or pollution. They could be detected in the energetic field, and be mistaken for an energetic manifestation of a physical disorder. For example, you might detect bad energy flow in the lower half of the left leg and ask, 'Do you have circulation problems here?' The client says, 'No, never.' On further questioning, however, you may find that the grandfather had gangrene in the left leg, which was amputated at the knee, and that the father got mysterious pains in the same area whenever he got tired. This is what is meant by miasms: the carrying forward of physical and emotional pain, albeit in reduced form.

Energies

There is no doubt that essential oils affect the aura and chakras. However, they have a different influence, depending on the person on whom they are used, and the person using them, in terms of how their vibratory rates interact with the fragrance. For example, if the fragrance is of a higher frequency than the person using or administering the oil at that particular time then the interaction is going to be slower and at a different rate than it would be with persons who are clear-minded and full of energy. The vibrationary level of a person could be reduced by stress, ill health or even a particular mind-frame.

The essential oils do not themselves directly harmonize the aura or energy fields. The aromatic molecule's energy interacts with the energetic and subtle anatomy of the person; their fragrance molecules stirring, agitating, electrically boosting or in some other way stimulating the human energetic fields, allowing them to reorganize and harmonize *themselves*.

It could be that diffused oils also react in this way – weaving a way through the energetic field, affecting the physical through the olfactory nerves. Perhaps we smell with our energetic fields and, because of that, science finds it difficult to gather the information needed to decipher and decode how the sense of smell actually works, and how it has such a profound effect on our minds and spiritual sense of being.

Any treatment using energetics aims to align all bodily currents: physically, emotionally and spiritually. The physical affects the emotional and the psycho-spiritual connections, and the reverse is also true.

Healing the Spiritual Crisis

Many people today are suffering because of the psycho-spiritual aspects of life. Just getting from day to day is a major battle for many. And as time goes on life is getting harder, faster and more stressful. Life is no longer simple, and as we try to do the right thing by our family, friends, workmates and ourselves, we often find ourselves facing opposition from all manner of officialdom. How do we cope when half the world seems to be driven by non-spiritual factors?

All this often results in a psycho-spiritual crisis: 'What is the meaning of it all?' 'How can I go on?' A person might argue that their religion/movement/sect/belief has the answer. But, of course, in this day of global communication, there are many pathways to choose from.

Sometimes I watch TV and see programmes about the arms industry, or global warming, or people starving (when there is enough food to go around) and people dying through lack of medicines (when we could make more), and wonder if I am on the same planet as all this. We can say, 'We are all equal,' but in this real world, in many respects, we are not. Is it any wonder that we've all – every one of us – picked up on the vibrations and frequency of psycho-spiritual suffering? I see many people who feel a deep sense of help-lessness and powerlessness, no matter what their spiritual beliefs are.

So how are we to deal with it? There are some basic, preliminary steps, each one huge, and a great personal challenge:

1) Develop the core of love in our hearts so that it fills our being.
2) Forgive, as not to do so only hurts ourselves.
3) Release anger, as not doing so only sets up the body for disease.
4) Remove ourselves from any source of abuse, which depresses the spirit.

No spiritual crisis can be healed by another person. We can be guided, certainly, but ultimately only we can heal our own spiritual crisis by taking time to really enter into our inner-being, our inner-self. For me, essential oils have always been, in their own way, a reference point for focus. They allow me time and space for an inner search, and I use a special blend, unique to myself, to contemplate, think, forgive, and make the spiritual connection.

Fragrances help concentrate the mind, and change it from a confused cacophony of negativity into a stilled surety of harmony and peace. There within us is this quietude, and it can expand. We can even get beyond our own everyday concerns and perspective and see another's point of view. Moreover, fragrances are healing. The natural, God-given, fragrant plant material helps heal the psycho-spiritual connection and can allow us, if only for a brief moment or two, to be free enough to reach out mentally to our higher selves, guiding us beyond this plane of existence to understanding and love.

One very practical aspect of this process is that fragrance can be carried with us, anywhere. I've sniffed my special spiritual aroma from a handkerchief on rush-hour underground trains and on aeroplane flights. Wherever I am, and whatever is going on, I can immediately enter that place of super-awareness, far quicker than by any other route.

Finding a fragrance or making a blend you particularly enjoy is not hard. There are many essential oils to choose from, and finding a fragrance that has a special spiritual effect may take a little time but it's worth it.

Some people are afraid of the aromas, almost as if they fear connecting into their true selves, because aromas can be very illuminating and revealing. It is always possible the reason for this is that they don't like the aromas available to them but if the right aroma for them can be found, they'll love it deeply. We are talking here of potential psycho-spiritual barriers, once expressed to me in the following way: 'Intuitively I knew the aromas would bring me to a place within myself, where body and spirit meet, and I was frightened to reach that place because I was ashamed that I'd been so horrible in my life, and was terrified of what I would feel if my defences were let down. I could imagine it would be wonderful, but what if it wasn't?' This person, Allan, decided after a while that he did love the smells after all, and, having had a wonderful experience with them, chose a focusing spiritual oil blend for himself; to give comfort and to help him make contact with his higher self.

Choose your oils from the essential oil profiles, blend carefully or, to start off with, enlist the help of someone who has blending experience. Once discovered, keep the formula to yourself, because each blend, like each individual, will be unique – a personal refuge and connection to the fragrant heavens.

THE SEVEN MAIN CHAKRAS

FIRST CHAKRA

Modern name:
(Root or) Base chakra

Sanskrit name:
Muladhara or Guda chakra

Situated: Back of the rectum, coccyx

Colour: Red

Petals: Four energy vortexes

Element: Earth or solids

This chakra needs to be cleansed and purified both emotionally and physically before any of the others; it's the first to be activated.

The support chakra.

Physical Associations:
Kidneys, excretion, spine.

Associated Gland:
Adrenal glands.

Associated Emotions:
Fear, obsessive/compulsive behaviour, protective instincts.

Weakness:
Non-attachment, nervous instability.

SECOND CHAKRA

Modern name:
Sacral chakra

Sanskrit name:
Indra or Swada or
Svadasthan chakra

Situated: Near the sacral bone
(above first lumbar)

Colour: Orange
(Some older texts
say yellow)

Petals: Six energy vortexes

Element: Water

It controls the creation of the physical form.
Sexual energy and all its desires.

Physical Associations:
Sexual reproduction.
Balance between oestrogen, progesterone, testosterone.
Liquids within the body: blood, urine, lymph, mucus, semen.

Associated Glands:
Gonads: ovaries, testicles.

Associated Emotions:
Desire, jealousy.

Weakness:
Lust, addictions, anger, pride, aggression.

THIRD CHAKRA

Modern name:
Solar Plexus chakra

Sanskrit name:
Manipurak or Nabi chakra

Situated: Near the solar plexus at the umbilicus, seventh and eighth thoracic vertebrae

Colour: Yellow

Petals: Eight energy vortexes **Element:** Fire

Suggestive of the sun, which is also needed for the metabolism of plant and human life.

Physical Associations:
Stomach, digestive system, spleen.
Metabolism: keeps the balance between anabolic-katabolic (the building-up of simple material into complex substances and the breaking-down of complex substances into simple ones).
Heat regulation control.
Endocrine digestive processes, sugar metabolism, production of insulin.

Associated Gland:
Pancreas

Associated Emotions:
Warmth, nurturing, fiery nature.

Weakness:
Emotional instability, skin eruptions.

FOURTH CHAKRA

Modern name:
Heart chakra

Sanskrit name:
Anahata

Situated: Between the breasts, fifth thoracic

Colour: Green

Petals: Twelve energy vortexes
Element: Earth (air)
The protector and distributor of energy for the lower chakras.

Physical Associations:
Heart, blood circulation, lung, respiration, the immune system, thymosin hormones.
Touch/sensation.

Associated Gland:
Thymus

Associated Emotions:
Love, compassion, protectiveness.

Weakness:
Heart problems, over-protective, attachment, greed, anger.
Hyper-immune reactions including rheumatoid arthritis.

FIFTH CHAKRA

Modern name:
Throat chakra

Sanskrit name:
Kanth or Vishudhi chakra

Situated: Near the cervical plexus, third cervical vertebra

Colour: Blue

Petals: Sixteen energy vortexes

Element: Fire/Water/Air (ether)

It has an energy field known as *akash*, which keeps the lower energy-currents running smoothly and energizes rational thought.

Where intelligence focuses in creativity, especially of the spoken/written word.

Genital/reproductive system can be worked on from this centre.

Physical Associations:
Vocal cords, pulmonary and bronchial systems, nervous system.

Associated Glands:
Thyroid and parathyroid.

Associated Emotions:
Honesty or dishonesty, criticism.

Weakness:
Imbalances of all kinds: vertigo, allergies, anaemia. Menstrual problems. Sore throats, laryngitis.

SIXTH CHAKRA

Modern name:
Brow chakra

Sanskrit name:
Ajuna or Do Dal Kanwal chakra

Situated: Between the eyes in the middle of the forehead.

Colour: Purple or violet

Petals: Two energy vortexes

Element: Ether

'The third eye' – where mind and spirit meet, within the physical context.

The energy from this point spreads into every cell of the body.

All other chakras are dependent upon, and ruled by, this.

Cognition: consciousness and subconsciousness.

This area links the subtle energy field for the whole body.

Physical Associations:
The sense of smell. Brain, eyes, nose, ears.

Associated Glands:
Pituitary, pineal.

Associated Emotions:
Imagination, idealism, love.

Weakness:
Pessimism, self-pity. Migraine, sleeplessness, catarrh, sinus problems, hayfever.

SEVENTH CHAKRA

Modern name: Crown chakra

Sanskrit name: Sahasrara

Situated: Top of head, approached via base of skull

Colour: White or white-gold

Petals: Twelve energy centres

Element: None: Some say magnesium, speech or spirit

All energies running through subtle meridians in our bodies – such as *ch'i* and prana – stop here. It is thought meridians and the acupuncture points or nadirs were discovered through opening of the crown chakra and higher consciousness.

Physical Associations:
Malfunctions of pituitary gland.

Associated Glands:
Pineal, pituitary.

Associated Emotion:
Emotional imbalance.

Weakness:
Coma, epilepsy.

THE FRAGRANT SYMPHONY

Sound and fragrance are expressions of vibration, as is colour. All three have a similarity in that these vibrations can be put together, creating something that is more than the sum of the parts. Musical notes can be put together to create chords and melody; and several pigments can be put together to create new colours and beautiful pictures. Fragrance is similar: several aromas can be put together to create the fragrant symphony.

Blending is an art, accomplished in the world of fragrance by G. W. Septimus Piesse, author of *The Art of Perfumery* in 1856. He introduced the idea of thinking of fragrance in terms of musical notes and created a comparative scale, the 'Gamut of Odours':

Treble or G Clef		Bass or F Clef	
F	Civet	C	Rose
E	Verbena	B	Cinnamon
D	Citronella	A	Tolu
C	Pineapple	G	Sweet Pea
B	Peppermint	F	Musk
A	Lavender	E	Orris
G	Magnolia	D	Heliotrope
F	Ambergris	C	Geranium
E	Cedrat (Lemon)	B	Stocks and Pinks
D	Bergamot		(Pinks = Carnations)
C	Jasmine	A	Balsam of Peru
B	Mint	G	Pergalaria
A	Tonka Bean	F	Castor
G	Syringa (Mock Orange	E	Calamus
	Flower)	D	Clematis
F	Jonquil	C	Santal (Sandalwood)

E	Portugal (Orange)	B	Clove
D	Almond	A	Storax
C	Camphor	G	Frangipani
B	Southernwood	F	Benzoin
A	Vernal Grass (new hay)	E	Wallflower
G	Orange Flower	D	Vanilla
F	Tuberose	C	Patchouli
E	Acacia		
D	Violet		

Piesse wrote:

Scents, like sounds, appear to influence the olfactory nerve in certain degrees. There is, as it were, an octave of odours like an octave in music; certain odours co-incide, like the keys of an instrument. Such as almond, heliotrope, vanilla, and orange blossom blend together, each producing different degrees of a nearly similar impression. Again, we have citron, lemon, orange peel, and verbena, forming a higher octave of smells, which blend in a similar manner. The metaphor is completed by what we are pleased to call semi-odours, such as rose and rose-geranium for the half note; petty grain, neroli, a black key, followed by fleur d'orange . . .

Piesse then quotes a magazine article which made the following points: music follows a mathematical law dependent on nature, which doesn't waste power and becomes more simple the better it is understood. The final hypothesis was that 'the whole of the pleasures of the sense of smell will be found to depend upon cognate laws'.

In the future, as the science of vibrational aroma expands, we may discover new aromatic laws which can guide us when blending two or more fragrances –

in proportions that follow these underlying principles – to create a perfect harmony. In the meantime, we rely upon our deep knowledge and appreciation of individual aromas; our tuning in to their vibration and tone; and our knowing what can be joined together without there being a discordant note, or a smothering of one by another.

Think of an insensitive drummer, sitting behind a band, crashing away noisily, drowning out the other instruments. Essential oils can do the same thing – drown out the sounds of others in a blend. We did not invent or create essential oils, but when blending them, we are the composer, the conductor and the sound engineer. It is up to us to know the capacity and beauty of each instrument in our orchestra, and to know when it is time to bring each beautiful tool of the heavens into our symphony.

Chapter Ten

ENERGETIC AROMATHERAPY

Essential oils both give and receive energy. We've seen this in the PIP aura pictures of essential oils taken by Harry Oldfield, and some of us know it from our own experience. Essential oils can also be energetically measured by more conventional means – in megahertz – each MHz equalling 1,000,000 oscillations per second: the frequency of their vibrational motion. However, the MHz number arrived at by using specialist equipment does not really tell us very much because the frequency of any one essential oil is changed dramatically when it comes into contact with other energies – people, for example.

I took some essential oils to Bruce Tanio, an agricultural scientist and inventor, who has the apparatus to test these things. The reading from a rose bulgar was 28MHz, but after I'd held the bottle for a short while, its reading was 202MHz. That's quite a difference! Another bottle of rose bulgar, from another source, and held in another hand, might produce two readings dissimilar to my own. As Bruce remarked, 'There is no consistency in the frequency of essential oils.'

The vocabulary of energy work is expanding. Bruce

talks, for example, of 'a symphony of frequencies occurring in the cells', and a 'resonant harmonic factor'. As we know from the work of Dr Valerie Hunt, the energy field of a person extends outside the confines of the physical form. That field, and the body it encloses, can be changed by the introduction of other energy forces.

Sometimes these are not good for us, and there has been a great deal of publicity about the negative influences on human cells and psyche by, for example, cellular phones, microwaves and power cables. Another electrical influence on us is ions in the atmosphere – put simply, negative ions make us feel good and positive ions make us feel bad. Positive ions can be created seasonally in certain geographic locations, when a strong wind comes into contact with a mountain range with a particular shape. This happens for a month each year in Geneva, Switzerland, and with the Santa Ana winds in California, for example, and it makes people feel irritable, even aggressive, and sometimes unwell – particularly with headaches, migraines, allergies, digestive and respiratory problems. Working at the University of California, Dr Hunt had the chance to record the fact that when the Santa Anas were blowing, the human energy field became small. She writes, 'It is as though the negative auric field splits away from the body, attracted by the high positive charge of the atmosphere.'

A high incidence of negative ions makes us feel good: vitalized and with a positive frame of mind. We can inhale negative ions while taking a shower, or when near a waterfall or sea, or on mountains, and discharge positive ions into the ground when walking barefoot on the grass. We can even purchase negative ions, or at least the 'ionizers' that create them. Dr

Hunt took some measurements with subjects on a mountain and near the sea and found the energy field expanded, and hypothesizes that this is due to the increased negative ions in the atmosphere there.

There is another way to positively affect the human energy field: by using essential oils, those vibrational marvels of nature. Many healers have been discovering this, and incorporate them in their practice. This is what this chapter is about: using essential oils for healing. The principles of working with energetic aromatherapy outlined here will apply to any healing modality.

If not trained in aromatherapy, don't use essential oils directly on the body of another person. When working with energy, there is absolutely no need. There are many other methods of using essential oils which are very effective for energy work, and are described throughout the following sections.

All aromas have the potential to evoke memories in a person, depending on what has happened to them in the past. The healer has no way of knowing which aromas may invoke a memory, and the clients themselves may not even know until they smell it. Those memories may not always be happy ones, and may be associated with someone the patient knows and has a hard time with, or even with someone who has passed on and for whom they are still grieving. Memories, either the clients' or healer's may alter the energetic response. The aromatic environment needs, then, to be either bland, or guided by a sensitive, conscious mind.

The haphazard or thoughtless introduction of aroma into the healing room can occur through the products we use on a daily basis – such as perfumed soaps, hand creams, deodorants, perfume, hair products – and through soap powders and fabric conditioners, in linen or towels for example. In some healing modalities, two or three people may be involved in the energetic work, and in these cases, aromatic overload could become a problem. Clients may in addition have an aversion to certain unnatural product ingredients and aromas. There are now many natural unfragranced personal-care products on the market, including glycerine soaps, and these could be used when healing.

A few people go to healers as a preventative 'work out' rather than because there is anything wrong with them. Most, however, go for a specific reason, or two. When choosing essential oils to work on a particular client, these reasons – their physical, emotional, mental or spiritual needs – must be taken into consideration. Energy work aims for flow and inter-action, and anything which facilitates this is welcome. Please refer to Chapter 11, where the therapeutic, emotional and spiritual qualities of essential oils can be found in their individual profiles. There are many oils to choose from. Before commencing, put a drop or just a smear of your chosen essential oil on the end of a smelling strip and ask the patient if they like it, or at least do not have an aversion to it.

Essential oils can also be used in another way: on the healer to increase their ability to work energetic-ally. Points and practical suggestions are made about this in the following different sections. Clearly though, if there is more than one healer, they will have to be consulted on the choice of essential oils used in room diffusers.

The refreshing tree essential oils – such as pine, spruce, fir and cypress – can be good in a waiting area, especially if electrical equipment is nearby, such as computers, clocks, radios, photocopiers, microwaves and the ubiquitous mobile phones. If using essential oils in a diffuser in the waiting room, consider the patients you are seeing that day, refer to the profiles, and then make a sensitive choice. Use only small amounts to create a light and gentle fragrant background.

ESSENTIAL OILS AND SPIRITUAL HEALING

Spiritual healers who 'lay on hands' may or may not actually touch the body. Most work in the auric field with their hands a few inches away from the surface. However, healers always say that the healing energies come from outside themselves, and that they are merely a channel for them. Most usually, the source of this healing energy is said to be God, universal energy or the cosmic intelligence. Essential oils can be incorporated into any form of subtle healing technique, by working within the subtle bodies of a person. As with all energetic aromatherapy, there is no need to apply essential oils directly on the skin.

When approaching any client, have nonjudgemental loving intention and clarity of thought – a clear idea of what you are setting out to achieve and how you are going to do it. You should know what physical, emotional and spiritual needs the client has from the client records, and will have your repertoire of hand positions and other particular healing practices. Using essential oils adds another layer to this energetic work, and on that level you also need to know how you are going to achieve your aim by learning about the oils in terms of their physical, emotional and spiritual properties – and the profiles in the next chapter will help you there. To intuit an essential oil, one first needs a wealth of information maintained in the psyche from which that inspirational knowledge can evolve.

Healers will be acutely aware that physical dysfunctions can be caused by intense anxiety and stress, for example, and there are enough essential oils to choose from that one can be found that will help with the emotional cause and physical symptom concurrently, allowing the spiritual to shine through. Not all illness is mind or emotion based. People get ill for all sorts of reasons that have nothing to do with them; such as toxic contamination at work, which might be chemical or electromagnetic and encountered recently or a long time ago; and accidental injury, which might be recent, or hardly remembered it was so far in the past.

You may want to consider spiritually cleansing your essential oils before using them. Please refer to Chapter 7. There are three main ways to use essential oils in spiritual healing:

- in the room (healing room or waiting room);
- in the auric field of the client;
- on yourself, the healer.

These involve different methods:

The Room

If you feel that using essential oils in the treatment room will interrupt your concentration, consider using them in the waiting room. The aromas will relax and open the hearts of people, making them more receptive to healing.

The usual type of diffuser or burner has a candle,

which should be extinguished if the room is left un-attended. Also available are electrical ceramic and fan models. Two or three drops are usually sufficient to provide the subtle fragrant background. Unless you want the energy to be very grounded, don't use myrrh or the other base vibrational or 'heavy' oils in a wait-ing room.

It's generally unnecessary to use blends while giving spiritual healing, which has its own dynamic flow. The essential oils are being used to facilitate that flow, by creating that space in which healing can take place, and singular oils have a simplicity and clarity which is appropriate now. The choice of singular oil can, of course, change over time.

In the Auric Field of the Client

Making an appropriate essential oil choice for the client from their general demeanour involves, as far as the individual healer's abilities allow, constructing a mental light-image of their physical, emotional and spiritual well-being, their subtle bodies, chakras, and aura. When this broader overview has emerged, and an increasingly broad knowledge of essential oils gained, more appropriate choices of essential oil can be made.

Choose one of the following method options, before commencing healing:

- Put 1 drop of essential oil on a small piece of white paper or cloth. Place it in the centre of the palm of a hand, then cover with the other hand. Rub the hands together lightly, then discard the paper.
- Wash your hands as usual before commencing treat-ment. Then half-fill a sink or bowl with water, add a drop or two of essential oil, and swish it around.

Rinse your hands in this, and lightly pat them dry.

- Have a prepared floral water. See Chapter 2 for Methods of Use. Spray your hands with it.
- Essential oils can be put on the floor under the treatment couch, in line with one or more chakras. They could be put in small bowls of water, or on small pieces of white paper or cloth.

On the Healer

The healer can use essential oils to open their energy channels. The choice of oil is an entirely personal matter. Only you can say which is in tune with yourself. Oils can also be chosen on the basis of their being in tune with the energy that uses you as a conduit. Choose one of the following methods:

- Put 1 drop of essential oil on two small pieces of white adhesive paper, and attach them to the soles of your shoes, under the centre of the soles of your feet.
- Use the spray method, as above, but on the feet.
- Put a small smear of essential oil on each foot, at the uppermost point of the inner bend or arch of the foot (underside of the metatarsal bone). This will have an effect along the whole spine, and on the chakras, and will help to clear your energetic field.

ESSENTIAL OILS AND DISTANT HEALING

Distant healing involves a person or persons transmitting healing thoughts to the receiving person, who is perhaps many miles away, even on another continent. The recipient may or may not be aware that healing prayers on their behalf are taking place. It is sometimes called 'absent healing' because the person receiving the healing is absent from the room in which healing is instigated.

We are talking now not about auric fields or energetic bodies, but about the huge cosmic space of the universe. It's known that people on opposite sides of the world can think of each other simultaneously. They might telephone each other at the very same moment, and find the other engaged . . . phoning them. This is a real mystery: thoughts seem to have no boundary. To thoughts, distance is nothing.

Whatever mechanism is involved in absent healing, and whatever space lies between sender and recipient, thoughts negotiate a way through all the invisible energies that now fill the airwaves, beaming down from satellites and aimed at us from radio and TV transmitters. The modern atmosphere is full of invisible informational traffic, like people's mobile-telephone conversations, which might not be entirely full of love and light. Aside from this, we have all manner of rays coming out at us from computers and microwaves, which further clutter the natural energetic environment through which, no doubt, our ancestors also sent each other their mental messages.

Because vibration attaches to vibration, the single most important thing to send is love. It may be the most important element of absent healing, giving the recipient the support and strength they need to resolve their own troubles.

The methods to choose for absent healing are the spray or diffuser methods. Only very small amounts are needed, around 3–4 drops. If you feel that cleansing is important, use the spray method with salt. This clears the atmosphere of elements that can impede the thoughts travelling on their way. Dissolve half a teaspoon in 250ml of warm water, in a spray mister, swish it around, then add 3–4 drops of essential oils and shake. Spray high into the air, trying to avoid letting the droplets fall on polished wood surfaces and other delicate materials.

As you spray, imagine the water-essential oil molecules clearing a path for your loving thoughts and the beautiful healing energy – creating a time or space-tunnel that charges through the air, land or ocean, to the destination of your healing thoughts.

Distant healing may have nothing to do with distance or space, but concentration is certainly needed to actually send the message. Essential oils can give light and clarity to the process of bringing the person at the end of the tunnel, so to speak, into your mind and thoughts.

The essential oils can be used on a diffuser in the room while the distant healing is being projected. The lighter vibratory oils appear to be more suitable for distant healing than those with heavier elements – by which I mean those with a heavy pungent aroma. Beyond this, you need to consider whether your thoughts are more concerned with a physical, emotional or spiritual need, and choose oils that are appropriate. If you are sending healing for a specific condition, choose an essential oil that amplifies the healing thought being sent with its corresponding specific healing frequency.

Thought forms and healing prayers seem to travel very well on the light particles of fragrance that transmit love across the universe. The higher vibratory essential oils would be good choices to start with:

• Rose bulgar – for universal love of the heart.

- Neroli – for the light that shines within it.
- Chamomile Roman – a humble flower that heals the spiritual connections.

If sending healing for a particular illness, disease or disorder, and you'd like to use an essential oil that has healing qualities in relation to it, choose an appropriate oil by looking at the healing properties sections in the profiles, and add that to one of the above three.

Healing Lists

Quite often, when people see there is a 'healing list' operating somewhere, they think of someone in need and ask for them to be put on the list. The person to receive the healing may know nothing about it, perhaps, until months later when they're told. It is always possible that the recipient may not want to go on a list; to have people they don't know knowing their name and details of their ailments. Perhaps people should be asked whether they want to go on a list before placing them there.

It is very difficult, if not impossible, to use essential oils with healing lists that involve more than a couple of people. The essential oils have to be chosen individually, taking several things into consideration, and if too much decision-making is necessary, it detracts the focus – which is primarily on sending love and healing energy.

ESSENTIAL OILS AND ENERGY WORKERS

It would be impossible to write individual sections for all the different forms of energy work as there are so many of them. There is in any case no need, as the principles of using essential oils in energy work are covered throughout this chapter.

It is particularly important however, to choose essential oils that are compatible with this type of work, and which have the same vibrational energy as the energy worker. The physiological and psychological condition of the client should also be considered. Please refer to the essential-oil profiles in Chapter 11.

Essential oils can be incorporated into energy work in one of several ways:

- Diffused in the room.
- A drop of essential oil can be placed on the end of a smelling strip which is then passed over the body in a pattern that mirrors the particular energy work being carried out. Do this before energy work begins.
- Put 1 drop of essential oil on a small piece of white paper or cloth. Place it in the centre of the palm of one hand, then cover with the other hand. Rub the hands together lightly, then discard the paper.
- Apply 1 drop on a fingertip, and spread over all fingertips.
- Apply 1 drop to any instruments used, such as a pendulum or crystal.
- Cut small paper circles and put one drop of essential oil on each. Place them at connection points, polarity points, energy points or chakras, either on the body or on the clothes.

ESSENTIAL OILS AND REIKI

The word 'Reiki' comes from the Japanese *Rei*, meaning universal, and *Ki*, life energy, and refers to the universal life energy which heals and brings the body into balance, as discovered by Dr Mikao Usui in the early 1900s. Reiki is a system of energy-activating attunements – using non-tactile hand movements and symbols – that unlock a person's ability to use the Reiki power, either on themselves or on another person.

Reiki is said to have its roots in ancient Tibet, although its home is said to be Japan, and it's generally thought of as a Japanese system. For this reason, it might be appropriate to use it with two Japanese essential oils: hinoki cypress or pine; and yuzu which comes from the rind of a citrus fruit. Reiki was received while in deep contemplation on a mountain outside Kyoto, surrounded by magnificent pine trees – which are so deeply embedded in, and inspirational to, Japanese spiritual thought. The burning wood is used in many traditional Shinto ceremonies, such as for cleansing. Hinoki essential oil has a woody-turpentine aroma. Using it while doing the attunements or studying the symbols might help form an energetic link to the original Reiki energy and thought form, which could be useful not only to the healer but to the energy itself.

The yuzu tree was introduced into Japan from China over a thousand years ago. This hardy citrus tree, which grows up to fifteen feet, can grow in surprisingly cold weather. It produces a yellow-green fruit with a thick, pithy skin, which is used in the essential-oil production. The oil is light, refreshing and universally liked.

The combination of hinoki pine and yuzu essential oils, in low volume in a diffuser, would provide a good subtle-energy environment for Reiki practice. If you wish to explore the deeper energetic history of Reiki, you might like to try using juniper essential oil, as juniper is the quintessential spiritual plant of Tibet.

The above suggestions may be useful particularly when there are two or three practitioners working on a client at the same time, because all would have to be consulted on, and in agreement concerning, any essential oil(s) planned to be used. A hinoki and yuzu combination might appeal to all.

For Reiki, use essential oils:

- In a diffuser
- In a water spray
- In water to wash the hands
- In water to wash the feet

Spraying the room, with hinoki or another pine or cypress essential oil diluted in water changes the ionic balance in the room to a more positive (that is negative ion) one. If the client is Japanese, hinoki will immediately remind them of home.

At the entrance of Shinto temples all over Japan, there's a special water-trough where a person can wash before entering the grounds. There's a big ladle at the trough from which water is poured down over the hands. Some people also ladle the water over their feet, or drop water from the ladle into their mouths – without actually touching the ladle with their lips – then rinse their mouths and spit the water out. Then shake the ladle under the water, rinsing their energies off.

Such washing rituals can be adopted with essential-oil use as a preliminary to Reiki practice. Put a couple of drops of essential oil in a bowl of water, swish them around, and use a ladle to pour the water, spoon by spoon over the hands, allowing the water to fall down over each one in turn.

ESSENTIAL OILS AND CRYSTAL AND GEM THERAPY

Crystals hold energy and memory. They can both amplify or de-amplify and can increase or decrease energy. Nobody knows how these mechanisms work, although there are plenty of scientists trying to find out. The largest amount of information can be held on a ruby.

Crystals have an intriguing symmetry, being either cubic, rhombic, hexagonal, tetragonal, monoclinic, triclinic or trigonal, reflecting the arrangement of the atoms or ions they are made of. All rocks are made up of crystals packed tightly together, but when there's a little space crystals can grow and be seen visually. Granite is full of these little pockets of grown crystal, and also happens to be the rock which most holds radioactive energy. Perhaps because granite causes interesting mental effects, it was used in the construction of many neolithic dolmens, from Korea to France. Dolmens are shelters made by putting two or three large flat rectangular stones upright and one over the top to form a roof. The religious statues and walls of many ancient buildings were made of granite, including the inner surfaces of the King's Chamber in Cheop's Pyramid in Egypt – where I spent a night and can vouch for the fact that very strange visionary events can occur.

There is no doubt that ancient folk had a great deal of respect for the properties of crystals and gems. In Exodus 28:15–30, God gave detailed instructions for the making of a 'breastplate of judgement', which had four rows of three gems, set in gold. There are different versions of which gems were to be used and their arrangement, depending on which bible you read. Below are three examples of differences in the relevant verses, 17–20:

The Holy Bible
King James Version
London: Collins (1997)

sardius	topaz	carbuncle
emerald	sapphire	diamond
ligure	agate	amethyst
beryl	onyx	jasper

The Holy Scriptures
according to the
Masoretic Text
Philadelphia: Jewish Publication Society of America (1976)

carnelian	topaz	smaragd
carbuncle	sapphire	emerald
jacinth	agate	amethyst
beryl	onyx	jasper

The Holy Bible
New Internationalist Version
London: Hodder and Stoughton (1985)

ruby	topaz	beryl
turquoise	sapphire	emerald
jacinth	agate	amethyst
chrysolite	onyx	jasper

Details about the breastplate can be found at The Temple Institute museum in Jerusalem, from where I took the following information practically verbatim. When it was used, a piece of parchment would be tucked into the breastplate, upon which was written the ineffable name of God – Urim V Tumim. It drew down the spiritual energy from above and caused the stones to light up. Each stone represented a letter. The breastplate was consulted in decisions that couldn't be reached any other way by the king (David) and the high priest. The high priest wore the breastplate, and only he could decipher the code of the letters through a spiritual form of prophesy.

Garudas, channelled through Kevin Ryerson in volume one of *Gem Elixirs and Vibrational Healing*, is asked whether the breastplate emitted a brilliance. He said yes, the stones had auric properties and there was a blending with the priest's consciousness and aura, activating 'a physical source of light merging with the auric and the real properties of the gemstones. This amplified the piezoelectric effect of the stones ... This effect was further amplified by the use of incense and essential oils with the breastplate.' The piezo-electric effect is a very interesting property of life, affecting many things including crystals, DNA and the crystalline mineral apatite which is found around collagen fibres in the bones and tissue. Basically, the piezoelectric effect is about electrical energy being pro-duced when pressure is exerted on the electrons of a thing. That pressure, or tension, can be provided by many things. Apparently, essential oils are one.

Exodus 28:21 states: 'And the stones shall be accord-ing to the names of the children of Israel, twelve, according to their names.' The arrangement of these names is shown in a painting at the Temple museum, along with colours which presumably represent the gem, as follows:

Levi: smoky	**Simeon:** green	**Reuben:** red
Zebulun: clear	**Issachar:** violet	**Judah:** green
Gad: clear	**Naphtali:** pinky-mauve	**Dan:** purple
Benjamin: opalish	**Josef:** black	**Asher:** bluish-green

Apparently, only vessels made from stone were used at the ancient Temple in Jerusalem as stone does not transmit ritual impurity, which is called *tumah*. Metal and wooden vessels were not used.

Working with gems and crystals is a very physical thing, involving energies that are found in the rocks under our feet and in the cells of our bodies. There are microtubules, for example, within the cytoplasm of cells and along the length of nerve axons. These packets of crystals move different chemicals up and down nerve axons, from the cell body to the synapses. How one crystal communicates energy and information to another is a scientific mystery, but it is a fact of physical life. The body also contains trace elements of minerals, such as gold and silver, which are, again, crystalline. Gems and crystals may also have an etheric body, and energy interactions happening in addition to the known properties, which are themselves amazing.

Crystals and many other gems are changed in colour depending on the minerals they have absorbed. Amethyst, for example, has absorbed iron. Colour thus tells us something about the history of the stone, and about its mineral make up, factors that need to be taken into consideration when working with gems and crystals.

Some people using essential oils in conjunction with gem and crystal therapy choose them on the basis of their *perceived* physical colour: for example, rose essential oil with rose quartz, and myrrh with the resinous amber. For those who wish to know the colours of essential oils, a complete list is below. This cannot be a definitive chart because the colour of essential oils varies, not only between species, but within one species, when they're grown and produced under different circumstances. The variables are: the season when grown, the location, soil, altitude and, most importantly, the temperature of distillation, the pressure of the steam, and the length of time of distillation. For example, a plant distilled under high temperature and pressure in a short time may have a different colour to one distilled under low heat and pressure over a longer time.

General Guidelines to the Physical Colours of Essential Oils

COLOURLESS	COLOURLESS WITH GREENISH TINGE	COLOURLESS WITH BLUEY TINGE
Angelica Seed	Cumin	Chamomile Roman
Aniseed	Rose Otto	
Balsam Fir		
Camphor		
Dill		
Elemi		
Eucalyptus Radiata		
Nutmeg		
Ravensara		
Rosemary		

COLOURLESS TO PALE YELLOW	PALE YELLOW	YELLOW
Basil (French)	Amyris	Bay
Black Pepper	Basil	Cananga
Cardamom	Carrot Seed	Cassie
Clary Sage	Cedarwood	Celery Seed
Coriander	Clove	Cinnamon Leaf
Cypress	Ginger	Galangal
Eucalyptus Citriodora	Hinoki Pine	Gardenia
Eucalyptus Globulus	Lime	Mandarin
Fennel	Litsea Cubeba	Manuka
Frankincense	Melissa	Opopanax
Hyssop	Neroli	Orange
Juniper	Oregano	Ormenis Flower
Lavender	Petitgrain	(i.e. Chamomile
Lemon Verbena	Star Anise	Maroc)
Manuka	White Birch	Spikenard
Marjoram	Ylang Ylang	Tonka Bean
Peppermint		Turmeric
Pine		Yuzu
Rosewood		
Sage		
Sandalwood		
Silver Fir		
Spearmint		
Tea Tree		

PALE YELLOW TO PALE GREEN	GREENISH-YELLOW	GREEN
Cubeb	Bergamot	Angelica Root
Galbanum	Geranium	Boronia
Grapefruit		Inula
Lemon		Valerian
Mimosa Leaf		Violet Leaf
Palma Rosa		
		GREEN TINGE
		Linden Blossom

AMBER TO OLIVE	BROWNISH-GREEN	LIGHT AMBER
Mastic	Oakmoss	Buchu
Vetiver		Carnation
		Pimento
		Tuberose

YELLOW TO LIGHT AMBER	YELLOWISH TO REDDISH-AMBER	RICH AMBER
Caraway Seed	Ambrette	Benzoin
Cinnamon Leaf	Cistus	Jasmine
Citronella	Styrax	Jasmine Sambac
Helichrysum	Tagetes	Myrrh
Lemongrass	Thyme	Patchouli
		Peru Balsam
		Rose Maroc
		Thyme
		Vanilla

REDDISH-ORANGE	DEEP ORANGE-REDDISH WITH GREENISH TINGE	DARK BLUE
Rose Maroc	Hyacinth	Chamomile German
	Narcissus	Yarrow

ESSENTIAL OILS AND CHANNELLING

The New Age area in bookshops is full of volumes purporting to be channelled from beings living in another dimension. These voices are said to come from 'ascended masters', 'angels', 'guides', 'spirit guides' and 'beings from other planets or stars'. Invariably, they bring messages of love, light, forgiveness and understanding. I was curious to know what these wise beings had to say about essential oils and, in particular, if they would all say more or less the same thing.

This was treated as something of an experiment, with all persons doing the channelling being offered the same bottles of essential oils, which were not named, only numbered. The channels, then, were responding to the exact same aroma, and did not have a verbal or written indication of what was in the bottle. Both they and I may have, from the aroma, known what some bottles contained, but as there were sixty-five oils in the set there was plenty of scope for olfactory confusion – especially as some of those used are rather rare, and little known by name, let alone aroma. The essential oil was put on the end of a smelling strip, which some channels chose to hold in their outstretched hands and some put to their noses. Some adopted particular hand movements while channelling, and asked me to hold the strip under their nose. Sessions were recorded, and later transcribed, and an observer was present to take notes of the order of events, any physical movements and indications made, and to ensure procedures were followed to maintain the anonymity of the oils.

The following are extracts of what six channels said about the same neroli essential oil, when asked to comment on its spiritual properties:

Channel A: It is one of moving through difficulty, a herb of transition from one state of awareness to another. You could use it in a catalytic way, as a carrier of consciousness from one state of frequency to another . . . Its colour is much more radiant and clear than the previous ones that we have discussed and it is tinged with a very electric clear white blue.

Channel B: To be used with care because will inflame the passions. The passions are not only when

252

we are in embrace, we also are angry.

Channel C: This will bring the sense of learning; what you would term the acquisition of knowledge is carried within the atoms herein. The ability, capability of input, that the capability from this is to be divided into three factors. Comprehension, assimilation, and the ability to, as it were, discard that which is of no importance to that particular incarnative quality. In the realms this is known as 'the heavenly touch'.

Channel D: This is a very light floral extract and we feel that this should be used on its own. It should not be mixed with any other of the extracts. It would then lose its subtlety.

Channel E: The distillation is fine but there's something at one end, I'm not sure if it's the beginning or the end of the process where the energy goes a bit wonky ... and should be in a recipe of three to four smells, aromas or whatever.

Channel F: This is more subtle, calming. I feel a lot of peace.

Neroli is the essential oil distilled from the flowers of the orange tree. It is very expensive, and in shops is often sold already diluted in vegetable oil. Many of the so-called 'pure essential oil' of nerolis are of inferior quality, and their aromas are dissimilar to the high quality sample offered to the channels. Neroli was chosen as the example in this section because it is, for the above mentioned reasons, not an oil commonly recognized, while it is one of the most spiritually active essential oils in the set used.

Some of the channels were clearly deluding themselves, despite having a striking air of authority. Channel B, for example, said neroli inflames the passions, which it does not do. There were conflicting opinions between channels, as between channel D who

253

said 'it should not be mixed with any other of the extracts', whereas channel E said it 'should be in a recipe of three to four aromas'.

On the other hand, channels could make some very impressive observations. Channel A, for example, who provided information on sixty-three different aromas, only made one comment regarding myself, saying of an oil I have a particular liking for, and affinity with (which of course she did not previously know), 'For you, Valerie, this oil has a special personal significance, for we see that it is fully aligned with your aura.'

Some of the channels were 'bringing through' the voices of beings who were supposed to have lived in particular historical times and locations. As there is a very long aromatic tradition, one would expect these beings to be familiar with certain aromas regularly used during 'their' time and place on earth, and I made a special point of offering such particular aromas in these cases. However, it often proved that these aromas did not 'click'; that the being did not recognize the aroma specific to the culture of their former incarnation. One 'ascended master' from biblical times, for example, did not recognize aromas we know from historical records he would have been familiar with. Even if the physical aroma did not reach this 'master', he should perhaps have been able to recognize it from its spiritual qualities.

It was made clear to the channel before each session that I was not asking for information on the physical properties of the individual essential oils, yet much information came forward in this respect – most of it wrong. The giving out of inaccurate medical advice is a very dangerous activity, especially when it is accompanied with an air of great wisdom and authority, sometimes by people who say they channel characters known from spiritual literature – whose 'channelled' advice some gullible people might follow word for word.

In *The Meeting of Science and Spirit*, John White says, 'I estimate that perhaps nine out of ten channels are "bringing through" nothing more than a fabricated subpersonality of their own creation.' I'd agreed with this. A channel, then, might, instead of guiding you on your spiritual journey, deflect you from the course of true knowledge. In terms of general guidance this is bad enough, but when the guidance involves essential oils, which have powerful physical qualities, it is quite another matter. My advice is to tread very carefully. They might tell you to use this oil (or herb, or homeopathic remedy), when it is ill-suited to your needs; or tell you not to use that oil, when that may be the very oil you need.

The experience of seeing many channels and asking them the exact same questions was, at times, hilarious or ridiculous. At other times it was interesting because of the concepts that emerged; the different ways of looking at things from a spiritual perspective. On a very few occasions, I came away wondering if I had, indeed, been listening to an 'ascended master'. Clearly, when planning to visit a channel for a personal consultation, great discrimination is required.

There's nothing new about people speaking in voices that are not like their usual selves. It's been going on for millennia, not as 'channelling' perhaps, but as 'oracle-giving', and even 'prophesy'. At least today channels say they are just that, a channel, and do not claim to be the source of the information that breaks through – sometimes without any warning or desire on the part of the speaker. In the past, some people who found themselves speaking in another voice may have deluded themselves, or others, that they themselves were of an essentially higher intelligence, or in some way chosen or special. Indeed, making the distinction between true and false 'prophets', or 'ascended masters', has been a problem since time began.

Essential Oils for Channelling

Essential oils do open the channels of communication, both with the higher self and with higher spiritual elements in the universe. Among those who work in channelling, the following essential oils have been found helpful to that process:

ESSENTIAL OILS FOR CHANNELLING	
Angelica Seed	Marjoram
Bay	Mimosa
Benzoin	Myrtle
Carnation	Narcissus
Cedarwood	Osmanthus
Chamomile Roman	Petitgrain
Champaca	Pimento Berry
Cypress	Pine
Fir	Rose Maroc
Frankincense	Sage
Galbanum	Sandalwood
Hyacinth	Spruce
Jasmine	Tuberose
Linden Blossom	Violet Leaf

ESSENTIAL OILS AND COLOUR HEALING

Colour is not static, it's dynamic. Colour is changed by heat, oscillation and chemical reaction. A red cabbage might be red, but it's turned green by washing soda, and back again to red with vinegar. That's chemistry at work. The brown gas nitrogen dioxide, when heated, becomes increasingly lighter. When it's colourless, if the heat is turned down, it becomes brown again. The human eye can detect ten million shades of colour, which is a dynamic of light, vibration, heat and chemistry.

Essential oils are a complex blend of many natural chemical components, with some having a 'contents list' of 300 or more. Molecules have a vibration, an oscillation. And essential oils are often heated, by means of diffusers, warm water or the human body. They are dynamic energetically, in just about every way you can think of, which means that when trying to ascertain their colour, we're going to have to try and consider many variables.

When we see colour, through the deciphering equipment of the eye, we're registering the wavelengths produced by light. Red has the longest wavelength; blue and violet have the shortest. White light is produced by the blending of equal wavelengths. Wavelength is changed by heat, which is why grey metal, when increasingly heated, will change in colour to red, then orange, yellow, and eventually 'white-hot'.

When we see the colour of an object, we see the wavelength that has *not* been absorbed. Inula essential oil is 'green' because it absorbs nearly all the colours of the light spectrum except green. The *reflection* of green is what we are seeing, not the absorption of it. Something that is yellow has absorbed blue light, and reflects the mix of red and green; magenta absorbs green and reflects a mix of red and blue; cyan absorbs red light, and reflects – is seen as – a mix of blue and green. In colour terms, things are not as they seem!

The light from the sun has all the colours in it; and they can be seen as a rainbow effect reflected on a wall or piece of white paper if you hold a prism, such as a clear water-crystal, in the sunlight. The prism splits white light into its component parts, wavelengths; the refraction is what we see. Red light is reflected least, and violet the most.

Plants absorb minerals from the ground, and essential oils contain trace elements of them. The type and amount of trace mineral depends on the uptake of the different species, and the particular growing environment. When burnt, minerals give off different colours. For example, potassium compound creates a purple or lilac flame; sodium an orange flame; copper makes it green-blue; and with lithium it's red. Heat agitates electrons in a thing, and they give off more light.

The man who discovered why the sky is blue, John Tyndall (1820–1893), also discovered that essential oils absorb infrared rays. Indeed, essential oils are extremely dynamic in terms of taking in and giving out infrared and electricity, as well as in terms of light refraction, chemistry, vibration and minerals – all of which depend on other factors, such as where the plant material was grown and distilled, under what conditions, and who has been handling it. As for colour, that varies too. The first essential oil in the following list, for example, ambrette, might be yellow-ish or reddish-amber depending on growing and distilling conditions, but we don't know what colour it is when it's heated by hands, body, warm water or diffuser.

There is no one 'colour' for any particular, individual essential oil. This is very clear when looking at their etheric colour or, for example, their aura pictures. The dynamic, *physical*, multicoloured aspect of essential oils can be seen at home, if certain conditions are just right. Put a large white container full of warm water on a counter, in front of a window which is receiving a lot of sunlight. Put one or two drops of an essential oil on the surface of the water, and adjust the position of your body to see, on the surface of the water, ripples of colour rather like those seen on a soap bubble or on an oily patch of water. Catching this effect is not easy and may require several goes. This effect is known as 'light interference', and is the result of there being two light-reflections – from the top surface and the underneath surface – of the essential oil. Where the light rays meet, there is an interference causing some colours to cancel each other out, and others to combine into bands of colour, the familiar 'rainbow effect'. In the case of essential oils, each one produces different combinations and strengths of colour and, even more surprisingly, different energy patterns which can be seen in the way the colours swirl and intertwine – fast or slow, moving inwards or outwards, towards or away from each other. If you can catch the light at just the right angle, wonderful colours can be seen – gold, silver, blue, green, red, magenta, yellow, orange and violet – in all different shades and hues, from the very deep to the lightest of translucent colours.

This light-print may be the true physical colour of an individual essential oil, and it bears no obvious, visible relation to the colour of the oil when it's in bottle or drop form. The etheric colour of an essential oil, its 'halo-colour' if you like, is also different to its aura picture colours, as revealed by the PIP moving video pictures. (And although both are dynamic – they have a different energy-action 'fingerprint' – they are dynamic in a different way.) When considering the colour of an essential oil, then, it's a difficult task because there are so many colours to choose from – even when talking about just one essential oil!

Some colour therapists, when using essential oils, consider the plant species that the essential oil is distilled from – the colour of the flower it produces or the colour of the part of the plant used. This information is provided in the following chart, but should be considered in view of lightwave absorption or reflection. The chart also includes information about the etheric colour of essential oils, but if working with them on a person, their colour field must be taken into consideration. For example, if a person is suffering a great deal of inflammation, a blue oil (containing azulene) is usually applied and, indeed, blue absorbs red – the traditional colour of inflammation. However, blue also absorbs green. A green oil, inula, will absorb blue and is useful for respiratory tract infections which cause excessive mucus and dampness within the body, usually associated with blue. But green also absorbs small amounts of red which is associated with warmth. You can begin to see how complex the subject of energetic colour really is.

In the early 1980s I experimented with coloured oils, producing combinations of essential oil, base oil and natural pigments. To see how long they would retain their colour in ideal storage conditions, a collection of these coloured-oil bottles was put away in a box. Taking them out recently, they were almost as vibrant and colourful as the day they were made. I encountered some difficulty in finding oil-soluble, organic, natural tints or dyes, but eventually was successful. The greater challenge was in marrying up the three components – essential oil, base vegetable oil and colour source – in terms of their compatibility with the physical condition of the person, or the condition of the chakra to be worked on. When working with actual people, there are a great number of things to consider.

If creating coloured oils, considerations must include all aspects of the colour of the essential oil to be included, as well as the colour of the vegetable oil in which it is to be diluted. As these two components are blended, a new colour may emerge. Any tint or dye should be from a natural organic source, and have the same physical attributes as the essential oil. You can immediately see that if using a coloured oil to counteract inflammation, say, the tint or dye should also come from a plant known by traditional herbalism or phytotherapy to serve that purpose. Each of the three components could also be considered from the point of view of their effect on chakras and the whole person – not only physically, but emotionally and spiritually. Although some people might think using coloured oils is an easy option, a science of aesthetics or even 'instinct', to be used therapeutically it's a science that can only evolve from a very broad knowledge base.

For those who wish to experiment, the following chart may help. The third column on the left shows the colour of the part of the plant used in the making of that particular essential oil, which could be grass, fruit, seeds, leaves, root, wood, bark, resin, flowers or flowering tops. Most species have a 'flower', even if that is a tree cone or grass spikelet, and the fourth column shows the colour of that 'flower'. The column for the colour of the essential oil is followed by a small section showing the density of that colour: 'C' indicates clearness or clarity; 'M' that it is of medium density; and 'D' that it is dense. The etheric colour is difficult to explain by means of a few short words which cannot convey the dynamism of these colours, their aliveness and their degree of sparkle.

THE COLOURS OF ESSENTIAL OIL PLANTS AND OILS – PHYSICAL AND ETHERIC

ESSENTIAL OIL	LATIN NAME	PART USED: COLOUR	FLOWER: COLOUR	OIL: COLOUR	DENSITY	ETHERIC COLOUR
Ambrette	Abelmoschus moschatus	seed: brown	red with yellow centre	yellowish to reddish-amber	M	reddy orange into gold, tinged with green
Amyris	Amyris balsamifera	wood chippings: tannish-brown	white	pale yellow	C	light yellow, orange, green
Angelica Root	Angelica archangelica	root: light green	greenish-white	green-blue	M	deep green and gold
Angelica Seed	Angelica archangelica	seed: green	greenish-white	colourless	C	light lime green with pink and gold
Aniseed	Pimpinella anisum	seed: light brown tan	creamy-white with yellow tinge	colourless	C	yellow, blue, green
Balsam de Peru	Myroxylon balsamum	leaves: green wood: brown	white	pale amber, orange	D	rich, deep purple, orange, gold
Basil	Ocimum basilicum	leaves and flowering tops: light green	white	yellow, pale green to colourless	C	green, blue, violet, silver
Basil Linalol (French)	Ocimum basilicum	leaves and flowering tops: light green	white	colourless to pale yellow	C	blue, violet, light silver, magenta, deep gold
Bay Laurel	Laurus nobilis	leaves: dark to mid-green	grey-white with yellow tinge	yellow with green tinge, orange	D	orange, blue, green, gold
Bay	Pimento racemosa	leaves: dark green	white with yellow tinge	dark orange	D	blue, orange/red

Key: C = clearness or clarity; M = medium density; D = dense

ESSENTIAL OIL	LATIN NAME	PART USED: COLOUR	FLOWER: COLOUR	OIL: COLOUR	DENSITY	ETHERIC COLOUR
Benzoin	*Styrax benzoin dryander*	resin: milky, light yellow	white	rich amber	D	orange, red, deep amber gold with a little blue
Bergamot	*Citrus bergamia*	fruit rind: deep yellow	white tinged with yellow	yellow to green	C	deep greens, blues, magenta, orange
Black Pepper	*Piper nigrum*	berries: green/red/ black	white	clear to slight green tinge	C	red, orange, blue, green, gold
Boronia Absolute	*Boronia megastigma*	flowers	yellow tinged with red	deep green	D	yellow-red, light green swirls
Buchu	*Barosma betulina*	leaves: olive-green/ bluish	white tinged with yellow	light amber	M	reddish orange-gold
Camphor (White)	*Cinnamomum camphora*	bark: orange twigs: light greenish/bluish leaves: dark green	white, red berries	colourless	C	silver/blue, green, yellow
Cananga	*Cananga odorata*	flowers	greenish-yellow	bright yellow	M	green, gold, orange
Caraway	*Carum carvi*	seeds: light brown (sometimes green)	white/pink	light amber	C	deep yellow, amber, red to green/blue
Cardamom	*Elettaria cardamomum*	pods: green	white (waxy) tinged orange/red	pale yellow to colourless	C	green, blue, gold, pink, violet
Carnation (Absolute)	*Dianthus caryophyllus*	flowers	pink	dark amber	D	rich pink-mauve, blue, gold-silver with green flecks
Carrot seed	*Daucus carota*	seeds: light brown	white	yellow and amber	M	orange, yellow, red, light green

Key: C = clearness or clarity; M = medium density; D = dense

ESSENTIAL OIL	LATIN NAME	PART USED: COLOUR	FLOWER: COLOUR	OIL: COLOUR	DENSITY	ETHERIC COLOUR
Cassie	Acacia farnesiana	flowers: golden yellow	golden yellow	dark yellow	D	red-gold tinged with purple
Cedarwood	Cedrus atlantica	wood chippings: dark pink/light tan	green cones	pale yellow	M	blue-green tinged with deep orange and purple
Celery Seed	Apium graveolens	seed: light brown	white	rich yellow	M	green, yellow, orange
Chamomile German	Matricaria recutita	flowers	white petals	deep, dark blue, green	D	deep blue, gold, yellow, deep green
Chamomile Maroc	Ormenis multicaulis	flowers	yellow/orange	pale yellow to deep yellow-brown	M	orange-yellow with green tinge
Chamomile Roman	Anthemis nobilis	flowers	white	pale translucent blue	C	turquoise, bluish-purple, green, gold, silver, white
Cinnamon Bark	Cinnamomum zeylanicum	orange/ reddish-brown	white	amber/mid-yellow	D	red, orange, gold, magenta
Cinnamon Leaf	Cinnamomum zeylanicum	dark green and slightly reddish underneath	white	yellowish	M	red, green, orange, blue
Cistus	Cistus ladaniferus	gum-resin: orange	white or yellow/maroon splashes at centre	deep orange, amber	D	purple, orange, silver/gold
Citronella	Cymbopogon nardus	leaves: deep green	spikelets: brownish green	yellow, amber	M	tannish-orange tinged red, yellow
Clary Sage	Salvia sclarea	flowering tops and leaves: green	pinky mauve/blue	colourless to pale yellow with green tinge	C	deep blue, gold, yellow, magenta

Key: C = clearness or clarity; M = medium density; D = dense

ESSENTIAL OIL	LATIN NAME	PART USED: COLOUR	FLOWER: COLOUR	OIL: COLOUR	DENSITY	ETHERIC COLOUR
Clove	*Eugenia caryophyllata*	buds: red	pink orange into yellow corolla	pale yellow to dark yellow	M	orange, red, violet tinged with green and gold
Coriander	*Coriandrum sativum*	seeds: light green	pinkish-white	colourless	C	blue, white, green, yellow, magenta
Cubeb	*Piper cubeb*	berries: green/red/ pink	white	pale greenish-yellow to colourless	C	yellow, green, blue, red
Cumin	*Cuminum cyminum*	seed: brown to black	white tinged with pink	colourless with greenish tinge	C	orange, pink, green, blue
Cypress	*Cupressus sempervirens*	needle: light green twigs: light tan	nuts: light brown	pale yellow	M	orange, gold, deep green, red
Dill	*Anethum graveolens*	seed: light brown herb: green	yellow	colourless	C	light blue flashes with green and pink
Elemi	*Canarium luzonicum*	wood resin: rich amber, slight greenish-grey tinge	white	colourless	C	bright orange, reddish tinge into yellow, green
Eucalyptus Citriodora	*Eucalyptus citriodora*	leaves: deep olivy-green	white, yellow	pale yellow	C	blue, gold, red orange, white
Eucalyptus Globulus	*Eucalyptus globulus*	leaves: green to greyish-bluish	white, creamy	colourless	C	blue-green tinge, orange
Eucalyptus Radiata	*Eucalyptus radiata*	leaves: green to silvery-bluish	white, creamy	colourless	C	blue-green tinge, yellow

Key: C = clearness or clarity; M = medium density; D = dense

ESSENTIAL OIL	LATIN NAME	PART USED: COLOUR	FLOWER: COLOUR	OIL: COLOUR	DENSITY	ETHERIC COLOUR
Fennel	*Foeniculum vulgare*	seeds: light tannish green	yellow	colourless	C	yellow, green, light green, reddish
Fir Balsam	*Abies Balsamen*	oleoe-resin: greeny-yellow	cones: mid-green to light tan	colourless	C	lime green into gold and silver tinged with red
Frankincense	*Boswellia carterii*	resin: light amber	pale pink, deep in middle	pale yellow to colourless	C	silver-gold/yellow turning into a silvery mauve/blue with deep blue
Galangal	*Alpina officinauram*	root stock: deep amber		yellow	M	orange, blue/green
Galbanum	*Ferula galbaniflua*	resin-gum: clear	white, creamy yellow tinge	pale yellow to olive green tinge	M	yellow, green, white, mauve/blue
Gardenia (Absolute)	*Gardenia jasminoides*	flowers	white (waxy)	deep yellow	D	blue, mauve/purple, gold, pink
Geranium	*Pelargonium graveolens*	leaves: mid-grass green	pink/mauve	green to greenish-yellow	M	pink-green, gold
Ginger	*Zingiber officinale*	root stock: yellow	yellow/purple white	pale yellow	C	rich blue, orange, yellow tinged with green
Grapefruit	*Citrus paradisi*	rind: bright deep yellow	creamy-white (waxy)	mid-yellow	C	green, violet, yellow, gold flakes, magenta
Helichrysum	*Helichrysum angustifolium*	flowers and tops: silvery green	yellow	pale yellow to amber	M or D	red, orange, yellow, blue
Hinoki Pine	*Chamaecyparis obtusa*	needles: green	cones: green-brown	colourless with yellow tinge	C	white, orange, mauve, silvery-green

Key: C = clearness or clarity; M = medium density; D = dense

ESSENTIAL OIL	LATIN NAME	PART USED: COLOUR	FLOWER: COLOUR	OIL: COLOUR	DENSITY	ETHERIC COLOUR
Hyacinth (Absolute)	Hyacinthus orientalis	flowers	blue	deep orange, reddish, greeny-brown	D	deep purple, blue, green, deep gold
Hyssop	Hyssopus officinalis	flowering tops leaves: mid green	blue-mauve	colourless to pale yellow with green tinge	C	blue, pink, gold, green/orange
Inula	Inula graveolens	leaves: deep green roots: brownish green	yellow	green	D	green, blue, yellow, pink
Jasmine (Absolute)	Jasminum officinale	flowers	white	mid-red, amber	D	gold, blue, pink, green, violet, silver
Jasmine Sambac	Jasminum sambac	flowers	white	mid-red, amber	D	gold, blue, orange, green, violet
Juniper	Juniperus communis	berry: green, deep indigo	green	colourless	C	silver, white, blue
Lavender	Lavundula angustifolia	leaves: silver tops: green	purple, mauve, violet	colourless, pale	C	silver-gold, blue-green
Lemon	Citrus limonum	fruit rind: light/ bright yellow	white with green/ yellow tinges	sharp yellow	C	green, yellow/goldish, slightly violet
Lemon Verbena	Lippia citriodora	leaves and flowering tops: light lime-green leaves	white	pale yellow	C	green, blue and yellow

Key: C = clearness or clarity; M = medium density; D = dense

ESSENTIAL OIL	LATIN NAME	PART USED: COLOUR	FLOWER: COLOUR	OIL: COLOUR	DENSITY	ETHERIC COLOUR
Lemongrass	Cymbopogon citratus / flexuosus	leaves: green to mid-yellow	spikelets: brownish-green	dark yellow, amber to orange, red	D	purple, red, orange, green
Lime	Citrus aurantifolia	peel: dark green, lime	white (waxy)	pale yellow	C	green, gold, blue, magenta
Linden Blossom (Absolute)	Tilia vulgaris	flowers	creamy white/ yellow	light amber, orange to green	D	blue, mauve, light opalescent silver
Litsea Cubeba	Litsea cubeba	berries: green	white	pale yellow	C	green, yellow tinged with magenta orange
Mandarin	Citrus reticulata	rind: bright orange	greeny-white tinged slightly yellow	deep orangey-yellow	M	blue, violet
Marjoram (Sweet)	Origanum marjorana	flowering tops	white	pale yellow to yellow	C	green/yellow, orange, amber/red
Mastic	Pistacia lentiscus	resin: brown	–	amber to yellow	D	gold, red, green, blue
Melissa	Melissa officinalis	leaves: green	white	pale yellow	C	deep blue/orange/red, green-gold into light blue
Mimosa Leaf	Acacia decurrens	leaves: green	bright yellow	pale yellow to pale green	D	gold, orange, greenish-blue, into deep amber
Myrrh	Commiphora myrrha	resin: light brown	white	deep orange/red, yellow	D	red, brown, orange with touches of blue/deep green
Myrtle	Myrtus communis	leaves: deep green twigs: brown	white	pale yellow to dark yellow	M	green, gold, pink

Key: C= clearness or clarity; M = medium density; D = dense

269

ESSENTIAL OIL	LATIN NAME	PART USED: COLOUR	FLOWER: COLOUR	OIL: COLOUR	DENSITY	ETHERIC COLOUR
Narcissus (Absolute)	*Narcissus poeticus*	flowers	white/yellow tinged with red	pale orange to greenish, tinged with deep green	D	blue, purple, silver, gold, deep emerald green
Neroli	*Citrus aurantium*	flowers	white with yellow tinge (waxy)	pale yellow	C	white/blue, purple, clear, gold
Nutmeg	*Myristica fragrans*	nut-seed: brown/tan	yellow	colourless	C	red, orange, yellow, blue with green tinge, purple
Oakmoss	*Evernia prunastri*	lichen: bright green	–	dark green brown	D	deep orange/red and green
Opopanax	*Commiphora erythraea*	resin: dark reddish-brown	white	deep yellow	D	red, brass-yellow, deep green
Orange	*Citrus sinensis*	peel: bright orange	white with yellow tinge (waxy)	deep yellow, orange	M	purple, gold, silver, white
Oregano	*Origanum vulgare*	flowering tops	pinky mauve	pale yellow to amber	M	red/orange, gold, yellow
Palma Rosa	*Cymbopogon martini*	leaves: mid-green	spikelets: greenish with yellow tinge	deep yellow with olive tinge	M	magenta, green, dark yellow, pinkish
Patchouli	*Pogostemon cablin*	leaves: green	purple/white	amber to dark orange/red	D	red/orange, violet tinged with purple-gold
Peppermint	*Mentha piperita*	leaves: mid-green	pinky white	pale yellow to colourless	C	pinky green, silvery blue

Key: C = clearness or clarity; M = medium density; D = dense

270

ESSENTIAL OIL	LATIN NAME	PART USED: COLOUR	FLOWER: COLOUR	OIL: COLOUR	DENSITY	ETHERIC COLOUR
Petitgrain	*Citrus aurantium*	leaves: dark green small twigs: pale green budding fruit: sharp bright green	white with yellow tinge (waxy)	pale yellow	C	greenish-yellow, orange
Pimento Berry	*Pimento officinalis*	berry: green	white with yellow tinge	orange to yellow	D	red, green, magenta/gold
Pine	*Pinus sylvestris*	needles	cones: brown	colourless	C	green, silver, blue, yellow
Rose Maroc (Absolute)	*Rosa centifolia*	flowers	reddish	reddish orange	D	emerald green tinged with magenta and gold
Rose Otto	*Rosa damascena*	flowers	pink	colourless to pale yellow with slight bluish-green tinge	C	pink, green, blue, gold, silver
Rosemary	*Rosmarinus officinalis*	leaves and flowering tops	blue to mauve	colourless to pale yellow	C	spring green, blue, silver
Rosewood	*Aniba rosaeodora*	wood chippings: reddish	yellow	pale yellow to colourless	C	greeny-orange going into bright red and magenta
Sage	*Salvia officinalis*	leaves and flowering tops: silver-green	purple/mauve	pale yellow to colourless	C	yellow, green, orange
Sandalwood	*Santalum album*	heartwood: light yellow/tan	pinky purple	pale yellow to colourless	C	orange-pink, purple, green

Key: C = clearness or clarity; M = medium density; D = dense

ESSENTIAL OIL	LATIN NAME	PART USED: COLOUR	FLOWER: COLOUR	OIL: COLOUR	DENSITY	ETHERIC COLOUR
Silver Fir	*Abies alba*	needles: mid-green	cones: light green turning brown	colourless to pale yellow	C	silvery blue-green with light white
Spearmint	*Mentha spicata*	leaves: bright green	pink	pale yellow to colourless, green tinge	C	blue, green, yellow, silver
Spikenard	*Nardostachys jatamansi*	root stock: light brown	pinky-violet	from deep orange to deep yellow	D	amber, gold, mauve/blue, rich magenta-white
Star Anise	*Illicium verum*	seeds: brown	white	pale yellow	C	orange/amber, red, green
Styrax	*Liquidambar orientalis*	resin: brownish-green	white	white, yellow amber	D	orange, reddish-gold with blue tinges
Tagetes	*Tagetes minuta*	flowers	orange and red	dark orange	D	red, dark brown with gold fringe
Tea Tree	*Melaleuca alternifolia*	leaves: green	yellow with mauve tinge	pale yellow to colourless opalescent tinge	C	yellow, green, reddish
Thyme	*Thymus vulgaris*	flowering tops	pink-pale mauve	light reddish-orange/yellow to dark yellow	D	reddish, orange/blue, deep green/yellow
Tonka Bean	*Pipteryx odorata*	beans: dark brown	purple	deep yellow	D	rich red/orange gold
Tuberose (Absolute)	*Polianthes tuberosa*	flowers	creamy-white	dark orange	D	deep blue/green, gold, deep yellow
Turmeric	*Curcuma longa*	roots: yellow	yellow	deep yellow	D	deep orange, green, red, gold, yellow

Key: C = clearness or clarity; M = medium density; D = dense

272

ESSENTIAL OIL	LATIN NAME	PART USED:	FLOWER: COLOUR	OIL: COLOUR	DENSITY	ETHERIC COLOUR
Valerian	*Valeriana officinalis*	root: yellow to pale greenish	purple/white	green to brown	D	deep blue/green, gold
Vanilla	*Vanilla planifolia*	beans: green, blackish-brown	white	dark amber	D	orange, gold, green
Vetiver	*Vetiveria zizanoides*	roots: whitish-brown	spikelets: green	dark brownish-orange/yellow	D	deep green and yellow with orange tinge, blue
Violet Leaf (Absolute)	*Viola odorata*	leaf: light to dark green	purple/mauve	very dark green	D	green, orange, yellow into purple, gold
White Birch	*Betula alba*	young leaves: pale green	catkins: pale green turning to brown	pale yellow	M	red–deep orange, green, silver
Yarrow	*Achillea millefolium*	leaves and flowers: dark green and white, tinged with pink	white tinged with pink	blue	D	blue-mauve into silver, moving into gold
Ylang Ylang	*Cananga odorata*	flowers	creamy yellow tinged pale pink or violet	pale yellow	M	gold, magenta, green, purple
Yuzu	*Citrus junos*	rind: orange-yellow	white (waxy)	bright rich yellow	M	green, red, yellow/gold

Key: C = clearness or clarity; M = medium density; D = dense

273

Chapter Eleven

THE ESSENTIAL OIL SPIRITUAL PROFILES

> When the soul approaches the
> mysteries; when it tries to rally to
> the great spiritual principles, the
> perfumes are there.
>
> MARGUERITE MAURY,
> *The Secret of Life and Youth:*
> *Guide to Aromatherapy*

The use of fragrance in making the spiritual connection is one of the most ancient and enduring of human activities. In some cultures, fragrance has also been used for what we might term 'energetic healing', although for most people in history, and still in many parts of the world today, there was no separation between body and spirit, and thus all healing was 'energetic' or spiritual.

The following profiles include information not only about the spiritual character and potential of each individual essential oil, but also about their therapeutic properties as used in physical healing, and their benefits to the mind and emotions. All three aspects of an essential oil could be considered, as each person has themselves a profile including their physical, emotional and spiritual aspects.

Essential oils are about vivification, the process of being enlivened in the spiritual sense. Each individual person is unique, however, and is touched by each essential oil in a different way. Just as we meet people with whom we are in harmony, and who enliven our souls, so too we can discover in the superabundance of essential oils those which release our spiritual potential.

The section in the profiles entitled 'Emotional Healing' shows those emotional qualities which that particular essential oil will help to bring out in a person. The section 'Physical Healing' contains the therapeutic properties, a glossary for which can be found before the profiles.

WHAT ARE ESSENTIAL OILS?

- Essential oils exist only in certain parts of aromatic plants, from which they are distilled or otherwise extracted.
- Only some species of the aromatic plants are used – there are approximately 700 varieties of geranium, for example, but only ten produce an essential oil which could be used in aromatherapy.
- Only specific parts of the essential oil-producing plants are used. Depending on the species, the essential oil might be extracted from the petals, or flowering tops, leaves, twigs or stems, roots, rhizome, grass, resin, bark, chopped heartwood, fruit or seed.
- The essential oils are found within the plant parts

in specialized cells, buds, canals, cavities, ducts, vittae or glands. Some plants produce their essential oil within 'oil hairs' or glandular trichomes, extending from the surface of the leaves.

- Most usually, essential oils are extracted from the relevant part of the plant by steam distillation. Essential oils in fruit peel – their zest – is extracted by cold-pressing or 'cold expression'. Enfleurage or solvent extraction is often used with flower petals, as steam distillation is usually too 'rough' a process for them.

- The essential oil in petals is often first extracted with enfleurage, then by extraction of the resulting concrete or pomade – using natural solvents or CO_2. The end result is called an absolute, and contains the heavier molecules, as well as the lighter ones that are extracted through the more usual steam distillation. Absolutes contain additional components, including waxes, colour pigments, fatty acids, vitamins and minerals, making the absolute smell just like the flower itself.

Capturing the Fragrance of our Favourite Flowers – What to do if You Don't Have the Essential Oils

When using fragrance for spiritual use, we do not always have to use essential oils – some of which can sometimes be difficult to find or afford. The extraction method called maceration captures the fragrance of aromatic plant material, especially petals, and can be used at home. It produces an oil that can be used as a body oil or added to the bath.

Simply put as many fragrant petals as you can into an airtight container and cover them with a vegetable oil, such as almond. Leave for a couple of days, then strain off the oil, keeping it in a clean jug or cup. Throw the old petals away, but keep the oil and add fresh petals to it. Leave it again for a couple of days. Keep repeating this process until the oil has taken on the strength of fragrance you like. Methods like this have been used since very ancient times, and basically involve the vegetable oil drawing out from the petals their fragrant molecules – the essential oils.

For spiritual use, it is the fragrance of aromatic plant material we use, and this comes from living plants which are often available in our own gardens or in flower shops. The living plants or flowers can be brought into our home and their aroma inhaled. We can even go into flower shops specifically to inhale our favourite spiritual aroma. Flowers such as pinks (carnations), hyacinths, narcissi and tuberoses can easily be grown in the garden or as a pot plant inside.

Spiritual fragrances are all around us. We can break the rind of citrus fruits and inhale the fresh zest – the essential oil. We can find spices in our own larder. And if taking a walk in a pine forest, stop to pick up some of the dark green needles, crush them between your hands and inhale their delicious fragrance. Fragrance is a gift of Heaven, there for us all to enjoy – any time, any place and in any way we can.

Glossary of Therapeutic Properties as Itemized Under the Heading *'Physical Healing'*

Analgesic: reduces sensation of pain.
Antibiotic / anti-bacterial: prevents bacterial growth.
Anti-fungal: prevents fungal growth.
Anti-infectious: prevents uptake of infection.

Anti-parasitic: acts against insect parasites.

Anti-putrescent: acts against putrefaction.

Anti-sclerotic: prevents hardening of cells and tissues.

Antiseptic: destroys microbes and prevents their development.

Anti-spasmodic: prevents or relieves spasms, convulsions or contractions.

Anti-sudorific: prevents sweating.

Anti-tussive: relieves coughs.

Anti-viral: prevents viral growth.

Balsamic: soothing to sore throats, coughs etc.

Calmative: sedative, calming agent.

Carminative: relieves flatulence, easing abdominal pain and bloating.

Cholagogue: promotes the evacuation of bile from gall bladder and ducts.

Cicatrisive: promotes the formation of scar tissue, thus healing.

Cytophylactic: promotes cell turnover, thus healing.

Depurative: cleanser, detoxifyer; purifies blood and internal organs.

Diuretic: promotes the removal of excess water from the body by urine.

Emmenagogue: induces or regularizes menstruation.

Emollient: soothes and softens skin.

Expectorant: promotes removal of mucus from the body.

Febrifuge: an anti-febrile agent; anti-fever.

Galactagogue: induces the flow of milk.

Haemostatic: stops bleeding.

Hepatic: acts on the liver.

Immuno-stimulant: stimulates the action of the immune system.

Mucolytic: breaks down mucous.

Nervine: acts on nerves; relieves nervous disorders.

Pectoral: beneficial for diseases or conditions of the chest and respiratory system.

Rubefacient: a counter-irritant producing redness of the skin.

Sedative: reduces mental excitement or physical activity.

Soporific: induces, or tends to induce, sleep.

Stimulant: increases overall function of the body.

Stomachic: good for the stomach; gastric tonic, digestive aid.

Tonic: invigorates, refreshes and restores body functions.

Vasoconstrictor: causes narrowing of the blood vessels and therefore a decrease in blood flow.

Vasodilator: causes widening of the blood vessels and therefore an increase in blood flow.

Vermifuge: expels intestinal worms.

Vulnerary: heals wounds and sores by external application.

Amber
Pinus succinifera

Through the veil of time, through the incarnations of man, this fragrance has remained, until washed up upon a shore or found buried deep in the forest. Such a fragrance has the ability to take us to the beginning of forever.

It can assist us in knowing where we have been, and to complete the cycle of where we are going. If time is circular, then amber holds the key. What spirit cannot be enthralled with such knowledge, such wisdom? As it is breathed in, it holds the mystery of the birth of the planet and of the universe; the creation of life, the garden of Eden, the clay which formed mankind; the walk of the giants, the mysteries of the prophets, the masters who came to earth. All have known this fragrance from the start of the world.

PHYSICAL HEALING

calmative, analgesic, antispasmodic, expectorant, febrifuge

AROMA

resinous, warm, smoky, with faint citrus/floral undertone

Combines well with
geranium, pine, spruce, cedarwood, myrrh, galbanum, frankincense, cypress, clove, aniseed, lemon, orange, cistus, rose absolute, hyacinth, yuzu, carnation, benzoin

EMOTIONAL HEALING

To encourage harmony, balance, inspiration, visions and inner knowing.

Angelica Root
Angelica archangelica

Encaptured within its powerful fragrance is the possibility to draw close to us those angelic forces that are receptive to our needs. It is the revealing sword of Michael cutting through pretence and falsehoods, bringing into the light shadows that we have denied within ourselves. Yet, in this disclosure, it has compassion and an understanding of all our failings, and of our longing for spiritual completion.

PHYSICAL HEALING

anti-spasmodic, expectorant, diuretic, depurative, emmenagogue

• Avoid during pregnancy.

• Should not be used on the skin if being exposed to sunlight or ultraviolet rays.

AROMA

earthy, herby-green, rich

Combines well with
bergamot, lemon, orange, grapefruit, lime, lemongrass, juniper, rosemary, eucalyptus, vetiver

EMOTIONAL HEALING

To encourage strength, stamina, comfort, focus, solidity, grounding and inner visions.

Angelica Seed
Angelica archangelica

With angelic virtues, its fragrance spreads to all around and in so doing spreads the protectiveness of the Creator, and etherealness; the lightness of being imbued with the might of the heavens. With gracefulness, angelica seed gently persuades the spirit to partake in the feast of the universe. It can shelter the vulnerable from intrusions into their thoughts and prayers, whilst allowing the guardians to give their reassurance.

PHYSICAL HEALING

carminative, digestive, diuretic, stomachic, depurative, general tonic

- Avoid during pregnancy.

- Try to avoid using on the skin if being exposed to sunlight or ultraviolet rays.

AROMA

clear, spicy, peppery

Combines well with
bergamot, cardamom, carnation, clary sage, coriander, fennel, geranium, hyacinth, jasmine, lemon, rose otto, sage

EMOTIONAL HEALING

To encourage inspiration, creativity, focus, concentration and inner vision.

Aniseed
Pimpinella anisum

One night a plant deva dared the aniseed plant to be strong and defiant. It protested, and ever since has assisted those who insist they have no need for prayer and are unbelievers. In defiance of what they know deep inside themselves to be true, they travel life's highway saying they have no need for a deity, that they believe in nothing. Yet when aniseed is given, perhaps as a medicine to calm the nerves, something else takes place – a puzzlement, a conflict. It can be dismissed, or a step can be taken to examine it further. And if that one small step is taken, then aniseed has completed its task: to make the conscious mind aware, even if protesting, that there is a conductor of the universe, and we are all part of the same orchestration.

PHYSICAL HEALING

antiseptic, anti-spasmodic, carminative, expectorant, stimulant, galactagogue

• Can cause irritation to sensitive skin.

AROMA

typical of aniseed: spicy-sweet

Combines well with
bay, clove, cinnamon, ginger, fennel, lemon, grapefruit, mandarin, peppermint, spearmint, geranium, myrrh, frankincense

EMOTIONAL HEALING

To encourage upliftment, stimulation, fearlessness, harmony, balance and to dispel timidity.

Balsam de Peru
Myroxylon balsamum

*This is a sweet aroma, soft like the innocence of a child
yet with an unconditional love and empathy which
stems from an understanding of the human state of
being. Its soft, warm fragrance fills the spaces which
have remained cold, untouchable and unreachable,
allowing the opening up of the heart without
recrimination, in trust and without judgement.
When in sorrow, the fragrance travels into the psyche
to give comfort and relief from pain. It softly
embraces us, spreading its fragrance around us like a
cloak of velvet, smooth to the touch and gentle to the
heart, cushioning us against emotional storms which
may impede our spiritual voyage.*

PHYSICAL HEALING	AROMA	EMOTIONAL HEALING
antiseptic, balsamic, expectorant, stimulant, pectoral, anti-tussive	vanilla-like resin	To encourage warmth, calm, comfort, peacefulness, and the feeling of being soothed.
• Can cause irritation to sensitive skin.	**Combines well with** rose absolute, ylang ylang, sandalwood, patchouli, petitgrain, clove, cinnamon, hyacinth, tuberose, orange, grapefruit, mandarin, cardamom, coriander	

Basil
Ocimum basilicum

Basil allows enlightenment to be absorbed by the physical mind-body, acting as a conduit, grounding at the same time as balancing subconscious thought and conscious reaction. It is then, a fragrance of reality — the reality of both physical and spiritual existence. It soars through all the realms, holding them together, allowing integration. It is a fragrance that not only harmonizes the many aspects of the person, allowing the light of the spirit to be held within, where it can illuminate the soul, it also stimulates recognition of those many aspects. It uplifts, awakens and clarifies, and in this respect is particularly useful for those who, through life's emotional circumstances, have become numbed to the wholeness of human existence.
For those who have lost their self through constant sacrifice to others, basil offers an opening of the heart, and a view of the universal whole.

PHYSICAL HEALING

restorative, general stimulant, anti-spasmodic, emmenagogue, stomachic, digestive tonic, intestinal antiseptic, anti-infectious

• Avoid during pregnancy.

AROMA

warm, rich, fiery, sharp, peppery, aniseed-like

Combines well with
bergamot, black pepper, cedarwood, clary sage, coriander, cypress, fennel, geranium, ginger, grapefruit, jasmine, juniper, lemon, niaouli, orange, palma rosa, pine, rosemary, sage, tea tree, thyme linalol

EMOTIONAL HEALING

To encourage positivity, purposefulness, concentration, assertiveness, decisiveness, straightforwardness, trust, integrity, enthusiasm, clarity, cheerfulness and strength.

• Can cause irritation
to sensitive skin.

• Not to be used
undiluted in baths.

In modern Greece, basil is venerated because it sprung up
at the place where it is said St Helen found the true cross
of Jesus. It's also associated with Saint Basil, and much
used during the Festival of St Basil, on 1 January.

'Holy Basil' (*Ocimum sanctum*) is known in India as *tulsi*.
Sacred to Krishna and Vishnu, some say also to Shiva, it's
thought to deter demons from coming near, and thus
became the protective plant of the house and of the spirit
of the family. It's said that every good Hindu places a basil
leaf on his/her chest when resting; also that basil, planted
on a grave, will help the soul pass to heaven.

In Nepal, basil is said to hold the spirit of Lakshmi,
consort of the god Vishnu.

Bay Laurel
Laurus nobilis

*This is the fragrance of victors and poets who have
used imagination and inspiration to attain their
goals. It encourages the gift of prophecy and
creativity, able to go beyond the normal activities of
the brain and in so doing bring forth tales of the
future and of destiny.
A scent fired by the sun, protective and preventative –
preventing the hold of unwanted forces upon the spirit
and clearing the confusion away. This is a fragrance
to use when the way ahead seems uncertain or
fraught with danger, when impoverished thoughts fly
silently through the night, to disturb our dreams and
our waking consciousness. To protect, yet give
inspiration, in the darkest hours when the mind
interferes and tells us that all is lost in the challenge
to conquer the shadows.*

PHYSICAL HEALING

antiseptic,
analgesic,
anti-neuralgic,
anti-infectious,
general
stimulant

• Avoid during
  pregnancy.

• Can cause
  irritation to
  sensitive
  skin.

AROMA

spicy, sweet, fresh,
balsamic

Combines well with
benzoin, bergamot,
black pepper,
cardamom, cinnamon,
clove, coriander,
cypress, frankincense,
geranium, ginger,
lavender, grapefruit,
juniper, lemon,
mandarin, orange,
rosemary, ylang ylang

EMOTIONAL HEALING

To encourage
confidence,
fortitude,
inspiration,
protection,
direction and
creativity.

287

'... resisteth witchcraft very potently, as also all the evils old Saturn can do to the body of man, and they are not a few ... neither witch nor devil, thunder nor lightning, will hurt a man in a place where a bay-tree is.'

Culpeper's Complete Herbal, 1649

In ancient Greek and Roman times, bay leaves were symbolic of great accomplishment, in sports as in literature. Thus, victors at Olympic games were crowned with bay leaves, and the term 'poet laureate' persists today.

Clouds of burning bay leaves were inhaled by the oracle of Delphi, to help induce her oracular powers of divination.

Benzoin
Styrax benzoin dryander

A gentleness of heart can sometimes grip the spirit and senses in an untold knowing, without words of explanation. No matter what touches the spirit, the soul must be allowed to speak, to be able to penetrate to the core of being. How misunderstood is this deep resin which is the holder of the energies and fire of sunlight, one of the joyous gifts of the universe. Persuasive and direct, it will open the heart and mind to receiving gifts which have been denied; allowing the spirit to receive from the soul, in feeling, in knowing, in just being.
Benzoin can be a pathway to understanding when all is confusion. It can assist in the choices which must be made with the heart, and be the softness needed when all contact with the self has been lost, helping guide us home to that place within, the inner sanctum of the soul. Life in this world is never easy and yet we have help awaiting, if only we ask for it. With our conscious minds we can forget those unseen who wait to assist us.

Benzoin tells us not to dismiss things which are difficult – the outcome to situations we may not want – but to hear the messages and be guided by them. Some things can be difficult to accept, but as the years advance, we may gain understanding of the teaching of our lessons. In this, benzoin gives us its shedded tears to use for guidance in that understanding, and for peace, on the pathway to inner enlightenment.

PHYSICAL HEALING

antiseptic, antidepressant, vulnerary, expectorant

• Avoid during pregnancy.

• Can cause irritation to sensitive skin.

AROMA

warm, balsamic, chocolatey-vanilla

Combines well with bay, bergamot, black pepper, cardamom, coriander, frankincense, ginger, geranium, grape-fruit, lemon, litsea cubeba, jasmine, nutmeg, orange, patchouli, palma rosa, rose absolute, sandalwood, ylang ylang

EMOTIONAL HEALING

To encourage comfort, elevation, peace, determination, while being soothing, cushioning and protective.

There are many types of benzoin, and wherever it occurs, it's used to produce a spiritually protective fragrance. For example, in Costa Rica *Styrax argenteum* is used as incense in churches, in Brazil they use *Styrax camporum*, while in Malaysia *Styrax tonkinense* is often mixed with myrrh or chocolate.

In Malaysia, it is burnt to deter bad spirits, especially during rice-crop ceremonies.

In Java, fishermen burn benzoin before entering the dark coastal caves where shoals of fish gather.

In Mali, it is used by shamans to facilitate transformation into other life-forms.

In India, it is used in Hindu worship, and in China in Taoist elixirs to prolong lifespan.

Bergamot
Citrus bergamia

The high frequency of bergamot works well in the auric field and also in that area of the light field which is closest to the body. It is an amplifier of light energy, energizing and magnifying, opening the heart to cosmic joy.

Bergamot lightens the shadows of the mind, bringing illumination and laughter. With this, it brings eternal youth and happiness, even to those who have put aside their problems, ignoring them until they have become so overwhelming that the person feels they cannot ask for help.

Bergamot teaches that the help of the angelic realms is ever there, all we have to do is reach for it. We may cry inside, our hearts aching, but bergamot will lighten the heart, and dispel self-criticism and blame.

To any soul, bergamot brings freshness and illumination, lifting us from stagnation, bringing an awareness that the light will rescue us and take us ever forward to the realms of peace and joy.

PHYSICAL HEALING	AROMA	EMOTIONAL HEALING
antiseptic, anti-spasmodic, stomachic, antidepressant, calmative, febrifuge, vermifuge	sweet, fruity, citrus with spicy-floral undertones	To encourage concentration, confidence, balance, strength, joy, motivation, good cheer, harmony and completeness.
• Should not be used on the skin if being exposed to sunlight or ultraviolet rays.	**Combines well with** all essential oils, including: black pepper, clary sage, cypress, frankincense, geranium, helichrysum, jasmine, lavender, mandarin, nutmeg, orange, ormenis flower, rosemary, sandalwood, vetiver, ylang ylang	

Birch (White)
Betula alba

A high-spirited essence of instruction and advice. It is there for whenever a clear pathway is needed for communication. It is a protective spirit which guards and guides, clearing away thought pollution or debris that may be lingering in the mind. It can stop unwanted energies being transferred into our environment, not unlike the wind clearing away clouds so the light can shine through.
If violation has occurred in any form, then this is the essential oil to use in a sacred space before using other more spiritually connecting fragrances. It is the celestial dustcart, sweeping up the misdirected and misguided thought-forms.

PHYSICAL HEALING	AROMA	EMOTIONAL HEALING
antiseptic, diuretic, tonic	balsamic, woody, green	To encourage protection, focus and concentration.
• Not to be used during pregnancy.	**Combines well with** cedarwood, cypress, frankincense, myrrh, black pepper, cinnamon, clove, myrtle, rosemary, eucalyptus, thyme	

Black Pepper
Piper nigrum

*This fragrance is strength and fortitude, giving us the
bravery to venture forth into places unknown and
unseen. Fearless in our progress, with no questions
but instead a deep faith and certainty in the
knowledge that we will be protected and guided every
step of the way. Strength is often needed: strength of
spirit to hold fast against adversity; ingenuity to
avoid making decisions that may not be in our best
interest and which we intuitively know is not the road
we wish to take; and the ability to hold fast to our
dreams and aspirations when everyone around us is
advising us in our choices.*

*Black pepper enables us to listen to the inner voice of
inspiration, and to take chances knowing that,
whatever happens, we alone have taken them.*

PHYSICAL HEALING

analgesic, antiseptic,
expectorant, tonic,
febrifuge,
aphrodisiac, anti-
catarrhal, digestive,
moderate rube-
facient, diuretic

There are over 900
species of pepper
but only about ten
are used in
medicines.

• Can cause
  irritation to
  sensitive skin.

• Not to be used
  undiluted in
  baths.

AROMA

strong, warm,
peppery

**Combines well
with**
bergamot, clary
sage, clove,
coriander, fennel,
frankincense,
geranium, ginger,
grapefruit,
lavender, juniper,
lemon, lemongrass,
lime, mandarin,
marjoram, myrrh,
orange, palma rosa,
rosemary, sage,
sandalwood, tea
tree, ylang ylang

EMOTIONAL HEALING

To encourage
fearlessness,
strength,
stamina,
endurance,
motivation,
flexibility and
comfort.

Camphor
Dryobalanops aromatica

*No timidity surrounds camphor, a fragrance of the
warrior angels. For freedom of the spirit and enlightenment camphor protects the soul. It is not the
sweetest smelling fragrance belonging to the angelic
world, yet camphor may be involved in our salvation.
With the might of the angelic realms and the heavens
behind it, camphor brings cleansing and purification,
and has done so for aeons. For longer than we can
imagine, the camphor tree has been guarding the
passages of life, a spiritual protector and guardian
of rebirth.*

PHYSICAL HEALING	AROMA	EMOTIONAL HEALING
analgesic, anti-spasmodic, antiseptic, carminative, tonic	camphorous balsam	To encourage upliftment, stimulation and liberation.
• Not to be used during pregnancy.	**Combines well with** rosemary, lavender, marjoram, peppermint, lemon, thyme, ravensara, cardamom, black pepper, orange, spearmint, tea tree, yarrow	
• Can cause irritation to sensitive skin.		

Sometimes referred to as 'borneol'.

Native to Borneo and Sumatra, this resin has long been
highly prized as an incense ingredient, believed to keep
away malevolent spirits.

Throughout south-east Asia, the wood of the various
camphor trees is used in temple building, and in the making of religious icons. Many large Buddhas have been
made from this wood.

Cardamom
Elettaria cardamomum

*Sweet cardamom, bringing the mysteries of the Orient,
a fragrance to stimulate the memories from the cycles
of incarnation, and the creativity and abundance
emanating from our higher selves. Cardamom gives us
wisdom when we are overburdened with responsibili-
ties, when we need to tap into our generosity of spirit to
allow our hearts to be open and expansive in order to
be gracious in our dealings with others. Also, it gives
encouragement when we need to take a step forward to
offer a hand of friendship when we see that a person is
in need. Cardamom assists in stimulating the spiritual
senses, awakening us to the bountiful in nature, and to
the beauty there is in seeing with our hearts the often
hidden virtues in all mankind.*

PHYSICAL HEALING	AROMA	EMOTIONAL HEALING
antiseptic, digestive stimulant, carminative, stomachic, diuretic, anti-spasmodic, expectorant	fresh, sweet green, spicy, balsamic **Combines well with** bay, bergamot, black pepper, cedarwood, cinnamon, clove, coriander, fennel, ginger, grapefruit, lemon, lemongrass, mandarin, litsea cubeba, neroli, orange, patchouli, palma rosa, petitgrain, sandal-wood, vetiver, ylang ylang, jasmine	To encourage clarity, concentration, direction, motivation, straight-forwardness, enthusiasm, confidence and courage.

'. . . the cardamom seeds illustrate the bifold structure of
maya or veiling. Mystics of all faiths have affirmed this
duality in every aspect of life, pointing to it as the source
of all creative activity.' Omar Garrison, *Tantra*

Carnation (Absolute)
Dianthus caryophyllus

Carnation soothes the soul, rejoicing in the rebirth of the spirit. It allows long forgotten memories to merge in a symphony of being, of oneness with the universe. It touches inner feelings buried through circumstances, which, in turn, enables messages from the spirit to comfort and cajole. Such joy is held within the fragrance that even the shyest aspects of self can be brought forth into the sunlight, to rejoice in the glory of Heaven. We do not need always to voice our needs and blessings, yet we may have a yearning to understand them. Carnation allows us to luxuriate in the knowing of the experience. The uplifting experience of reaching higher realms brings untold gladness to the heart and soul.

PHYSICAL HEALING

calmative, sedative, neuro tonic, soporific

Only very small amounts of absolute oil are used in blends as these oils can be very strong.

Bay essential oil and synthetic aromatics such as eugenol, isoeugenol, and phenyl ethyl alcohol are sometimes used to adulterate carnation oil.

AROMA

rich, floral, spicy, honey-clove

Combines well with
rose absolute, clove, lemon, black pepper, bergamot, geranium, orange, neroli, ylang ylang, sandalwood, jasmine, clary sage, chamomile roman, coriander, cardamom, hyacinth, yuzu

EMOTIONAL HEALING

To encourage self-worth, communication, creativity, independence, tenderness, cushioning, openness and release.

Cedarwood
Cedrus atlantica

*Steadiness is the message of the spirit of cedarwood.
It is the spirit of integrity, of stability, of solidarity in
all things. It has qualities which are often needed
when the spirit is weakened by living too much,
loving too hard, and being unable to forgive. It
encourages the strength we need to continue on our
pathway, and urges us to hold fast to our dreams,
helping bring our hopes to reality.
It can bring understanding from a non-emotional
standpoint, while allowing compassion to be ever
present. Its spirit has the energy to allow us to
continue with a job or task that may seem distasteful
to us, and it gives us the strength not to feel revenge-
ful. Cedarwood is the spirit of the ancients; the vigour
and might of the universe; its elders holding fast the
earth while living through many incarnations of the
human soul. It allows us to look into our past while
looking forward to the future in strength of heart,
wisdom and the security of love.*

PHYSICAL HEALING

antiseptic, tonic, anti-spasmodic, regenerative

Several different types of essential oil are distilled from other species of cedar, for example, *Juniperas virginiana* and *Cedrus libani* (Himalayan cedar).

AROMA

warm, sweet, soft, woody, balsamic

Combines well with
bay, bergamot, cardamom, chamomile roman, clary sage, cypress, fir, frankincense, geranium, grapefruit, juniper, lavender, marjoram, orange, neroli, palma rosa, petitgrain, pine, rosemary, sandalwood, ylang ylang

EMOTIONAL HEALING

It encourages strength, focus, balance, fortitude, persistence, confidence, protectiveness and concentration.

'The trees of the Lord are full of sap; the cedars of Lebanon, which He hath planted.' Psalms, 104:16

'. . . in (India) a fire is kindled with twigs of the sacred cedar, and the Dainyal or sibyl, with a cloth over her head, inhales the thick pungent smoke till she is seized with convulsions and falls senseless to the ground. Soon she rises and raises a shrill chant, which is caught up and loudly repeated by her audience.'

J. G. Frazer, *The Golden Bough*

Used by the ancient Egyptians for mummification and, as by other ancient cultures, for sarcophagi, palace and temple building material. According to Dr Christian Ratsch, author of *The Dictionary of Sacred and Magical Plants*, 'The cedar ... played a central role in the Egyptian tree cult; since it arose from the god Osiris, it became a symbol of eternal return. For this reason, its wood, but especially its oil, was thought to contain magical powers which the proper magical formulae could call forth.'

The Native American Nations use cedar extensively, both for medicine and for spiritual purification. The Guarani, for example, hold the cedar as sacred, using both wood and oil in their shamanic practices, saying the sap is a part of eternity. Cedar was the first tree their god, Nanderuvuzu, created, and it still stands in their paradise.

Chamomile German
Matricaria recutita

*When used with purpose and direction, the fragrance
of the blue chamomile assists in seeking spiritual
understanding. Its petals open with the sun, and it
pulls down the energy from the heavens and the solar
system. When inhaled with purpose, it can allow a
deeper knowledge of the working of the universe, and
of certain angelic orders who work close to the earth.
When confusion seems to have become prevalent in a
person's spiritual life, and the laws of the Creator
seem to have no meaning to the life we live on earth,
then the fragrance can often help us to understand.
As we all already know the answers, it is that we need
a stillness to react to the wisdom stemming from God
which can be found by meditation. It can help the
transference of prayers, and gives clearer understanding of God's work, energies and laws.*

PHYSICAL HEALING	AROMA	EMOTIONAL HEALING
calmative, analgesic, anti-spasmodic, febrifuge, anti-inflammatory, immuno-stimulant, emmenagogue, digestive, hepatic, vulnerary	sweet, straw-like, herby **Combines well with** bergamot, chamomile roman, clary sage, lavender, cypress, frankincense, geranium, marjoram, lemon, grapefruit, niaouli, pine, ravensara, rosemary, tea tree	To encourage communication, relaxation, understanding, organization, empathy, patience, calm and to soothe.

Chamomile Roman
Anthemis nobilis

Harmonizing, peaceful, soothing to the spirit.
Chamomile roman resonates beyond the auric, and
beyond the seven rays. It operates in the realm of light
and connects with the light body.
Connects with the inner child in us, allowing us to come
closer to the spiritual realms for comfort and uniting.
Use for gentleness, when the spirit is sad.
The petals open their arms in prayer as the sun rises,
giving thanks to the Creator, sending their fragrance
into the heavens where angels capture each tiny mole-
cule and hold it close to their heart – to send back to the
children of the earth in times of need.

PHYSICAL HEALING

analgesic,
anti-spasmodic,
calmative,
antiseptic,
antibiotic,
anti-inflammatory,
anti-infectious,
vulnerary,
immuno-stimulant,
sedative,
anti-neuralgic,
nervine,
antidepressant

AROMA

fruity, sweet, fresh,
herbaceous, rather
apple-like

Blends well with
lavender, geranium,
lemon, grapefruit, rose
otto, neroli, jasmine,
clary sage

EMOTIONAL HEALING

To encourage
stillness, calm,
softness,
gentleness,
relaxation,
serenity,
spiritual
awareness,
emotional
stability, inner
peace,
understanding
and
co-operation.

'*Chamomile anthemis palaestina* has scented aromatic leaves and white, downy flowers . . . would very likely have been growing around and about our Lord's feet as He was speaking.'

W. E. Shewell Cooper, *Plants, Flowers and Herbs of the Bible*

In preparation for passing to spirit, a variety of chamomile was used on the body of Rameses II in *c.* 1224 BC – possibly as a scented oil.

In Tutankhamen's tomb, statues of the gods were garlanded with leaves and flowers, including 'mayweed', a type of chamomile – *Anthemis pseudocotula.*

Cinnamon
Cinnamomum zeylanicum

Love, in all its many guises, speaks through cinnamon to touch those hidden areas of the self that we have denied love access to. Bringing into our hearts the ever-understanding love and oneness, it invites love from higher realms; even if at first, inner love is often difficult in the human state of being, the warm glow of cinnamon radiates through all space and time, transforming sorrow into happiness. It brings the realization that love is always there, if we tune into its warm vibration.

PHYSICAL HEALING	AROMA	EMOTIONAL HEALING
anti-infectious, antiseptic, analgesic, stimulant, anti-spasmodic, emmenagogue • Not to be used during pregnancy. • Can cause irritation on sensitive skin.	warm, spicy, sweet **Combines well with** clove, nutmeg, ylang ylang, mandarin, orange, lemon, grapefruit, benzoin, rose absolute, bay, carnation, coriander, cardamom, geranium, ginger, lemongrass, patchouli, petitgrain, yuzu	To encourage invigoration, benevolence, strength, energy, confidence, motivation and generosity.

Cinnamon has been recorded as being used in China in 2700 BC, and was known to the Egyptians by 1500 BC. According to Lise Manniche, a papyrus recording the offerings made by Rameses III to the god Amun amounted to 'one whole log, 246 measures and 82 bundles'. She says there is no evidence of the ancient Egyptians having burnt cinnamon in offering to their gods.

In Exodus 16, after being in the wilderness of Shur for three days without water, Moses and the people of Israel arrived at Marah, but the waters were 'bitter' and undrinkable. Moses appealed to God, 'and the Lord shewed him a tree, which when he had cast into the waters, the waters were made sweet'. As only date palms grew there, Dr de Waal has suggested that Moses used cinnamon bark. Two hundred and fifty shekels of 'sweet cinnamon' were included in the holy anointing oil of Exodus 30:23.

Clary Sage
Salvia sclarea

The abundance within this fragrance is captivating, full of prosperity of the spirit. It has benefits for both the physical and psychological aspects of mankind, while also promoting contentment in a loving heart.
Clary sage teaches us to be satisfied with our achievements, and brings the realization that most of our problems exist in the imagination, and that issues which affect us will be resolved eventually. Instead, whispers clary sage, be at ease, and focus on contacting the inner spirit.
Clary sage carries spiritual timelessness within itself – a second could be a year, a year a second – and brings the realization that it's how much love we can pour into a second that counts.

PHYSICAL HEALING

antiseptic, calmative, tonic, emmenagogue, anti-infectious, nervine

AROMA

nutty, warm, light, musky, herbaceous

Combines well with geranium, lemon, grapefruit, lavender, sandalwood, cypress, mandarin, jasmine, juniper, rose absolute, bergamot, bay, black pepper, coriander, lime, patchouli, tea tree

EMOTIONAL HEALING

To encourage calm, confidence, grounding, regeneration, tranquillity, revitalization, balance and restoration.

The name 'salvia' is derived from the Latin for 'good health', and has come to mean wisdom, as in 'the sages'.

Clove (Bud)
Eugenia caryophyllata

Stirring the spirit, clove has no time for contemplation, only for action. Such is the message of clove: move forward, make things happen, achieve as much as your spirit can, without harming another. This is sometimes the most difficult aspect of what we have to encounter – not hindering others on their journey, nor giving them pain, while moving ourselves forward.

Clove assists in the awakening of the senses, and in our striving for completion and oneness. It passes to us the sensitive confidence we need to be unafraid. This fragrance discourages inhibiting thoughts and encourages progressive deeds, making it easier to ride the waves while weathering the storms.

PHYSICAL HEALING

antiseptic, stimulant, analgesic, anti-neuralgic, anti-spasmodic, carminative, anti-infectious, tonic

• Not to be used during pregnancy.

• Can cause irritation to sensitive skin.

AROMA

rich, warm, sweet, spicy

Combines well with lemon, geranium, lavender, grapefruit, chamomile roman, ginger, palma rosa, ylang ylang, sandalwood, mandarin, jasmine, clary sage, bay, benzoin

EMOTIONAL HEALING

To encourage stimulation, regeneration, inspiration, trust and inner warmth.

304

Some commentators have suggested that the *'onycha'* mentioned in the recipe for the holy 'perfume' in Exodus 30:34, can be translated as 'nail', and indicates the use of dried clove buds.

In parts of Central America, it is believed that clove will dispel the demons of disease.

Coriander
Coriandrum sativum

Its fragrance is fresh, as if seeking new horizons. It's cool, it's hot – ever changing, depending upon the receiver's mood. The seeds are sweet, the flowers deli- cate – like a lacy cloud atop a green field. Fragrant yet subtle is this plant – like its action upon the human spirit. Gentle and compassionate, it inter- twines with the inner depths of the nature of man. For seekers who wish to experience all things, before they feel sure of themselves and of the future thoroughfare to their soul. Who can understand the changing heart better than our guides? How can we change, yet still be true to ourselves and not stray too far from the joy of being at one with the universe? In this fragrance lies the challenge of change, helping us to go forward, even if timidly, rather than staying behind for ever wondering: 'what if?'

PHYSICAL HEALING	AROMA	EMOTIONAL HEALING
sedative, anti-spasmodic, carminative, stimulant, tonic, stomachic, depurative, regenerative	sweet, warm, spicy **Combines well with** amber, bergamot, clary sage, black pepper, cardamom, cinnamon, clove, cypress, frankincense, geranium, ginger, grapefruit, lemon, neroli, nutmeg, orange, palma rosa, petitgrain, pine, ravensara, sandalwood, vetiver, ylang ylang, jasmine	To encourage creativity, imagination, good memory, confidence, motivation, optimism, sincerity, expressiveness and enthusiasm.

'And the manna was as coriander seed, and the colour thereof as the colour of bdellium.' Numbers 11:7.

Coriander seeds have been used for thousands of years. They were found in Tutankhamen's tomb.

Cypress
Cupressus sempervirens

*Cypress is often associated with the passing of a soul
into the deity's presence, bringing comfort to those left
behind, who will continue to hold their loved one in
their hearts. Cypress has frequencies that are in
transition between the physical and the spiritual,
which is why it can be used to assist in the passing
over of a spirit.*

*Cypress has the ability to connect strongly with
human frequencies and thought-forms. With great
direction, cypress helps connection with the wisdom of
the universe.*

*It empathizes with suffering, the energies that
emanate from a life in sorrow. It offers strength and
energetic protection to those who need protecting, and
those who are feeling vulnerable and insecure, or have
lost their purpose. Cypress can be used to move on.*

PHYSICAL HEALING	AROMA	EMOTIONAL HEALING
astringent, anti-spasmodic, anti-sudorific, diuretic, restorative, cicatrisive, vasoconstrictor, respiratory tonic, calmative	woody, warm, slightly spicy **Combines well with** bergamot, clary sage, lemon, lavender, orange, lime, juniper, pine, marjoram, chamomile roman, mandarin, sandalwood, rosemary, geranium, eucalyptus, frankincense, cedarwood, pine, rosemary	To encourage comfort, change, assertion, understanding, balance, stillness, confidence, inner peace, wisdom, stability, patience, trust, incorruptibility, willpower and straightforwardness.

The cross of Jesus, and Noah's ark, are thought to have been made of cypress.

The ancient Egyptians used cypress to make coffins, while other ancient peoples used it in their funeral pyres. Cypress trees are often grown in Muslim graveyards.

The wood was used by goddess worshippers to make images.

Dill
Anethum graveolens

*We can find devotion and love in the smallest thing,
because all of Creation is an act of love. A flower or a
seed shine with love. A tree or a meadow have love
flowing through them in the energy of the plant life.
The majesty of the rocks and mountains has the spirit
of protection and strength. The smallest seed is a
powerhouse of energy, whether spilling into the body of
the world, or existing within ourselves. The fragrance
of dill is so sweet one is reminded of the wonder
in the world.*

*The joy of Creation is encapsulated in dill, as is the
taking in of spiritual nourishment from the heavens,
bringing closeness with the angelic realms. Dill
reminds the human spirit that the body is fragile, and
indebted to the earth. With purity and optimism, dill
shows a clear way to complete the tasks we undertake
on our journey.*

PHYSICAL HEALING

anti-spasmodic,
emmenagogue,
stimulant,
carminative,
digestive

AROMA

unique sweet, herby
spice

Combines well with
coriander, cardamom,
peppermint,
spearmint, orange,
nutmeg, bergamot,
clove, mandarin,
pimento berry,
juniper, bay, aniseed,
lemon, myrtle, fennel,
ginger, geranium

EMOTIONAL HEALING

To encourage
tenderness,
transformation,
harmony,
soothing, calm
and cushioning.

309

Elemi
Canarium luzonicum

Emptiness fills the mind, silence creeps softly over the heart, and stillness enters. For elemi is a fragrance of placidity, of the quiet need to hear our own soul speak from deep within.

Elemi awakens the knowing which is hushed in the waking dream of reality. It speaks to the inner being, lulling the quickened heart and mind, steadying us that we can complete what we have begun. Wrapping us in a cloak of sympathy when our spirit is most in need of comfort, elemi is soothing yet strong; supporting our humanity, offering strength, and also the upliftment we need to reconnect all parts of our being – our mind, body and spirit.

PHYSICAL HEALING

antiseptic, cicatrisive, expectorant, tonic

AROMA

spicy, citrus, fresh balsam

Combines well with frankincense, hyssop, rosemary, cistus, lavender, cinnamon, clove, orange, lemon, ormenis flower, ginger, lemongrass, marjoram, petitgrain, sandalwood, benzoin, bay

EMOTIONAL HEALING

To encourage soothing, calm, stillness, contentment, compassion and peace.

One variety of elemi, *Canarium schweinfurthii*, called 'African elemi' or 'elemi of Uganda', is used as incense in African churches.

310

Eucalyptus Radiata
Eucalyptus radiata

*Ancient hearts dance to the beat of the eucalyptus.
Fully aware of the past, eucalyptus is yet a fragrance
of newness, renewal and the seeking of new horizons.
The fortitude it gives lies in its long existence as one
of the earth's early healers, and the experience of
generations of others who have taken eucalyptus's
healing gift, often when no other help could be found.
We see with clear vision the power of healing, and the
many levels upon which it occurs, and with a final
whisper, eucalyptus awakens the spirit of our own
healer within.*

*Eucalyptus is a precursor to the fragrances that exist
on an angelic frequency. Its role is to encapsulate the
spirit within the physical form.*

PHYSICAL HEALING	AROMA	EMOTIONAL HEALING
antiseptic, anti-infectious, expectorant, pectoral, tonic	woody, camphorous, with faint peppermint undertone	To encourage emotional balance, concentration, centring and rationality.
	Combines well with lavender, rosemary, chamomile german, peppermint, thyme linalol, lemon, grapefruit, geranium, ginger, juniper, cypress, pine, tea tree, basil, camphor, frankincense, helichrysum, hyssop, myrtle, fir	

Fennel (Sweet)
Foeniculum vulgare dulce

*Although humble and unflamboyant, fennel is strong,
resonating with the infinite energy of the aeons. With
great fortitude and strength it brings the light of
solution into the shadows of difficulty. Its
extraordinary power boosts the spiritual, recharging
and amplifying, so it floods into the physical and mental bodies. This subtle strength clears and purifies the
auric field of people, and the environment beyond, giving protection from outside influences. Fennel brings
the infinite light within it into the hidden shadows that
may surround us, allowing our spirit to expand
and soar.*

PHYSICAL HEALING

carminative,
galactagogue,
depurative,
diuretic,
stimulant,
anti-spasmodic,
antiseptic,
vermifuge

AROMA

warm, sweet, aniseed-
like, peppery

Combines well with
juniper, geranium,
lavender, bergamot,
black pepper,
cardamom, cypress,
ginger, grapefruit,
lemon, marjoram,
rosemary, sandalwood,
ylang ylang, spearmint,
peppermint, coriander

EMOTIONAL HEALING

To encourage
enlivenment,
motivation,
clarity,
perseverance,
reliability and
assertiveness.

Fir (White Spruce)
Abies alba

*The spirit of fir extends around the planet, encircling us
in its wide enveloping arms of protection, bringing
down the rainbow of heavenly lights that shine upon us.
Every soul knows the fragrance of fir, even if only in
the ancient heritage of their bones and spirit. The
fragrance is in the collective soul – a family member
we love to remember who is always familiar.
As we inhale the aroma of the sparkling green needles,
we remember deeply the heritage we have shared with
the trees, the plants, the animals, the stars and the
heavens. With the clarity of mind and spirit given by
this fragrance, we can know we are One.*

PHYSICAL HEALING	AROMA	EMOTIONAL HEALING
anti-depressant, expectorant, analgesic, antiseptic, tonic, stimulant	fruity pine	To encourage protection, steadiness, grounding, harmony, compassion, clarity, achievement, strength and inner unity.
	Combines well with pine, cedarwood, cypress, orange, bergamot, yuzu, geranium, lavender, rosemary, marjoram, lemon, peppermint, thyme, birch, myrtle, basil, camphor, hyssop, frankincense	

'I will set in the desert the fir tree, and the pine, and the
box tree together: That they may see, and know, and
consider, and understand together, that the hand of the
Lord hath done this . . .' Isaiah 41:19–20

'The beams of our house are cedar, and our rafters of fir.'
The Song of Solomon 1:17

313

Frankincense
Boswellia carterii

*This sweet protector of the heavens operates far
beyond the auric field, in the light realms. It is
adaptive – it will adapt to a person's spiritual state of
being, like an ever-watchful older friend capable of
offering support in a wide range of circumstances.
But, like a vigilant parent, it will not let us go where
we are not ready to go.
Holding the wisdom of the ages, it waits for what is
asked of it and can do all that may be required.
Watching, with infinite sight, if it encounters
malevolent energies attached to a person it has the
authority and power to assist in their removal. In cases
of spiritual shock or loss, when the spirit can step out
of the body, even for a brief moment, frankincense can
gently ease us back to our earthly home. Frankincense
is elevating, spiritual and meditative, and holds some
of the wisdom of the universe, that which is manifested
in the spiritual self.*

PHYSICAL HEALING

tonic,
stimulant,
expectorant,
cicatrisive,
pectoral, anti-
depressant,
antiseptic

AROMA

warm, sweet,
balsamic, spicy,
incense-like

Combines well with

cypress, orange,
mandarin,
sandalwood, vetiver,
pine, geranium,
lavender, neroli,
bergamot, rose
absolute, rose otto,
clary sage, coriander,
grapefruit, lemon,
patchouli, palma
rosa, ylang ylang

EMOTIONAL HEALING

To induce
feelings of
emotional
stability,
enlightenment,
protection,
introspection,
courage,
resolution,
fortitude,
acceptance and
inspiration.

314

'And the Lord said unto Moses, Take unto thee sweet spices, stacte, and *onycha*, and galbanum; these sweet spices with pure frankincense: of each shall there be a like weight: And thou shalt make it a perfume, a confection after the art of the apothecary, tempered together, pure and holy.' Exodus 30:34-35

Given to Jesus by one of the three wise men, on the occasion of his birth in Bethlehem.

Included in the incense used by Roman Catholic and Greek Orthodox Churches.

Frankincense is sometimes called olibanum.

Galbanum
Ferula galbaniflua

*A sacrificial fragrance which allows for the shedding
of old ideas and outmoded behaviour and attitudes,
resulting in total surrender to the Creator. It sheds
light on life's purpose, and on the inner-self. It
communicates with the deeper layers of self, allowing
a gradual unfolding of truth for those who have been
blinded by success and ambition, allowing a sense of
balance within the spiritual and physical self.
This fragrance should always be used with caution for
what it might unveil – sadnesses, wrongdoings,
untruthfulness and crimes against the soul. It should
only be used by those who have already travelled a
large part of their life's journey, and having perhaps settled in their ways, find an urgency for stronger beliefs
and the wish to walk in the light.
Be aware, galbanum brings with it all knowledge in
its many forms.*

PHYSICAL HEALING

antiseptic,
anti-
spasmodic,
analgesic,
emmenagogue,
expectorant,
cicatrisive

AROMA

green-pepperish, with a
green-woody, slightly
balsamic edge

Combines well with
(*use only small amounts
in blends*)
lavender, geranium,
pine, spruce, chamomile
maroc, clove, cinnamon,
amber, cedarwood,
cypress, frankincense,
myrrh, tuberose, lemon,
benzoin, grapefruit,
lemongrass, hyacinth,
linden blossom, rose
absolute, yuzu

EMOTIONAL HEALING

To encourage
calm, stability,
direction,
concentration,
fortitude and
focus.

316

Geranium
Pelargonium graveolens

*Geranium resonates with Mother Earth. It signifies
the archetypal energy of goddess culture, and
encompasses the energy of the feminine, of
reproduction, of birth and rebirth.
The frequency of geranium appears to allow energy to
become matter, and also allows the dispersion of
matter through the energetic field. It must always be
used with the great respect transformational energies
deserve. When the spirit is hidden, like a frightened
child, within, geranium offers its warm hand of
comfort, opening our hearts and memories and
healing the pain.*

PHYSICAL HEALING	AROMA	EMOTIONAL HEALING
astringent, haemostatic, diuretic, antiseptic, antidepressant, regenerative, tonic, anti-spasmodic, anti-infectious	flowery rose, sweet, soft, green	To encourage solace, adjustment, regeneration, balance, assurance, tranquillity, steadiness and the feeling of being cushioned, soothed, shielded and mothered.
	Combines well with lemon, grapefruit, lavender, rosemary, chamomile roman, peppermint, clove, clary sage, ginger, palma rosa, ylang ylang, sandalwood, mandarin, juniper, cypress, benzoin, bergamot, black pepper, fennel, frankincense, orange, rose absolute, rose otto, jasmine	

317

Ginger
Zingiber officinale

*Ginger is a fragrance of valour and courage. It brings
assistance to the faint-hearted and to the weak, giving
a sense of being capable and strong enough to carry
on regardless. With the courage encapsulated in
ginger's fragrant breath, we can utter that one crucial
word, or think that one crucial thought, that changes
our direction and starts the walk along a new and
brighter road. With courage, we can summon the
angelic realms when in need, or pray from the heart
without worrying what expectations of us that may
bring. Ginger provides a tool to break out of spiritual
apprehension which restricts our ability to be free
and soaring high.*

PHYSICAL HEALING

antiseptic,
stimulant,
analgesic,
carminative,
fortifying,
expectorant

• May cause
  irritation to
  sensitive skin.

AROMA

characteristic of ginger

Combines well with
lemon, grapefruit,
geranium, sandalwood,
palma rosa, mandarin,
ylang ylang, juniper,
eucalyptus, clove, rose
absolute, neroli,
jasmine, frankincense,
vetiver, patchouli,
cedarwood, coriander,
lime, orange, bergamot

EMOTIONAL HEALING

To encourage
warmth,
empathy,
courage,
assurance,
optimism and
liberation.

In India, it is said that ginger awakens *agni*, the inner fire
of divinity and creativity.

318

Grapefruit
Citrus paradisi

Grapefruit rouses the human spirit from slumber, giving it the impetus to pay attention to the guidance being given to mankind. Energizing and enlivening, it disallows the egocentricity of just living for the body, without making connection with the spirit. It can thus reconnect mind, body and soul.

While praying, grapefruit awakens the mind, allowing the prayers to be sung from the inner chambers of the emotional heart with force and mindfulness. Its purpose is not so much to help us connect with the angelic realms, but with the angelic within us. It reconnects the silken cords that may through genetic inheritance have become broken, allowing us to be completely in harmony so that when the spirit speaks, the body hears the message.

PHYSICAL HEALING	AROMA	EMOTIONAL HEALING
tonic, digestive, depurative, antiseptic, anti-infectious, restorative	warm, sweet, fresh citrus	To encourage joy, positivity, confidence, attunement, alertness, generosity, spontaneity, co-operation and upliftment.
	Combines well with ginger, juniper, cypress, clary sage, clove, palma rosa, ylang ylang, mandarin, lavender, geranium, rosemary, thyme linalol, peppermint, eucalyptus, fennel, black pepper, frankincense, patchouli	

319

Helichrysum
Helichrysum angustifolium

*A fragrance of the devic world, helichrysum opens
hearts to the unseen energies which affect our lives
here on earth. It has a special purpose for 'the
walking wounded' – those who cannot reminisce for
fear of the painful emotions that may be brought to
the fore. It is also for those who feel their physical self
has lost touch with their soul.
Who will understand their pain? Who will
understand why they feel shy and vulnerable when
exposed, and only wish to protect themselves from the
storm? Helichrysum's spiritual purpose is to make
self-exposure safe. It cannot heal the past, nor protect
the heart from future hurt.
Helichrysum allows a person to understand that to
love truly also involves the acceptance of the pain of
love – gladly, willingly, and without compromise.*

PHYSICAL HEALING

anti-spasmodic,
analgesic,
cicatrisive,
expectorant,
cholagogue,
stimulant

AROMA

powerful, fruity, fresh,
straw-like

Combines well with
bergamot, black pepper,
cedarwood, chamomile
german, clary sage,
cypress, frankincense,
geranium, grapefruit,
juniper, lavender, lemon,
mandarin, palma rosa,
pine, rosemary, sage,
thyme linalol, rose
absolute, rose otto, ylang
ylang, vetiver

EMOTIONAL HEALING

To encourage
calm,
acceptance,
dreams,
patience, per-
severance,
inner strength
and aware-
ness.

Hyacinth (Absolute)
Hyacinth orientalis

Carrying souls across the divide betwixt heaven and earth is the task of hyacinth. Its fragrance sits so closely with the guardians that its heady fragrance drifts easily into the heavens with whatever spirit it must carry. Gentle and with compassion, the fragrance emanates from the flowers' heads which balance like ballerinas upon a strong stem. So it is with the spirit. As the time draws near for us to depart this earth, the fragrance connects us with the divine deep within our soul. It becomes one with all that we are, and assists in the letting-go of earthly ties.

In meditation, it has a quality unlike any other – heady and dizzy to the point of visions and prophecy.

PHYSICAL HEALING

hypnotic, sedative, antidepressant, antiseptic, used for aroma-psychology

Only a small amount is used in a blend, diluted, as it is very strong.

Synthetics are sometimes sold as natural.

AROMA

powerful, hypnotic, green, deep, soft, floral

Combines well with
rose absolute, rose otto, lemon, bergamot, grapefruit, litsea cubeba, neroli, ylang ylang, frankincense, orange, cypress, sandalwood, petitgrain, geranium

EMOTIONAL HEALING

To encourage calm, forgiveness, self-esteem, perseverance, equilibrium, trust, faith and courage.

In spring the hills of Galilee are completely covered with the highly fragrant blue hyacinth, which is indigenous to the area. This perennial is part of the lily family and is thought by some to be the 'lily of the valley' mentioned in the Song of Solomon 2:1 and elsewhere.

321

Hyssop
Hyssopus officinalis

This holy herb uplifts the spirit to the realms of divine wisdom, the source of Creation, preparing the higher self for the final ascent into the heavens. It purifies and cleanses, awakening closed hearts and minds, bringing tolerance and understanding, unconditional love and acceptance, and the comprehension needed for the ultimate oneness with the universe.
A protective herb of the heavens, it is touched with the love and protection of the divine. Hyssop is a quintessential cleanser, enabling a clarity of spirit, and recognition of the divine beneficent power in the universe.

PHYSICAL HEALING	AROMA	EMOTIONAL HEALING
antiseptic, diuretic, emmenagogue, expectorant, anti-tussive, nervine, vulnerary	green, sweet, herby, spicy	To encourage awakening, acceptance, fulfilment, encouragement, leniency, direction, clarity, balance and harmony.
• Not to be used during pregnancy, or by those with epilepsy.	**Combines well with** rosemary, myrtle, bergamot, grapefruit, frankincense, geranium, cypress, cedarwood, eucalyptus, orange, lavender, marjoram, myrrh, clary sage	
• Can cause irritation to sensitive skin.		

'Sprinkle me, O Lord, with hyssop, and I shall be purified; wash me, and I shall be whiter than snow.' The *Asperges me*, said during the anointing of the sick (Pre-Vatican II Roman rite)

There are twelve references to hyssop in the Bible, most relating to cleansing rites, and there has been much discussion as to which species is being referred to. One of the most authoritative sources of information is the biblical landscape reserve in Israel, Neot Kedumim, near Jerusalem, and one of their publications says the following on this subject, quoting *Safra Metzora*, chapter 1,16:

'The Sages were very strict in ensuring that only the true hyssop, *ezov* (*Origanum Maru* or *Marjorana syriaca*) be used in this ceremony and not ezovion [in another version, Greek hyssop] and not blue hyssop and not Roman hyssop and not wild hyssop and not any other hyssop that has a descriptive name.'

Jasmine (Absolute)
Jasminum officinale, J. grandiflorum, J. sambac

*Jasmine softly embraces the spirit and heart,
bringing greater understanding of the conscious mind
and all its foibles. In its perfume, the wishes and
desires of the heart are reflected and in gentleness we
come to understand the subtle motives of the spirit.
Our aspirations may not always be what is required
to tread a spiritual path, and our wishes and dreams
for others may deflect them from their path. Jasmine
helps us to understand this and accept.*

*It is said that jasmine has the ability to call the angelic
realms close, and to be able to transmit our soul's joy
and love to the universe, if the intent and purpose is
carried from a clear and pure heart. In the world in
which we live, space is often needed for a moment's
reflection – to be able to consider the greater purpose
and to inhale the glory of Heaven, and feel the master
hand at work. Paths trodden are often a mixture of joy
and sorrow, but through it all we can survive – sometimes all it takes is another point of view.*

*Jasmine's purpose is to provide us with our personal
haven, where we can find a greater conscious
resonation with our higher self.*

PHYSICAL HEALING

anti-depres-
sant,
stimulant,
antiseptic,
anti-spasmodic,
cicatrisive,
sedative

AROMA

sweet, rich, floral

Combines well with
rose absolute, rose otto,
neroli, sandalwood,
palma rosa, geranium,
lemon, clove, grapefruit,
bergamot, mandarin,
orange, patchouli,
petitgrain, ylang ylang,
coriander, benzoin, bay,
ginger

EMOTIONAL HEALING

To encourage
upliftment,
optimism,
openness,
sensitivity,
harmony,
awareness,
profundity,
inspiration and
joy.

Juniper
Juniperus communis

Juniper's message is to complete the tasks and learn the lessons. Meanwhile, it clears obstructions on our pathway to the divine spirit. While facilitating the transmission of our thoughts and prayers, it offers itself as a protective shield, disallowing impure thoughts to pervade our mediations and conversations with the universe.

A cleansing and purifying action takes place when juniper's fragrance is inhaled, and subtle changes are made – physically, mentally and spiritually – as the unencumbered spirit can speak to the heart and mind.

PHYSICAL HEALING	AROMA	EMOTIONAL HEALING
antiseptic, diuretic, emmenagogue, depurative, tonic	fresh, fruity, woody	To encourage inner vision, upliftment, strength, vitality, sincerity, enlightenment and humility.
• To be avoided during pregnancy and by those with kidney problems.		

Combines well with
rosemary, geranium, lavender, cedarwood, sage, lemon, grapefruit, sandalwood, mandarin, cypress, clary sage, pine, eucalyptus, frankincense, vetiver, bergamot, fennel

Elijah '... came and sat down under a juniper tree: and he requested for himself that he might die; and said, It is enough; now, O Lord, take away my life; for I am not better than my fathers. And as he lay and slept under a juniper tree, behold, then an angel touched him, and said unto him, Arise and eat.' 1 Kings 19:4–5

The berries and twigs have been used in spiritual practice in many areas including North America, Europe, Egypt, Tibet and China. Juniper is universally considered cleansing and purifying, and is often used in fumigation.

In parts of central Europe, during the last three days of April, the smoke of burning juniper berries and twigs was used to cleanse the houses of evil influences, and juniper branches were fastened to the doorposts to deter such negative forces from entering.

To the ancient Germans, juniper was 'the Tree of Life', and branches were buried with the dead to facilitate their easy passage to their heaven, Valhalla.

In Siberia, shamans have traditionally inhaled the smoke of juniper to facilitate trance and visions.

At dawn in Tibet, every household burns a fragrant wood, usually juniper, in their ceremonial roof-stoves, *bsangsthab*.

Labdanum (Rock Rose)
Cistus ladaniferus

Labdanum is a fragrance of prophecy, of visions, of quests in the search for truth. It provides a vehicle to explore the knowing, and a means by which to acknowledge the existence of universal wisdom deep within. The emotions of mortals are touched by labdanum, and it can bring to the forefront of the mind access to the soul level of all living things.

Labdanum cannot provide answers, nor can it speak, but it stimulates the eternal knowledge that is intrinsic to all human beings. There are no words to express this knowing, as no words can fully express feeling, but in the knowing we tap into the source of all Creation, that which links us all.

Labdanum brings awareness that the universal spirit can be glimpsed and absorbed into our very being, although the complete merging with God must remain just out of reach while we fulfil our role here on the earth.

PHYSICAL HEALING	AROMA	EMOTIONAL HEALING
antiseptic, anti-tussive, emmenagogue, tonic	rich, musky, balsamic, herb	To encourage visions, dreams, pacification, centring, joy, balance and liberation.
• Not to be used during pregnancy.	**Combines well with** rose absolute, cypress, cedarwood, hyacinth, bergamot, ormenis flower, patchouli, orange, sandalwood,	
• Can cause irritation to sensitive skin.	galbanum, spearmint, lavender, juniper, jasmine, nutmeg, lime, lemon	

'A caravan of Ishmaelites came from Gilead, with their camels bearing spicery and balm and labdanum, going to carry it down to Egypt.' Genesis 37:25.

'And their father Israel said . . . carry down the man a present, a little balm, and a little honey, spicery and labdanum . . .' Genesis 43:11 (Masoretic Text).

In the mountains of Crete, monks gather the sticky resin emanating from the stems and leaves of a similar variety of white and yellow flower, *Cistus creticus*, to make incense.

Lavender
Lavandula angustifolia, L. officinalis

Lavender embodies the warm, protective love of Mother Earth. It is caring, cherishing and nurturing, and energetically very active in the auric field closest to the body, incorporating heavenly energies into the physical with great efficiency.

When deep sadnesses covers the spirit like a suffocating blanket, lavender gently lifts the weight. When the inner tears fall, lavender wipes them away. When depression clouds the psyche, lavender blows it asunder. And for those with worries that trouble the spirit, lavender lifts the veil of despair.

The mother of essential oils will not tolerate bitterness, malice or jealousy in her mortal brood, but with compassion seeks to bring out the best in us all, letting us know that we are all her precious children, and we all have our destiny of goodness to fulfil.

PHYSICAL HEALING	AROMA	EMOTIONAL HEALING
antiseptic, analgesic, cytophylactic, anti-spasmodic, tonic, cicatrisive, anti-inflammatory, restorative, calmative, sedative, anti-infectious	fresh, herbaceous, floral **Combines well with** chamomile roman, chamomile german, lemon, geranium, eucalyptus, thyme linalol, rosemary, tea tree, peppermint, grapefruit, clary sage, palma rosa, mandarin, juniper, cypress, pine, aniseed, angelica root, camphor, black pepper, marjoram, cedarwood, bergamot, lemongrass, ravensara	To encourage security, gentleness, compassion, reconciliation, vitality, clarity, comfort, acceptance, awareness and emotional balance.

It has been suggested that the 'spikenard' of biblical reference may refer to the 'spike' lavender, *Lavandula latifolia*, which grows in the Mediterranean region, or even to *Lavandula dentata*, native to Afghanistan and Iran.

For hundreds of years lavender has been a favourite plant grown in monasteries' gardens.

Lemon
Citrus limonum

Lemon clarifies everything through upliftment and focus. In this, there is centring and the impetus needed to send precious thoughts. Its fragrance enables our meditations to be deeper, and our prayers to take flight.
The spiritual cleansing of lemon enables the entire psyche to react to the positive in mortal, as well as divine, love. Lemon represents the fruitfulness of the earth, and life which is bitter-sweet.

PHYSICAL HEALING

carminative, diuretic, antidepressant, stimulant, antiseptic, anti-spasmodic

- Should not be used on the skin if being exposed to sunlight or ultraviolet rays.

- May cause irritation to sensitive skin.

AROMA

light, fresh, citrus

Combines well with
orange, rosemary, lavender, fennel, basil, nutmeg, dill, hyssop, peppermint, frankincense, bergamot, bay, ylang ylang, geranium

EMOTIONAL HEALING

To encourage clarity, direction, awareness, concentration and liveliness.

'And ye shall take you on the first day the fruit of the goodly trees . . .' Leviticus 23:40. The first of the four species that were directed to be taken to the temple in offering and gratitude for the gifts of the land during the Festival of Sukkot, is thought to be the citron, or *etrog* – *Citrus medica*. It is preferred that the citrus used in the modern ceremony has an elongated end.

Lemongrass
Cymbopogon citratus, C. flexuosus

In the quest to be free from desire and ego there can be no pretences. This fragrance, powerful through its simplicity, has nothing to hide and could never pretend otherwise. It clears regrets or shame, encouraging forgiveness of those who have dishonoured and discredited us. Plainly straight-forward, the spirit of lemongrass illuminates what has been with the statement, 'forgive then forget'. With the utter simplicity of truth, and in understanding gentleness, it reminds us that we are who we are, and that all life's experiences make the whole. With clarity we can see that the choices have been ours, and that freedom of choice is one of the many gifts the Creator has given us. Equally, comes the realization that the outcome of our following spiritual journey will depend on the choices we make.

PHYSICAL HEALING	AROMA	EMOTIONAL HEALING
antiseptic, carminative, nervine, tonic, calmative	citrus, fresh, straw-like	To encourage upliftment, calm, balance and integration.
• Should not be used on the skin if being exposed to sunlight or ultraviolet rays. • Can cause irritation to sensitive skin.	**Combines well with** rosemary, lavender, thyme, basil, bay, cardamom, frankincense, hyssop, geranium, lavender, nutmeg, cinnamon, clove, orange, mandarin, petitgrain, spikenard, yarrow, vetiver	

Linden Blossom (Absolute)
Tilia vulgaris

Love in all its many guises speaks through linden blossom. It touches those hidden areas of self we may have denied love access to, bringing into our hearts the ever-understanding expression of love and oneness.

A graceful fragrance, it manifests a graceful spirit; bringing a sense of grace to our prayers and meditations, and graciousness to all we do. A fragrance of mercy, it brings with it the ability to be merciful and non-judgemental in our dealings. It may appear impossible, in the times we live, to live in a state of graciousness, but this is within everyone's reach. The spirit of the linden tree is ever present in the fragrance whether emanating from the flowers or in the aroma of its essence. Linden can be used when things seem cold and people unfeeling; when life appears to be rough, harsh and uncaring; when the little niceties are gone and it seems as if no-one cares. It brings back a sense of respect for others and the enchantment of being kind, and helps us to accept the kindness shown – without expecting there to be ulterior motives for such actions.

PHYSICAL HEALTH

anti-spasmodic, antidepressant, nervine, tonic, calmative

AROMA

light, floral, sweet

Combines well with
frankincense, geranium, jasmine, rose absolute, rose otto, hyacinth, tuberose, carnation, lemon, orange, mandarin, neroli, petitgrain, sandalwood, ylang ylang, black pepper, clove

EMOTIONAL HEALING

To encourage relaxation, calm, self-confidence, security, balance, equilibrium, and the feeling of being soothed.

'There are references in more than one land to a Paradise among the mountains. It figures in the fairy stories of Central Europe . . . with its linden Tree of Immortality, the hiding-place of a fairy lady, its dancing nymphs and its dwarfs; the king of dwarfs has a cloak of invisibility which he wraps around those mortals he carries away.' Donald A. Mackenzie, *China and Japan: Myths and Legends*

The bark of the linden tree was once widely used, in woven form, as boat sails and clothing. Italian Renaissance paintings sometimes show the Virgin Mary wearing a skirt of linden bark.

Linden is often called 'lime tree' although no limes grow from it.

333

Mandarin
Citrus reticulata, C. nobilis

*The gentleness and sweetness of spirit is gathered in the
arms of this fragrance. But however gentle it may be,
there is a vigour and sprightliness in how mandarin stirs
the spirit. At times, when we feel fully connected to the
source of all Creation, and still enough to hear the
celestial music, we touch the spirit held within mandarin.
The elders gather where ancient fragrances play, and
although mandarin is young, it still attracts the attention
of the elders.
Mandarin can be inhaled whenever we feel the urge to
make the connection with other realms and hear the music
of the spheres.*

PHYSICAL HEALING	AROMA	EMOTIONAL HEALING
tonic, calmative, anti-spasmodic, antiseptic	sweet, light, floral, fruity, citrus	To encourage calm, upliftment, inspiration, soothing, integrity and tranquillity.

Combines well with
lemon, grapefruit,
geranium, clove, palma
rosa, ylang ylang,
juniper, jasmine, rose
otto, neroli, basil, black
pepper, chamomile
roman, frankincense,
patchouli, petitgrain,
sandalwood, cinnamon

Japanese myths regarding the 'fruit of the Everlasting
Fragrant Tree' are quite likely referring to mandarin.

Marjoram (Sweet)
Origanum marjorana

Marjoram calms the senses and allows peacefulness to come into a frantic world. It stills the mind long enough so that the still voice within that communicates with the soul can be heard. Its warmth carries with it the fire and sparks of the cosmos, with which we can make a connection to our own internal fire. With its warmth comes a deeply centred peace that has flowed with the tide of humanity's evolution, holding within its fragrance all that humanity has borne. Tread carefully it tells us, speak not of evil or be judgemental least you too may be judged. Try instead to forgive without judgement, without criticism, and for no other reason than to have a clear, untroubled heart.

PHYSICAL HEALING

analgesic,
anti-spasmodic,
vasodilator,
calmative,
expectorant,
digestive,
vulnerary,
anti-tussive,
anti-infectious,
emmenagogue

AROMA

warm, spicy, herbaceous

Combines well with
basil, bergamot, black
pepper, chamomile
roman, chamomile
german, cedarwood,
clary sage, cypress,
eucalyptus citriodora,
eucalyptus radiata,
fennel, juniper,
lavender, lemon, orange,
peppermint, pine,
rosemary, tea tree,
thyme linalol

EMOTIONAL HEALING

To encourage
calm, balance,
integrity,
perseverance
and sincerity.

According to some sources, a species of marjoram, *Origanum syriacum*, is the 'hyssop' of biblical reference. It grows abundantly in the Holy Land, and as it has very hairy stems, would have been an appropriate plant to use as a sprinkler in the biblical context.

Said to be the herb of the Egyptian god Sobek. Often used in the funerary garlands put around the heads of mummified bodies.

Used in unguents and perfumes in the ancient world since known records.

Melissa
Melissa officinalis

Melissa vibrates at a very high light frequency, and travels far. The energy it brings into the spirit comes from a place more distant than we can imagine, beyond the sun, beyond the stars. When the magnetic energy is at a low ebb, melissa supports our need with an understanding that defies words. Melissa is a spiritual conduit, and is thus a precious gift of the heavens at any time, but perhaps is especially appreciated before meditation or prayer.

PHYSICAL HEALING	AROMA	EMOTIONAL HEALING
antiseptic, calmative, antidepressant, stimulant	citrus, light, fresh	To encourage strength, revitalization, gentleness, peace, progressiveness and cheerfulness.
• May cause irritation to sensitive skin.	**Combines well with** chamomile roman, rose absolute, rose otto, neroli, petitgrain, geranium, frankincense	
	Most often used on its own.	

Myrrh
Commiphora myrrha

This deep fragrance resonates with the wounded healer – the wounds running deep, carrying the pain of others – for infinity. The fragrance enables the letting go of the need to battle for the just against the unjust.

The meaning of life – so often sought – has no meaning when the purpose of life is realized! This realization can come from deep within the heart after the emotional wounds have healed. Our spirit can also feel wounded, although it is always protected, but sometimes it seems outside our grasp. Myrrh, with all its submerged meanings, links with the pathway of the soul, standing at the very crossroads. It would be so easy to walk down any of the roads hanging on to our wounds, but myrrh helps us to realize the need to let go, that they are past and that it's time to move forward.

PHYSICAL HEALING	AROMA	EMOTIONAL HEALING
pectoral, antiseptic, antispasmodic, cicatrisive, expectorant, astringent, vulnerary	warm, slightly musty, earthy	To encourage fortitude, courage, peace, calm, sympathy, acceptance and mastery.

• Not to be used during pregnancy.

Combines well with
frankincense, sandalwood, cypress, bergamot, juniper, galbanum, geranium, grapefruit, lavender, lemon, palma rosa, patchouli, pine, hyssop, eucalyptus citriodora, ylang ylang, rosemary, chamomile german

'Moreover the Lord spake unto Moses, saying, Take thou also unto thee principal spices, of pure myrrh five hundred shekels . . .' Exodus 30:22–23

'(for so were the days of their purifications accomplished, to wit, six months with oil of myrrh, and six months with sweet odours, and with other things for the purifying of the women;)' Esther 2:12

'Who is this that cometh out of the wilderness like pillars of smoke, perfumed with myrrh and frankincense, with all powders of the merchant?' The Song of Solomon 3:6

Given as a gift to baby Jesus by one of the three wise men, at his birth in Bethlehem.

Used for over 4,000 years. The ancient Egyptians burnt it at midday, in praise of the sun god Ra; also used it in their *Kyphi* incense, and in embalming.

Myrtle
Myrtus communis

The fragrance of myrtle allows entrance to the pure and absolute; where ego has no entrance-pass; where all is one, and one becomes all; where there is no beginning or end. It tells of going forward carried within the spirit, reminding us that this existence is in preparation for another along the evolutionary cycle which we shall transcend.
Its spirit is energetic truth, and forgiveness, giving support to the unsupported and teaching that divine love embraces all living beings.

PHYSICAL HEALING	AROMA	EMOTIONAL HEALING
antiseptic, expectorant, tonic, calmative	sweet, camphorous, herbaceous, green	To encourage upliftment, comfort, forgiveness, acceptance, empowerment and harmony.
	Combines well with bay, orange, rosemary, geranium, basil, mandarin, galbanum, lemon, bergamot, ginger, eucalyptus, cardamom, cinnamon, clove, benzoin, helichrysum	

'And they answered the angel of the Lord that stood among the myrtle trees . . .' Zechariah 1:11

'. . . instead of the briar shall come up the myrtle tree: and it shall be to the Lord for a name, for an everlasting sign that shall not be cut off.' Isaiah 55:13

'Go forth unto the mount, and fetch olive branches, and pine branches, and myrtle branches, and palm branches, and branches of thick trees, to make booths, as it is written.' Nehemiah 8:15

The myrtle was a sign of immortality to the people living in the ancient Near East, perhaps because it remains fresh for several weeks after being cut. Known as *hadass* in Hebrew, myrtle is said to be the quintessential fragrant plant of Israel, and as such is incorporated into the spice-box used on the Sabbath evening, wherever possible.

Narcissus (Absolute)
Narcissus poeticus

*Narcissus is a keyholder of the doorway to realms
beyond inspiration and imagination; a fragrance on
which to dream of things untold, unseen and unheard of
by mortal beings, in the heavenly domain.
Protecting our fragility from fear and anguish,
narcissus keeps us soaring into infinity, bypassing
mortal conditions, linking us with the lore of worlds
which have no beginning nor end. Such is the effect
upon the spirit of one who inhales narcissus with
spiritual intent. It is not for the faint-hearted for no
mortal can say where it may take you.
Narcissus can assist in overcoming the blockages we set
on our pathway, and in attaining greater understanding
of the unknown.*

PHYSICAL HEALING	AROMA	EMOTIONAL HEALING
	heavy, green floral	
anti-spasmodic, sedative	**Combines well with** (only use in small amounts; principal use as perfume or room fragrance) jasmine, hyacinth, tuberose, clove, cinnamon, ylang ylang, sandalwood, bois de rose, ho-wood, lemon, grape-fruit, orange, mandarin	To encourage inspiration, creativity, stillness, inner vision.
• Not to be used during pregnancy.		

The soul of the ancient Greek flower-god, Narcissus, was
captured by the Titans by means of a magic reflecting
pool, the home of Echo and other water nymphs. With his
soul entrapped Narcissus died, but he reappeared as the
spring flower.

Neroli
Citrus aurantium, C. brigaradia, C. vulgaris

Neroli touches the realms of the angels, and anyone who uses it is brushed with the light of angels' wings. Neroli is one of the most precious essential oils, its vibration being one of the highest. It may be that it resonates with energy from another light-time in the universe, perhaps taking its light from another sun in the vast cosmos. Wherever its subtle and luminescent quality comes from, it is omnipresent.

Neroli is itself pure spirit, representing the purity in all things. It is always loving and peaceful. Neroli brings light into any day, but is especially useful whenever mistrust has overtaken reason, or during dark periods of deep depression.

Neroli has another purpose – to bring self-recognition and relief. Our pain and sorrow is sometimes brought about because we have not seen how we have affected others, and inadvertently caused a rift between us. Neroli allows the reflection which can throw light on the wounds which tie us to old patterns of relating. As truth is revealed, the self emerges into wholeness and unconditional love, stirring the spirit in ways that can be both unexpected and liberating. Then, the spirit can really soar.

PHYSICAL HEALING	AROMA	EMOTIONAL HEALING
anti-depressant, anti-infectious, tonic, cytophylactic, calmative, cicatrisive	highly radiant, sweet, floral **Combines well with** geranium, chamomile roman, coriander, frankincense, mandarin, orange, petitgrain, jasmine, rose otto, ylang ylang, yuzu, lemon, grapefruit, mandarin, lavender, sandalwood, juniper	To encourage lightness, the lifting of sorrows, completeness, joy, understanding, calm, regeneration, peace and to feel guided.

Nutmeg
Myristica fragrans

Nutmeg brings hopes, dreams and prayers to their right-ful home, and in so doing, the highest elements of the ego take their place within spiritual wonderment. When the ego has received many life-blows, is depressed, or unable to connect with the higher realms, nutmeg assists in the reconnection.

It is hard to see how our lives have affected others, and how sometimes we might have brought pain and sorrow. When there is recognition, however, there is also relief.

This opening of recognition is never accomplished without reflection, and is seldom easy. But the wounds and ties which hold us fast can deter us from finding our true selves, and as self emerges into wholeness, then a stirring of the spirit occurs which is liberating, and at times unexpected as it allows the spirit to soar.

PHYSICAL HEALING	AROMA	EMOTIONAL HEALING
analgesic, antiseptic, carminative, emmenagogue, tonic, nervine	spicy, light, warm, fresh	To encourage calm, peace, visions, dreams, unity, comfort and stillness.
	Combines well with clove, cinnamon, bay, orange, lemon, lime, geranium, rose absolute, jasmine	
• Not to be used during pregnancy.		
	Use small amounts only.	

Nutmeg is one of the oldest cultivated plants.

In Malaysia, nutmeg was given to people possessed by spirits, to drive them out.

In India, nutmeg was known as 'narcotic fruit', *mada shaunda*.

Orange
Citrus sinensis

Orange is imbued with the energy of sunlight and the radiance of the stars. Its fragrance has the adaptability required of such a high energy. So, at times it may be gentle, at other times it may give the determination needed to enliven the spiritual sense of being.

Orange contains the joy and magnificence of the light of the heavens. Bursting with vitality, it brings happiness to the heavy-hearted, and to those who seem lost. It brings newness and regeneration. It can kindle a spark long-forgotten and revitalize spiritual connections to a soul grown dim through living too hard, too fast, too painfully.

Orange conquers fears of letting go, and obsessions. The fragrance uplifts those with obsessions, so they can see the full spectrum of light.

PHYSICAL HEALING	AROMA	EMOTIONAL HEALING
calmative, sedative, stomachic, cholagogue, diuretic, tonic, anti-spasmodic, antiseptic, depurative	fresh, fruity, tangy, sweet **Combines well with** bay, benzoin, bergamot, black pepper, cinnamon, clove, coriander, frankincense, geranium, ginger, grapefruit, juniper, lemon, litsea cubeba, marjoram, neroli, patchouli, petitgrain, sandalwood, vetiver, jasmine, ylang ylang, rose absolute	To encourage joy, upliftment, light-heartedness, regeneration, creativity, positivity and self-confidence.

Ormenis Flower
(Chamomile Maroc)
Ormenis multicaulis

*This sweet-petalled flower, which closes as the dusk
sky changes into deep velvet blue, is often mistaken
for another. The fragrance sighs for those who have
been overlooked, those passed by in mistake, or
misunderstood by others. It is no coincidence that this
aroma is so often called by another name.
Those who have the gentlest of heart and spirit are
often overlooked in favour of those with a more
forceful spiritual nature. Yet this fragrance holds a
key to the telling of who you really are, in truth with
fortitude of spirit, neither meek nor mild.
It enables a person to be free enough to say, 'I am also
important, I too have a story to tell, and a destiny in
this lifetime. I shall not always be passed over for
those more flamboyant than I, those often mistaken
for being stronger than I.' This fragrance reveals the
true inner spirit yet, if required, will provide the
camouflage sometimes needed to hide a sweet and
tender-spirited heart.*

PHYSICAL HEALING

anti-infectious,
tonic,
emmenagogue,
anti-spas-
modic,
sedative,
calmative,
antiseptic

AROMA

balsamic, herby, sweet

Combines well with
bay, benzoin, bergamot,
cardamom, coriander,
frankincense, geranium,
grapefruit, lavender,
lemon, lemongrass,
mandarin, marjoram,
orange, patchouli,
petitgrain, ylang ylang,
yuzu

EMOTIONAL HEALING

To encourage
empathy,
courage,
relaxation,
mindfulness,
attentiveness
and centring.

345

Palma Rosa
Cymbopogon martini

*The fragrance of palma rosa hovers within the outer
boundaries of the physical form, in the auric field and
slightly beyond, energizing the human form, enabling
it to extend towards the heavens.*

*Its strength of purpose enables it to persuade the
mind to be gentle, and to love the form within which
it travels, knowing that all that is held in mindfulness will become a reflection of the heart. The
fragrance reminds us that strength lies in direction
and purpose, but that there is only one road – that of
the illuminated heart. Travelling this road, we can
overcome the impediments of the physical world,
learn to let go and walk with the spirit.*

*Palma rosa encourages us to be kind and gentle to
ourselves, not overcritical or judgemental, because
when we have learned to love who we are, we can love
others in the same way. It tenderly creates a space, a
garden, in which love can grow.*

PHYSICAL HEALING

antiseptic,
cicatrisive,
anti-
depressant,
stimulant,
tonic

AROMA

sweet, rosy, floral, lemony

Combines well with
geranium, grapefruit,
clary sage, ginger, ylang
ylang, sandalwood, man-
darin, juniper, lemon,
clove, rosemary,
chamomile roman,
rose absolute, rose otto,
bay, benzoin, bergamot,
coriander, frankincense,
lemongrass, lemon,
orange, petitgrain,
patchouli, clove

EMOTIONAL HEALING

To encourage
mildness,
growth, loyalty
and
enthusiasm.

Patchouli
Pogostemon cablin

Patchouli brings with it the sense of the sacredness of life. It is also a fragrance of action, knowing that no ideal will occur unless we take the first steps to make it happen. At the same time, patchouli reminds us that sitting quietly under a tree is good if there is purpose in it – the purpose of knowing and appreciating. Sitting under a tree represents the contemplation of what we can do for ourselves and others in the way of caring. As the thought of caring for others enters our spirit, so too does the thought of caring for the tree which harbours us, and caring for all else besides. Such is the scope of patchouli's liberation from boundaries.

PHYSICAL HEALING	AROMA	EMOTIONAL HEALING
tonic, cytophylactic, anti-infectious, antiseptic, antidepressant, calmative	smoky, herbaceous, earthy **Combines well with** bergamot, black pepper, frankincense, clove, geranium, grapefruit, jasmine, rose absolute, mandarin, neroli, orange, sandalwood, ylang ylang, coriander, ginger, lemongrass, cinnamon, litsea cubeba	To encourage far-sightedness, rapport, invigoration, reasonableness, lucidity, astuteness and stimulation.

Since ancient times, wherever it has been grown, patchouli has been used in incense and fragranced oils and widely traded.

Peppermint
Mentha piperita

Peppermint raises the spirit to fuller understanding and appreciation of the mysteries that will eventually fully unfold for us. It stimulates and soothes, uplifts and calms – whatever is needed, this fragrance can provide it. Those lethargic with thoughts that all is lost will be energized, and come back into touch with their inner-selves. Peppermint can also stimulate the dream time, using this time of physical stillness to bring information and understanding. The fragrance will not provide a shield of comfort in restlessness, nor lull the senses. It instead increases sensitivity, awareness and perception, bringing an alertness even in the dream state, so we can remember and take in the wisdom of other worlds.

PHYSICAL HEALING	AROMA	EMOTIONAL HEALING
antiseptic, anti-infectious, carminative, stomachic, anti-spasmodic, stimulant, emmenagogue, expectorant, analgesic, digestive	camphorous, minty fresh	To encourage regeneration, self-acceptance, concentration, vitality and vibrancy.
	Combines well with basil, pine, lemon, geranium, rosemary, tea tree, lavender, eucalyptus, grapefruit, juniper, spearmint, cypress, black pepper, niaouli, ravensara	

'Woe unto you . . . for ye pay tithe of mint and anise and cummin, and have omitted the weightier matters of the law, judgement, mercy, and faith . . .'
St Matthew 23:23.

According to Greek mythology the genus *Mentha* takes its name from the nymph Minthe who was seduced by Pluto and turned into a plant by his jealous wife, who trod Minthe into the ground. Pluto, however, turned her into a herb, knowing Minthe would then be appreciated by people for years to come.

Petitgrain
Citrus aurantium, C. brigaradier

Stability is often needed when we are at our most vulnerable, feeling fragile and taking everything a little too personally and emotionally. It's at times such as these that we need a delicate spiritual strength, a gentle outstretched hand to guide us through the days when tears seem ever-present.

The spirit of petitgrain is embodied in gentle strength, encouraging positive resolutions and outcomes at difficult times. It enables us to see ahead and to forge a link with our inner truth, understanding that in our personal truth comes strength.

The small twigs and little fruits from which petitgrain is made are themselves vulnerable and, in this perhaps, lies the empathetic connection that petitgrain has with the human spirit. 'Treading softly' also applies to our dealings with other people who might be feeling vulnerable, and are perhaps trying hard not to show it. In these circumstances, petitgrain can form a bridge across the divide that we may have created between us and them.

PHYSICAL HEALING	AROMA	EMOTIONAL HEALING
anti-spasmodic, anti-depressant, stimulant, tonic, calmative, anti-infectious, antiseptic, nervine	warm, sharp, woody, floral **Combines well with** rosemary, clary sage, basil, bergamot, benzoin, clove, cedarwood, cypress, eucalyptus citriodora, frankincense, geranium, jasmine, juniper, lavender, lemon, mandarin, marjoram, neroli, orange, palma rosa, patchouli, rose absolute, rose otto, sandalwood, ylang ylang, yuzu	To encourage harmony, upliftment, joy, inner vision, strength, self-confidence and expressiveness.

Pimento Berry
Pimenta officinalis

Do not try too hard or too forcefully, advises sweet pimento, for we cannot always change what has been ordained by God – accept gently, with compassion and thankfulness, that which has been given to us. But pimento does not teach complacency. It encourages us to attempt to change that which we feel is having a negative effect on the collective human psyche. It helps us search within, to speak out against injustice, and be strong in the face of adversity. Pimento softly reminds the spirit that the short time we have on earth is to be appreciated. Yet, we can both admire the beauty of the planet, and enjoy our time upon it, while still defending that which is right.

PHYSICAL HEALING	AROMA	EMOTIONAL HEALING
analgesic, carminative, stimulant, tonic, anti-depressive	spicy, warm, balsam	To encourage warmth, comfort, stimulation and energy.
• Not to be used during pregnancy.	**Combines well with** lavender, frankincense, rose absolute, jasmine, ylang ylang, patchouli, petitgrain, cinnamon, clove, bay, camphor, bergamot, lemon, orange, mandarin	
• Can cause irritation to sensitive skin.	Only use in small amounts.	

Pine
Pinus sylvestris

The pines watch humanity come and go, while they live on. Amongst them, below them, we inhale their powerful fragrance, which shoots through our spirit, and ends in an inner explosion of understanding. In doing so, we are brought within the large embrace of nature, and can inhale its presence, acceptance and wisdom.

Pine teaches that it is love and generosity of spirit that endures – in the hearts of those we have loved and known, and in our children. Our love is that which endures, through all weathers and seasons. With this comes the knowledge that we should not destroy that which is close to our hearts, for to do so is to destroy ourselves.

PHYSICAL HEALING

anti-infectious, antiseptic, tonic, pectoral, expectorant, stimulant, restorative

• May cause irritation to sensitive skin.

AROMA

crisp, clean, fresh, resinous pine

Combines well with
clary sage, cypress, lavender, rosemary, tea tree, juniper, lemon, grapefruit, eucalyptus, frankincense, marjoram, peppermint, ravensara, thyme linalol, bergamot, cedarwood, sandalwood

EMOTIONAL HEALING

To encourage humility, simplicity, assurance, perseverance, mindfulness, trust, direction and tenacity.

'The glory of Lebanon shall come unto thee, the fir tree, the pine tree, and the box together, to beautify the place of my sanctuary; and I will make the place of my feet glorious.' Isaiah 60:13

In parts of Poland and the Czech Republic, between Christmas and New Year, pine resin was burnt throughout the long nights, in the belief that the fragrant smoke would drive away any witches or other bad influences.

In Japanese myths, 'the Tree of Life' is sometimes associated with the pine. 'The Fungus of Immortality' is said to grow in the shade of holy trees, of which there are several, but most usually it grows in the shade of a pine.

In Japanese myths, spirit-lovers are sometimes said to inhabit pine trees, and to live to a very old age. In classical Japanese Kyogen theatre, the image of a large pine tree always provides the stage backdrop.

In China the dragon is often associated with the pine; the myth being that the pine changes into a dragon.

Rose Absolute
Rosa centifolia

The depth of this fragrance tells all who come near that this is soul perfume, or a perfume of the guardians or messengers that sometimes sally forth from the heavens, to guide us and stand by us in times of need or of joy. The etheric realms associate rose absolute with the desires of the human heart. It is completing a task perhaps for which it was born – to send forth the glory of Heaven. So in the smelling of the rose we can experience the subtleties of the universe. It touches and stirs the spirit, sometimes even awakening the acknowledgement of divine mysteries and of the glory of Heaven.

PHYSICAL HEALING	AROMA	EMOTIONAL HEALING
anti-infectious, tonic, stimulant, nervine, cytophylactic	deep, soft, hypnotic, honey-spicy rose	To encourage motivation, inner vitality, confidence, passion, co-operation, fulfilment, forgiveness and a sense of freedom.
Rose 'Maroc' and Rose 'Turk'* are both absolutes – and 'Rose Absolute' refers to both these, as well as 'Egyptian' rose.	**Combines well with** jasmine, neroli, geranium, sandalwood, clove, palma rosa, lemon, ginger, ylang ylang, mandarin, patchouli, frankincense, cardamom, coriander, bay, benzoin	
*Turkey also produces a rose otto, (distilled).	Often adulterated during extraction with other rose species, palma rosa or geranium.	

Rosettes are often seen on Arab, Turkish and Israeli gravestones.

In India, the 'Great Mother', the early goddess, was known as the 'Holy Rose'.

In ancient China, the red rose was called the 'Flower of the Goddess'.

Rose Otto
Rosa damascena

*The breath of rose otto is like the beating of angels'
wings. It operates with a light far brighter even than the
sun, with a frequency that cannot be measured but
which is still everywhere, and which we can feel if only
we stop to smell the rose. Rose otto vibrates with the
energy of universal love, operating in the light of
unconditional love and giving.*

*The rose offers itself in sacrifice for the love of the
human race, and the planet. While all plants used in
herbal medicine suffer in their sacrifice to help us, rose
otto is the quintessential fragrance of love, the love that
touches our very soul, and it is for the awakening of love
in us that it offers itself.*

*Rose otto eases the sorrow of the soul, bringing harmony
and comfort. It is gentle yet euphoric.*

PHYSICAL HEALING

tonic,
cicatrisive,
cytophylactic,
pectoral,
anti-
depressant,
calmative,
haemostatic

AROMA

flowery, rosy, lemony,
fresh

Combines well with

jasmine, neroli,
geranium, sandalwood,
lemon, chamomile
roman, amber,
mandarin, ylang ylang,
petitgrain, bergamot,
benzoin

EMOTIONAL HEALING

To encourage
contentment,
devotion,
inner vision,
happiness,
inner freedom,
acceptance,
completeness,
patience, love,
sensuality and
purity.

The Virgin Mary has been called the 'Rose', 'Holy Rose', the 'Rose Garden', the 'Queen of the Most Holy Rose Garden', 'Mystic Rose', 'Rose Garland' and 'Rose Bush'.

In ancient Greece, the rose was symbolic of the goddess Aphrodite. In later, Roman, times it was said the rose sprung from the blood of the god Adonis (while others still maintained it sprung from the blood of the goddess Venus, the Roman name for Aphrodite).

In Greece and Italy, in ancient times, graves were planted with rose bushes, and strewn with rose petals.

In Medieval Europe religious rites for the dead were often carried out in rose gardens or within the 'rose hedge'.

Rosemary
Rosmarinus officinalis

The hills are alive with the spirit of rosemary, which spills forth its fragrance at a signal from the midday sun. Carried upon the light of the human spirit, it sends forth messages from earth to the heavens, filling the atmosphere between with its aroma. Crushed underfoot the fragrance rises, and, as it is inhaled, it enables the human spirit to receive and understand the assistance descending to us from wiser beings, and from God. Rosemary helps us to remember who we are, and of our place in the evolutionary plan. It helps us to perform tasks which may be needed on our own spiritual pathway, and to assist others along theirs if we are asked to do so.

PHYSICAL HEALING	AROMA	EMOTIONAL HEALING
antiseptic, stimulant, analgesic, antidepressant, anti-spasmodic, vulnerary, carminative, emmenagogue, anti-tussive, decongestant	camphor-like, woody, herbaceous, powerful	To encourage energy, upliftment, confidence, clarity, concentration, stability, purification and awareness.
	Combines well with lemon, geranium, lavender, peppermint, tea tree, thyme linalol, grapefruit, clary sage, palma rosa, juniper, cypress, pine needle, bergamot, black pepper, cedarwood, eucalyptus, frankincense, mandarin, marjoram, ravensara, oregano, niaouli, litsea cubeba, basil	
• Not to be used during pregnancy. • To be avoided by those with epilepsy.		

In the European Tyrol, rosemary was amongst the fragrant plants used to fumigate and cleanse houses during the May Day festival.

Sage
Salvia officinalis

Sacred sage cleanses and purifies the spirit. The spirit of the different sages – for there are many – holds the wisdom of the spheres within its fragrance, while summoning the powers that heal and protect.
Sage is a protective spirit for those who are not afraid of the spiritual forces or of the force of the unseen beings.
The might of the heavens summoned by the sage is wisdom and power, standing fast in times of adversity. Sage's purpose is to provide all these things for humans; also it helps us to integrate a spirit that has the majesty of the heavens behind it – to call forth God and the celestial warriors, to defend, protect and heal the human spirit and Mother Earth.

PHYSICAL HEALING

antiseptic, anti-spasmodic, diuretic, emmenagogue, tonic

- Must not be used during pregnancy or by those with epilepsy.

- Rarely used in home aroma-therapy – best used in vapor-izing/ diffuser methods.

AROMA

warm, herby, spicy, camphorous

Combines well with rosemary, lavender, hyssop, cedarwood, cypress, lemon, orange, chamomile maroc, basil, myrtle, petitgrain, pine, peppermint, thyme, yarrow

EMOTIONAL HEALING

To encourage strength, courage, perseverance, grounding and protection.

357

There are many varieties of sage growing around the world, some of which have been attributed with spiritual powers and are an important component of religious ceremony. The ancient Romans called sage *herba sacra* – the sacred herb – and would have been referring to *Salvia officinalis*. Sage is today most commonly used for spiritual purposes by the Native American Nations, who use the word sage for several species of plant which would more properly fall into the botanical group, *Compositae*.

In Mexico the Mazatec people use *Salvia divinorum* for divination. The North American Paiutes use *Artemisia dracynculoides* in the costume of the medicine man, and in various spiritual practices and rituals, including the sun dance celebration. *Artemisia tridentata* is incorporated in the costume of Washoe medicine men and is also used in the making of the moccasins used during the sun dances. It is burnt at the start of all spiritual ceremonies, and is also an essential part of the ritual bathing ceremony.

Sandalwood
Santalum album

A fragrance that stretches out to the universe, into the hallowed space between heaven and earth, to contact the divine presence. Sandalwood brings our wisdom into a meditative state, quieting us so we can hear and rejoice in the choral singing of the universal soul. It brings us into the great cosmic prayer, the infinite meditation.
Sandalwood helps humanity to have strength of conviction when standing against adversity, as it rejoins all aspects of being. It rejoices in the physical aspects of mankind, while always being aware of the spiritual self.

PHYSICAL HEALING	AROMA	EMOTIONAL HEALING
antiseptic, anti-depressant, diuretic, tonic, calmative, anti-infectious, decongestant	warm, balsamic, rich, woody **Combines well with** black pepper, geranium, grapefruit, frankincense, fennel, myrrh, benzoin, patchouli, petitgrain, orange, clary sage, palma rosa, ylang ylang, mandarin, lavender, lemon, clove, chamomile roman, rose absolute, rose otto, neroli, jasmine	To encourage warmth, sensitivity, serenity, harmony, peace, wisdom, insightfulness and unity.

The oldest Vedic scripture, the fifth century BC *Nirukta*, mentions sandalwood, which has continued to be one of the most important fragrances used in Indian religious practice. Sandalwood was traded from the earliest times.

Sandalwood has been widely used in embalming. In Ceylon, princes were embalmed from the ninth century onwards.

Other species produce an oil which is similar in smell only (not in terms of therapeutic values) – the African *Osyris tenuifolia* plant, the Australian *Antalum spicatum*, and the West Indian *Amyris balsamifera*.

Spikenard
Nardostachys jatamansi

For the sweet depths of devotion. In preparation for the departure of the spirit to the heavens, spikenard allows us to release our fears of the unknown, to have the courage to step forward. Spikenard helps to reconcile all that has happened to us in this lifetime upon the earth, and to make peace with those who have hurt us. It is a fragrance of forgiveness offered with love. Also, a fragrance that carries with it the bonds of human existence; the chains that bind us to the emotions which we may be fearful of releasing. Its purpose is to release the past from the shackles of our own making, those which relentlessly bind us to repeating actions which affect the freedom of the spirit.

PHYSICAL HEALING	AROMA	EMOTIONAL HEALING
antiseptic, calmative, sedative, anti-infectious	heavy, warm, peaty, musty	To encourage forgiveness, fearlessness, calm, centring, balance and resolution.
	Combines well with lavender, pine, clove, lemon, clary sage, palma rosa, juniper, cypress, geranium, rose absolute, neroli, frankincense, myrrh, patchouli, vetiver	

Known in ancient times as 'nard'.

In Chapter 12:3 of the Book of John in the Bible it says, 'Then took Mary a pound of ointment of spikenard, very costly, and anointed the feet of Jesus'.

Storax (Styrax)
Liquidambar orientalis

*In meditation and prayer, the divine purpose of souls has
a voice through this fragrance. It unlocks doors leading to
unknown corridors in the furthermost reaches of the
mind, where there are windows to the souls of light.
This ancient and mystical fragrance brings us back to
the source of Creation – to the time when all was one –
helping us to understand the paths taken by the saints
and martyrs who sacrificed all for the love of God.
Answers come in their own time, but storax softly opens
and prepares each heart for that knowing.*

PHYSICAL HEALING	AROMA	EMOTIONAL HEALING
antiseptic, anti-tussive, expectorant, nervine	sweet, resinous, balsamic, vanilla-like	To encourage soothing, harmony, benevolence, compassion and unity.
• Not to be used during pregnancy.	**Combines well with** ylang ylang, jasmine, rose absolute, hyacinth, carnation, orange, lemon, geranium, lavender, cinnamon, clove, bay, ginger, helichrysum, cardamom, nutmeg	
• Can cause irritation to sensitive skin.		

Another species, with a very similar aroma, *Styrax
officinalis* – a big bushy shrub with white flowers – is
commonly thought to be the 'stacte' of the holy incense of
Exodus 30:34.

The name 'styrax' is sometimes given to *Liquidambar
orientalis*, storax.

Thyme
(Red and chemotype linalol)
Thymus vulgaris

There is fire within the soul of thyme, the fire to summon the most mighty angels to our assistance – the force within the compassion, the forgiveness in might, the enlightenment of the mind and spirit, the revealing of truth. In the power and might of the heavens, where pretence does not exist, we cannot hide – least of all from ourselves.

This fragrance joins with our guardians in assisting us in having strength and love for ourselves during times of reconciliation, when we strive to acknowledge the shadows and disrobe the outer shell of protection – the disguise which we may find difficult even to acknowledge.

PHYSICAL HEALING

analgesic, expectorant, antiseptic, anti-infectious, emmenagogue

• Not to be used during pregnancy.

• Can cause irritation to sensitive skin.

AROMA

sharp, woody, herbaceous
(The species known as thyme linalol is gentler, and has a softer, woody herbaceous aroma.)

Combines well with geranium, grapefruit, frankincense, clary sage, ormenis flower, ginger, mandarin, palma rosa, lemon, rosemary, hyssop, myrtle, orange, pimento berry, eucalyptus, cypress, pine, birch

EMOTIONAL HEALING

To encourage balance, tolerance, courage, supportiveness, alertness and warmth.

Tuberose (Absolute)
Polianthes tuberosa

Tuberose embodies forgiveness, and the refinding of self-love when the self is lost and the spirit low. When the ego has received many life-blows, and is depressed and unable to connect with the higher realms, tuberose assists in that reconnection. This is a perfume for reaching the true self in a world in which it is easy to be without hope. When all seems lost, it brings the ego into the spirit, in an event which brings balance and harmony.

It helps in transporting the spirit to places unknown, where it can dwell for a brief moment, finding comfort and knowing.

Tuberose is for the finding of truth in truths long-forgotten, to bring hopes and dreams and prayers to their rightful place, and in so doing, to integrate the highest elements of the ego within spiritual wonderment.

PHYSICAL HEALING

antidepressant, calminative, nervine, sedative

AROMA

sweet, heavy, spicy, floral

Combines well with hyacinth, rose absolute, jasmine, ormenis flower, bergamot, sandalwood, benzoin, balsam de Peru, orange, mandarin, narcissus

EMOTIONAL HEALING

To encourage motivation, enthusiasm, encouragement, sensuality, sensitivity, expressiveness and frankness.

In India, Malaysia and other Asian countries, the flowers are made into garlands and placed around the necks of religious sculptures, such as Krishna, Shiva and Buddha, and also given as offerings at home shrines.

In Egypt, garlands are made during religious festivals.

363

Vetiver
Vetiveria zizanoides

Sometimes deep secrets of the soul are hidden in the heart, buried so deep they do not disturb the waking dream of who we think we are. Vetiver can awaken those secrets, which often involve the realization that we are not alone in the universe. This awakening can be unsteadying, even unbalancing, but vetiver holds us fast. Vetiver stops the swirling of the mind, the turmoil of unanswerable questions. In many ways, vetiver helps us to remain calm when unsettling events affect the spiritual self, and when facing adversity.
Gently, and without disturbing the creative forces, vetiver steadies and calms any inner disquiet – and in that calmness may come the answers we seek.

PHYSICAL HEALING	AROMA	EMOTIONAL HEALING
antiseptic, tonic, emmenagogue, anti-spasmodic, nervine	soft, earthy, musty **Combines well with** sandalwood, orange, lemon, mandarin, grapefruit, eucalyptus citriodora, litsea cubeba, yuzu, melissa, geranium, ylang ylang, lavender, clary sage, jasmine, rose absolute, bergamot, black pepper, coriander, ginger, lemongrass	To encourage growth, integrity, wisdom, strength, honour, protection, self-esteem and grounding.

Violet Leaf (Absolute)
Viola odorata

Violet is for timidity of the spirit. There are those who have within them deep knowing, who silently marvel at the wonder of life and who, yet, are shy. They may fear venturing forth into worlds unknown, or fear the afterlife. They may be unable to voice the troubles of their heart and soul. There are those too who are unable to pray out loud, and instead silently offer a prayer from their heart, although sometimes wondering if it will be heard. Some are too timid to step into the light and feel its strength-giving warmth, that which gives courage to speak and be heard. And there are those too timid to accept the love offered by all realms. For all these shy, timid spirits, violet offers understanding and empathy, and a way into the great open void of love.

PHYSICAL HEALING	AROMA	EMOTIONAL HEALING
analgesic, anti-rheumatic, decongestant, diuretic, soporific	forceful, greenish with slight floral edge **Combines well with** rose absolute, tuberose, clary sage, lemon, grapefruit, tangerine, basil, hyacinth, jasmine, sandalwood, clove, bay, cinnamon, geranium, lavender Use only small amounts in blends.	To encourage security, courage, confidence, centring, gentleness and upliftment.

Yarrow
Achillea millefolium

This fragrance has long been an energetic messenger of the heavens, since it was first planted by the Creator. It delicately balances the flow between the yin and yang energies received from the sun, the moon and the stars. Once the balance and harmonization of yin and yang energy within a person has been completed, the fragrance acts as a conduit for the opening of intuitive perception and the acceptance of the hidden faculties of the mind. Although it at all times remains firmly attached to the earth plane, it intercepts and assists in the delivery of messages and prophecies from other planes of existence. A fragrance for dreaming, for visionary experiences, for travelling on the energy of the universe while being protected and nurtured.

PHYSICAL HEALING

anti-inflammatory, antiseptic, carminative, tonic, anti-spasmodic

• Can cause irritation to sensitive skin.

AROMA

herby green with a slightly spicy camphorous note

Combines well with
lavender, chamomile roman, clary sage, geranium, peppermint, eucalyptus, lemon, sage, myrtle, fennel, frankincense, ginger, helichrysum, marjoram, pine, rosemary, black pepper, cypress, birch, bergamot

EMOTIONAL HEALING

To encourage harmony, equilibrium, intuition, centring, dreams and visions.

A sacred plant to the North American Nations, and the Chinese, amongst others.

The long, wood-like dried stems of the yarrow plant continue to be used as the most traditionally correct tool for casting the *I Ching*, for prophecy.

Ylang Ylang
Cananga odorata

Ylang ylang is the tender-hearted one whose hanging petals dance in the wind, as if, through flexibility, it protects its tender heart from destruction. It shields and guides the passion of love and true emotion, whilst allowing a tender awakening of that sensual part of our being and spirit which can embrace all things. It will open our hearts to the pleasures which God has given to us as we walk our mortal path, and to the understanding that even Heaven and the angelic realms enjoy the passion of a spiritual being. It may soften the hard-hearted and allow those that use judgement against others to feel the soft seduction of Heaven. For those who have a yearning for completion.

PHYSICAL HEALING	AROMA	EMOTIONAL HEALING
sedative, antiseptic, aphrodisiac, nervine, antidepressant, calmative	sweet, intense, balsamic, floral **Combines well with** lemon, mandarin, palma rosa, yuzu, litsea cubeba, eucalyptus citriodora, clove, orange, ginger, sandalwood, jasmine, bergamot, chamomile roman, clary sage, patchouli, jasmine, rose absolute, petitgrain, vetiver, grapefruit	To encourage self-confidence, warmth, awakening, sensuality, upliftment, calm, joy and enthusiasm.

Yuzu
Citrus junos

Yuzu is purifying, strong and clearly focused. If feeling spiritually unsettled, yuzu gives the spiritual purification and strength needed to move forward, and the focus required as we take in new thoughts and feelings. It also has within it the facility of discipline, which is required so as not to allow our thoughts to stray or become unsettled and distracted by others.

Stillness and focus are the reference points which make invisible the many distractions that tempt us from the spiritual peace. Yuzu offers this, sweetly, kindly, and with a resolution that can withstand all storms, with a benign confident smile upon its face.

PHYSICAL HEALING	AROMA	EMOTIONAL HEALING
tonic, stimulant, anti-infectious, diuretic, calmative, antiseptic, analgesic • Should not be used on the skin if being exposed to sunlight or ultraviolet rays.	a unique blend of fresh citrus **Combines well with** basil, bergamot, black pepper, cardamom, cedarwood, clary sage, coriander, cypress, ginger, jasmine, lavender, marjoram, palma rosa, pine, ravensara, rose absolute, rosemary, sandalwood, ylang ylang	To encourage focus, concentration, strength, courage and centring.

It's used in religious ceremonies by some Shinto priests, for purification before prayer.

Chapter Twelve

THE AROMATIC TRADITIONS

Fragrance has played a very important part in the spiritual traditions of the world, with no other material substance being so universally employed in spiritual practice. We know fragrance can affect both body and mind, but it can also affect spiritual perceptions, and it is this reason, I believe, rather than any of the many philosophical/metaphorical/practical reasons that have been given, that ultimately explains its widespread use.

From a philosophical point of view, aroma is something both physical and ethereal, linking the realm of the known to the unknown. Fragrance is also transformational: with resin, for example, being changed from light, odourless rocks into fragrant smoke, rising to Heaven. The delightful nature of fragrance reminds people of the good things in life, of all they have to be grateful for, and they give thanks. By a simple analogy, death, decay and bad smells were equated with evil, and good smells with well-being, immortality and the spiritual realms. Burning fragrant material sent a 'smoke signal' to the gods, letting them know people were thinking of them and seeking their help. The medicinal qualities of many fragrant materials were used – in ancient Mesopotamia for example – in inhalations, medicated baths and poultices; and their beneficent properties must have been thought of as a blessing from the gods.

There are, then, many reasons why fragrance might have been thought to be the means by which to show appreciation to the deity. It is also the case, however, that fragrance affects the mind and spirit, and no doubt the peoples who used fragrance on a regular basis knew this too, as do those who continue to use it for that purpose today.

THE GODDESS OF THE SACRED TREES

The earliest known example of a building with a specifically ritual purpose, a place of communal worship, is 9,000 years old. It's at Novali Cori, on the Turkish-Syrian border. The people here, like all others known to archaeologists from this time, worshipped a goddess – at Novali Cori the goddess was associated with a tortoise. Goddess worship was known throughout Europe, the Middle East, India, Pakistan and North Africa from earliest times, possibly as early as 30,000 BC. Male gods only began to appear around 6000 BC. They started out as sons of the goddesses, then became their consorts and eventually took over the main role. However, it was a long process, which involved the prophets of the Old Testament fighting 'the queen of Heaven' and her 'idolaters', and the ancient Greeks, who as late as 500 BC were still arguing over who should have supremacy – the male (Zeus) or the female (Athene). Male gods eventually won.

The battle against worship of females is told in the Old Testament. For example in Jeremiah 44:16–17,

370

the people of Pathros told the prophet '. . . we will not hearken unto thee. But we will certainly do whatsoever thing goeth forth out of our own mouths, to burn incense unto the queen of Heaven, and to pour out drink offerings unto her, as we have done, we, and our fathers, our kings, and our princes, in the cities of Judah, and in the streets of Jerusalem: for then had we plenty of victuals, and were well, and saw no evil.' The Canaanites worshipped a goddess called Astarte, and put plaques with images ('graven images') of her on the backs of the doors so when the agents of the Israelite kings burst into the houses to check on their religious practices, as the doors were thrown open the images were hidden between them and the wall. The Canaanites also worshipped the goddess as a tree; pine, juniper or cypress, and where these were not available they substituted *asherah* – which were wooden poles made of tree trunks and placed in the ground.

Incense burning was a central feature of goddess worship in predynastic and later Egypt, in Sumeria and throughout the Middle East. As time passed and the authority of the goddesses became supplanted by that of male gods, the priestesses who had served the goddesses were replaced by male priests. Censers have been found in the graves of many women, humble as well as noble, and it's thought that many ordinary women took on the role of priestess within their local area. As the official power and authority of women in spiritual matters dwindled, their area of influence became confined to that of oracle-giving. This involved going into trance – often induced by inhaling the smoke of burning incense and other fragrant material – and apparently speaking in the voices of the gods or goddesses.

The most famous oracle was at Delphi in Greece, to whom national leaders went for advice, long after the male element had taken over official religions. Whoever was the oracle at any particular time was known as *Pythia*, 'the Pythoness' or snake priestess. The fragrant material favoured at Delphi was bay, which was burnt to produce a profusion of smoke. It's also been suggested that the roof of the central building at Delphi was made of branches of bay trees, and that the oracle ate the leaves. By the late Greek period, goddesses had more or less been softened and made sensual rather than all-powerful. Many continued to be associated with fragrance, such as Circe, Demeter and Aphrodite, also known as Venus.

ANCIENT EGYPT

It was ... in their grand religious processions that they made the most luxurious display of perfumes. In one of those described as having taken place under one of the Ptolemies, marched one hundred and twenty children, bearing incense, myrrh, and saffron in golden basins, followed by a number of camels, some carrying three hundred pounds weight of frankincense, and others a similar quantity of crocus, cassia, cinnamon, orris, and other precious ointments.

EUGENE RIMMEL, *The Book of Perfumes*

The ancient Egyptians didn't question whether there was a life after death. They were so convinced they spent half their lives preparing for it. Royalty and people of standing or wealth built tombs for themselves which were packed with all manner of possessions that would be needed in the afterlife, as the body itself would be packed with aromatic materials during mummification, to prevent decay.

The Egyptian civilization grew up along the banks of the River Nile, starting around 4000 BC, with the first walled cities around 3300 BC, the unification of the 'upper' and 'lower' valley kingdoms in 3200 BC, and the construction of the first stepped pyramid begun around 2650 BC. Egypt continued as an important cultural centre for another 2,600 years, until the defeat of Cleopatra in 30 BC by the Roman, Octavian-Augustus. Because there was such long continuity in the priestly tradition which recorded knowledge about plants, and because this evidence remains either in papyrus or stone, we can be very sure that fragrance in all its forms was lavishly used throughout the millennia.

The existence of the myrrh tree was explained as it being a tear of the god Horus, as other incense trees grew where the tears of the gods Shu and Tefnet fell. The gods were offered incense in return, usually in the form of little round pastilles or balls which the priest fed into the long censer, balanced carefully on one hand.

The sun-god Ra was offered some form of resin at dawn, myrrh at midday, and *kyphi* at sunset. This last incense was admired by many famous Greeks, including Galen, and has come down to us in the form of several recipes. Plutarch said it could heal the soul. There were at least sixteen ingredients, possibly including, as well as wine, honey and raisins, myrrh, cardamom, juniper, mint, cypress, spikenard, cassia and cinnamon. Within the temple complexes there were special areas for preparing incense for ritual use, and as this was carried out, priests would read aloud from sacred texts. A visual record of the making of *kyphi* can still be seen on the walls of the Temple of Horus at Edfu.

In the late 1960s, Dominique Mallet and other archaeologists excavated the tomb of a nobleman and high priest, Ptah Du-Auu at Saqqâra. Most items had been removed by graverobbers but they did find two used censers and some pots, one of which had 'B'rth Respeth incense' written on the side in ink, and contained about half a pound of resinous material; apparently including benzoin, sandalwood, myrrh, frankincense and juniper, along with lotus oil, fragrant rush, sweet gum bark and gum mastic.

In many temples, priests and priestesses would burn fragrant woods and resins throughout the day. However, as can be seen from the beautiful wall friezes left for us to enjoy, on important state occasions the king himself would lead the ritual, holding a censer in one hand and a spouted vase in the other. This vase may have contained wine, or possibly the perfumed oil which was poured on the altar or put on the statues of the gods.

The ancient Egyptians needed oils to keep their skin supple in the searing dry heat, and these were perfumed in various ways: by steeping the petals or other fragrant material in oil or fats; by putting the material in hot oils and straining; and by squeezing the essence out of plants using a press or by putting it in material which was then twisted very tightly using special equipment.

Embalming involved filling body cavities with copious amounts of fragrant material and resins such as cassia, cedarwood and myrrh, and much anointing of the body. Frankincense was reserved for use on the head. Vases of fragrant oils were placed with the mummy who, it was thought, would surely need them when the transition to the other world was complete. When buried, the body was first anointed and perfumed, and a crown of flowers was placed on the head. A prayer was then said, invoking the god Horus to favour the dead with his perfume and acceptance.

The Egyptians traded extensively to acquire the aromatics they required in both their spiritual and secular lives. Temples and homes were both fragranced, sometimes with a censer with a perforated cover. As well as the fragrant materials already mentioned, which are used today in the form of essential oils, spikenard, galbanum, and at a later date rose, were known to have been used.

As Egypt declined in power and importance, the knowledge of plants accumulated over the millennia was transferred to the many excellent schools of medicine and learning that emerged from the third century BC onwards. The most famous of these was at the busy northern port of Alexandria. It became the centre of alchemical research which aimed to sublimate matter and give body to that which is spiritual. Alchemists sought to capture the essential spark of divinity in plant and mineral matter. As part of this quest, essential oils were distilled, or 'transformed' from raw plant material, giving rise to the enduring idea that essential oils have *quintus essentialis* or life force.

In an Alexandrian text from the first century AD, called *The Gold Making of Cleopatra* (not the queen), we find the first illustration of a distillation unit, the invention of which is ascribed to 'Maria the Jewess'. Alongside are two other images. One is a serpent holding its tail in its mouth and the inscription 'All is one'; the other is a disc within which are the words, 'It is towards oneness that all phenomena tend'. Pliny, the first-century Roman writer, visited the perfume factories of Alexandria, noting twenty-eight different varieties and describing how the workers had to remove their clothing before leaving in the evening because the costly perfume materials may have adhered to them. Fragrance was precious indeed.

MESOPOTAMIA

I poured out a libation on the peak of the
    mountain
Seven and yet seven kettles I set up
Under them I heaped up sweet cane, cedar,
    myrtle,
The gods smelled the savor,
The gods smelled the sweet savor
The gods gathered like flies over the sacrificer.

Epic of Gilgamesh, 2000 BC

Mesopotamia is the name given to the area between the two great rivers, the Euphrates and Tigris, which run southeast from the mountains of Turkey, through Syria and Iraq, to the Persian Gulf. Around 3500 BC the first city-states appeared in the south, which came to be known as Sumeria. Ur, Uruk and Lagash grew prosperous on an agricultural economy, greatly aided by vast irrigation schemes. The temples dominated the city physically. At Ur, for example, the vast ziggurat rose to the heavens by three steps, the lowest of these

376

being forty-five-feet high. Ritual was at the centre of social activity. The temple owned much of the land, and controlled most foreign trade, which went west to Egypt and east to the Indus Valley. The need to keep records of the crop surplus, and the import and export goods, gave impetus to the invention of writing. These cuneiform records make it possible to accurately ascertain events of the past. One tablet, for example, tells us that 5,000 years ago, people were placing orders for 'oils of cypress, myrrh and cedar to be obtained from abroad'.

As time went on, city-states such as Kish, Nippur and Babylon, further northwest upriver, became more prominent. This more northern region is generally known as Babylonia. The city of Babylon became an important centre of trade, as did the northerly rain-fed Nineveh; and their economic and political importance continued into Assyrian times. Much of the trading was in spices of various sorts, which were used for ritual, cleansing, medicine, perfuming and cooking.

The Mesopotamians liked to perform their rituals as high as possible – on a mountain top, or atop a very high clay-brick construction – where huge amounts of incense would be burnt to attract the gods and goddesses. The fragrant materials available included juniper, myrtle, calamus, pine and fir resins, as well as cedar, cypress, myrrh and, certainly by the later period, around 600 BC, frankincense and sandalwood. Many other fragrant plants may have been used, as a herbal dated at 2200 BC lists 250 species, as well as giving recipes for perfumes and ointments.

Anointing had great significance in several contexts. Oil was rubbed on statues of deities and on stones meant to represent ancestors; poured on the head of a girl as a sign she was chosen to be married, or on the head of a vassal king; and used to confirm a contract or oath. How much of this anointing oil was fragranced is difficult to tell, but we do know that Babylon was renowned for its scents, which were traded far and wide. Liquid essences were stored in alabaster or glass bottles, while ointments were kept in boxes made of porcelain or chalcedony.

In Babylonian religious literature the mother-goddess Ishtar has a son, Tammuz, who 'dies' each year to be reborn; symbolizing the 'death' of nature, and its rebirth in spring. In one text, *The Descent of Ishtar to the Underworld*, it says of Tammuz 'wash him with clean water, anoint him with perfumed oil, dress him in a red cloth . . .' Commenting on this in *The Golden Bough*, J. G. Frazer says that religious songs or chants were made over an effigy of the dead god 'while the fumes of incense rose into the air, as if to stir his dormant senses by their pungent fragrance and wake him from the sleep of death'.

The cuneiform tablets frequently mention incense, and the censers which distributed the aroma around both temples and homes. It seems to have been used in some quantity, with a King Nabonnedos, for example, apparently 'filling the temple with the odour of incense'. Often censers would be mentioned along with incantations that were supposed to drive out evil spirits. Houses where there was sickness were fumigated with incense and torches of burning fragrant material to exorcize negative influences.

In Mesopotamia, plants were seen as the source of deity and immortality, with kings offering incense to the 'Sacred Tree', and the hero of the epic, Gilgamesh, going in search of 'the herb of immortality'. Being on the crossroads between east and west, the people had access to a variety of fragrant material, which was used in protective amulets, lotions, compresses, inhalations, medicinal baths and in massage oils. The fragrance molecules could have been extracted by steeping the raw material in oil or fat, although pots found at Tepe Gawra, near Nineveh, also suggest that some form of distillation method was in use.

THE HEBREW TRADITION AND THE KABBALAH

> As each commandment [of the Ten Commandments] was spoken by the Holy One, Blessed be He, the world filled with fragrance.

Shabbat 88b, RABBI YEHOSHUA BEN-LEVI

The first Jewish patriarch was Abraham, who lived in Mesopotamia around 1700 BC. As we can read in Genesis 12:1 – the Lord told him 'Get thee out of thy country . . . unto a land that I will show thee: And I will make of thee a great nation . . .' Abraham duly went with his wife, Sarah, and nephew, Lot, to Canaan, settling away from the already cultivated lands of the farming Canaanites, by the 'oak of Moreh'. In time, to prevent his flocks overgrazing the land, Abraham went to the hills of Hebron, and Lot went to Sodom, on the plain of Jordan. Years later, because of a famine in Canaan, Abraham's descendants went to Egypt, where they were enslaved for centuries, before being led out of captivity by Moses. They returned to Canaan, where people were already living in the fertile valleys, and settled in the forested, uninhabited hills. This was the land flowing 'with milk and honey'

– the milk came from the goats and the honey from the bees that fed on the many fragrant wild flowers growing amongst the wild undergrowth. The hills were cleared, terraced and planted with olive trees, figs, pomegranates and vineyards.

Moses was instructed by God, in Exodus 30, to make both a Holy incense and a sacred anointing oil. The practice of offering incense twice daily started with Aaron during the long flight through the wilderness from Egypt, and continued at the Temple in Jerusalem. In the Hebrew Holy Scriptures (according to the Masoretic Text), the ingredients are given as 'sweet spices, stacte, and *onycha*, and galbanum; sweet spices with pure frankincense'. The Temple Institute in Jerusalem told me that the full list was stacte, *onycha*, galbanum, frankincense, myrrh, cassia, spikenard, saffron, costus, aromatic bark and cinnamon. Some Christian bibles, along with the Hebrew, add 'seasoned with salt, pure and holy'. The 'salt' was probably saltpeter, a binding agent.

There is an ongoing and complex debate about the names given to plants and plant materials in the Bible. The cinnamon we know, *Cinnamomum verum* (formerly *C. zeylanicum*), only grew in the East, and although we know the Phoenicians and Arabs were trading in it perhaps as early as 500 BC, and may have been doing so even earlier, it's also possible that the 'cinnamon' of ancient texts has been translated incorrectly and that it refers to the bark of an Ethiopian tree, *Amyris kataf*. Similar problems of definition surround cassia, stacte, *onycha* and hyssop, amongst others. Even considering more local plants can be problematic. Stacte might have been, for example, *Styrax officinale*, *Liquidambar orientalis*, *Pistacia lentiscus*, or the sweetly fragrant resin that used to

380

exude spontaneously from *Amyris kataf* – the bark of which, in other opinions, is the biblical 'cinnamon'. You can see how complicated it all gets!

What is certain is that the hillsides of ancient Israel abounded with fragrant flowers, herbs and shrubs, that resins exuded from many species of trees – and fragrance was an important part of ancient Hebrew life. The medicinal properties of these fragrant materials was at least partly understood, and their purification and cleansing properties much appreciated. Fragrant incense accompanied offerings and prayers to God, while the fragrant holy oil – made of myrrh, cinnamon, calamus and cassia diluted in olive oil – was used to anoint the tabernacle, the ark, the table, the candlestick, the altar of incense and the altar of burnt offering, along with all their associated cups and containers.

When instructing Moses about the making of both the holy incense and oil, different texts say it should be made either 'after the art of the apothecary' or 'after the art of the perfumer'. At this time, of course, they were in a sense one and the same thing as perfumes – fragrance materials – which were central components in the apothecary's, that is the druggist's or pharmacist's, materia medica.

The ancient Hebrews also used aromatics as part of personal hygiene and cleansing practices: as body perfumes and clothes fragrancers; as pest-deterrent fumigations and fragrancers of bedding and linen; as seasoning for food and wine; for anointing the heads of guests in welcome to the house; and in their funerary rites. If fragrance was precious, it was also an essential part of daily life.

> And Hezekiah was glad of them, and showed
> them his treasure-house, the silver, and the
> gold, and the spices, and the precious oil . . .
>
> ISAIAH 39:2

The mystical aspect of Judaism is, in part, contained in the tradition known as 'Kabbalah'. These teachings aim to explore and explain, in both biblical and metaphysical terms, the relationship between God, the universe and mankind. Being very much an oral tradition, Kabbalah has changed over the years, and had different perspectives on the nature of things. In one medieval text, Eliphas Levi presented the following incense formulas, which he related to colours:

Colour	*Incense Composed of:*
Red	balm, ambergris, grains of paradise, saffron
Green	benzoin, mace, storax
Blue	roses, violets
Purple	saffron, cinnamon, red sanders
White	camphor, amber, aloes, white sandal, cucumber seeds

> Aaron shall burn thereon incense of sweet spices
> every morning and when he dresseth the lamps,
> he shall burn it. And when Aaron lighteth the
> lamps at dusk, he shall burn a perpetual incense
> before the Lord throughout your generations.
>
> EXODUS 30: 7–8

There has always been a strong connection in the Jewish tradition between fragrance and light; since Aaron was instructed to light the lamps at the same time as burning the incense on the altar. The 'lamps' are the seven-part candlestick known as the menorah, which has been the symbol of Judaism for 3,000 years, and the shape of which is modelled on a plant. There are so many highly fragrant plants growing in Israel which have the shape of the menorah, it's difficult to say exactly which species it was fashioned after, and the generic term *'moriah* plant' is applied to them all. *Salvia dominica* and *Salvia palaestina* are likely candidates. They are both varieties of the sage. On the evening of the Sabbath, Jews remember the lamps and incense of the Temple in Jerusalem, when blessings are made over the *havdallah* candle and spice box. Different spices are used, but myrtle has been called 'the quintessential fragrant plant of Israel' and is often preferred when available. Indeed, the spice box is called *hadass*, which means myrtle, by many Ashkenazic and Sephardic Jews.

Salvia palaestina

menorah

THE CHRISTIAN TRADITION

> . . . Mary Magdalene, and Mary the
> mother of James, and Salome, had
> brought sweet spices, that they might
> come and anoint him.
>
> ST MARK 16:1

From his birth to his death, Jesus knew about
fragrance. At his birth in Bethlehem, two of the three
wise men brought the gifts of frankincense and myrrh.
After his crucifixion and placing in the sepulchre, the
two Marys and Salome came to anoint him with 'sweet
spices', as was the custom at the time.

> But I have all, and abound: I am full,
> having received of Epaphroditus the
> things which were sent from you, an
> odour of a sweet smell, a sacrifice
> acceptable, wellpleasing to God.
>
> PHILIPPIANS 4:18

The word 'savour' in the Bible is often interchangeable with the word 'fragrance', depending on which
version you read. In biblical times, it often described
the smell of sacrifice, which in the tabernacle con-
sisted of both meat and incense. There were two altars
– of brass and gold – for this purpose. This practice of
making dual sacrifice can make reading Bible references confusing, as it's difficult to know whether
'sweet savour', which is pleasing to God, means the
aroma of the burning meat or of the burning incense,
or both.

The word 'savour' was also used to indicate 'sacrifice'

in its broadest sense, as here, when St Paul spoke to the Ephesians: 'And walk in love, as Christ also hath loved us, and hath given himself for us an offering and a sacrifice to God for a sweetsmelling savour.' To the Corinthians, he said: 'For we are unto God a sweet savour of Christ . . .' 'Savour' was so well understood to mean sacrifice that it was used metaphorically, so that *not* to have 'savour', according to *The Illustrated Bible Dictionary*, indicated insipidity or foolishness and lack of strength. It states: 'Something is missing from God's people or the worship of God when there is no "savour".'

> Is any sick among you? let him call for
> the elders of the church; and let them
> pray over him, anointing him with oil
> in the name of the Lord; And the
> prayer of faith shall save the sick, and
> the Lord shall raise him up; and if he
> have committed sins, they shall be
> forgiven him.
>
> JAMES 5:14–15

Oil was an extremely important commodity in biblical times. It was used not only for cooking and fuelling lamps, but for external application on wounds and, as an extension of those visible benefits, taken internally for illness. In most cases, simple, pure olive oil was used. Fragrance added another dimension to the oil, giving it a deeper and more spiritual connotation, and was incorporated in the Holy oil for anointing priests and sacred objects, for example. Fragranced or not, oil is associated with essential goodness. Psalm 23, which begins 'The Lord is my shepherd; I shall not want . . .'

later says 'thou anointest my head with oil; my cup runneth over.' And in Psalm 133, we read 'How wonderful it is, how pleasant, for God's people to live together in harmony! It is like the precious anointing oil running down from Aaron's head and beard . . .'

The Christian Church has taken different views on the subject of anointing, with and without added fragrance, and on the subject of incense. Those against its use say it's simply unnecessary, or that its use is quasi-magical. One can understand this position to a point, in that fragrance was used in some profusion by religious groups that stood in opposition to Christianity, and worshipped other gods with it, such as the Romans, and before them the 'idolaters' who so irked the Jewish prophets by continuing to pay homage to 'the queen of heaven'. Aiming to distance themselves from these other people, then, early Christians in particular eschewed the use of incense.

When it comes to anointing, the discussion becomes more complex as there are different elements to consider: its use in baptism, confirmation, healing, last rites, ordination of priests, consecration of churches and ritual objects, and the coronation of kings and queens. Over the years, and in different places, opinions have differed over which sacramental practices, if any, should involve the use of oil, and whether they should be perfumed or not. Objections have focused on the thought that nothing physical – such as oil – can represent in any way the blessing of God; God is above the physical, so no physical accoutrements are necessary. Or, as James Pilkington, a sixteenth-century Bishop of Durham put it:

What can their holy ashes, holy palms, holy crosses, holy bells, holy creams, relics, moulds,

chalice, corporas, fire, candles, beads, or that
which is that most holy relic, their oil, wherewith
they anoint their shavelings, priests and bishops,
do?
There is no creature which can give that holiness
to another which is in itself; this thing belongs to
Christ alone.

Over the centuries there's been endless debate over where to draw the line and, indeed, the Christian Church today finds itself splintered partly as a result of the differences in opinion. The Church of England does not generally anoint, with either plain or perfumed oil, those being baptized; yet a fragrant anointing oil is an important part of the ceremony when an incoming monarch is crowned. On the other hand, the Greek Orthodox Church uses pure olive oil in the sacraments of baptism and holy unction, and a perfumed chrism oil following baptism, or when a new convert is received into the Church.

Many commentators over the years have believed that oil, particularly the Holy chrism or perfumed oil, in some sense contained the Holy Spirit. But according to Eisenhofer and Lechner in *The Liturgy of the Roman Rite*, oil is merely a symbol for the imparting of grace. In a personal communication, Revd Allen Morris informs me that it is not Catholic doctrine 'that the oil undergoes substantial change such as does the bread consecrated at the Eucharist.'

On the subject of perfumed oil, he says:

The scent of chrism is particularly appropriate
for those anointings which lead to the person or
object anointed becoming significant of Christ in
a particular way. Thus, not only bishops and

priests at their ordination, but any person at their baptism, and altars consecrated for their sacred use.

One member of the Russian Orthodox Church, Gillian Crow, has kindly offered her personal interpretation of the use of fragrance in that tradition, as follows:

As a rule, Orthodox worship aims to be heaven on earth, and expresses the beauty of the fact of God's love. It therefore tries to be beautiful in every possible way, including fragrance. There is nothing in Orthodoxy that is suspicious of beauty ... The house of God therefore is expected to be sweet-smelling ... Because Orthodoxy understands the human being as a unique being of body and soul together, both loved by God, and both destined to rise to eternal life – as demonstrated by the Incarnation, life, death and Resurrection of Jesus Christ, God become human – it insists on the body sharing with the soul in the spiritual life, just as the soul shares with the body in the physical life. Therefore worship and prayer, like every aspect of life, is both a physical and spiritual experience in which body and soul take part. Worship, whether private or public, therefore involves all five senses, of which one is the sense of smell.

There are a variety of opinions on the use of fragrance in a spiritual context, none more so than in the Christian tradition. Opinions vary along the whole spectrum, from seeing it as a pointless indulgence, to believing it contains the Holy Spirit. For someone who is inexperienced in the potential effects of aroma, this disparity could be highly confusing. Where there is some hostility to the use of fragrance, this may be because aroma is little understood. For example, essential oils, which are contained in all natural fragrant plant materials, are often very medicinal. When vast clouds of fragrant incense smoke descend on a congregation, some might think, That'll purify the atmosphere in here, while another person, unaware of the vibrational and medicinal properties, might think it all a load of superstitious hokum. Similarly, I know essential oils can deeply affect spiritual perception and believe this was one of the reasons fragrance was used in such abundance in ancient, and indeed modern, times. Others may simply think 'it covers up bad smells', or offer a metaphorical or symbolic explanation for its use. Spirituality is, of course, a personal journey, but in time, perhaps, more credence will be given to the use of aroma in a spiritual context, especially in the Christian tradition.

ANCIENT GREECE AND ROME

Let the rich fumes of od'rous incense fly,
A grateful savour to the powers on high;
The due libation nor neglect to pay,
When evening closes, or when dawns the
day.

HESIOD, *Work and Days,* i.334
(eighth century BC)

The origin and use of fragrance was, in Greek mythology, attributed to the gods, who lost their monopoly on the secrets when one of Venus' nymphs, Aeone, was indiscreet. When Greek goddesses made an appearance on earth, there was always an associated fragrance, while in their heaven the gods and goddesses enjoyed special wonderful perfumes, not available to humans. Worshippers hoped to reach the Greek heaven, 'the Elysian fields', which were redolent with fragrance, as here described by Eugene Rimmel:

> In the midst of the Elysian fields they were to find a golden city with emerald ramparts, ivory pavement, and cinnamon gates. Around the walls flowed a river of perfumes one hundred cubits in width, and deep enough to swim in. From this river rose an odorous mist, which enveloped the whole place and shed a refreshing and fragrant dew. There were to be, besides, in this fortunate city, three hundred and sixty-five fountains of honey and five hundred of the sweetest essences.

No wonder the worship of gods and goddesses was invariably accompanied by sweet fragrance. At home, incense was burnt on the *thyterion*, the incense altar; while at gatherings where animal sacrifice was involved, it was put on an altar along with herbs, flowers and resins. Vegetarians, such as Pythagoras, just 'sacrificed' plant materials. As there were thousands of Greek gods and goddesses, there were many religious festivals, when fragrant materials were used in great profusion.

The first book entirely dedicated to fragrance, *Concerning Odours*, was written by 'the father of botany', Theophrastus, who was born in Lesbos in 370 BC. From him and other sources we know the Greeks used – amongst other fragrances – cassia, cinnamon, cardamom, spikenard, storax, iris, costus, saffron, myrrh, kyperion, ginger-grass, sweet flag, sweet marjoram, lotus, dill, rose, gillyflower, lillies (susinon), myrtle, oil of balanos, bergamot, bay, mint, thyme, hyacinth, violets and narcissus.

These were made into essences, and incorporated into oils and unguents using olive, sesame, castor and linseed oils. Wine was another popular 'carrier' of fragrant material. Apollonius of Herophilia wrote a *Treatise on Perfumes*, listing the best sources of particular ingredients and blends. He lamented the loss of a good source of frankincense 'unguent':

> Long ago there used to be a most delicious unguent extracted from frankincense at Pergamus, owing to the invention of a certain perfumer of that city, for no-one else had ever made it before him; but now none is made there.

The medicinal qualities of aromatic plants were much appreciated at this time, with Criton, Galen and Hippocrates all advocating the use of fumigations at the time of epidemics. Theophrastus wrote:

> It is to be expected that perfumes should have medicinal properties in view of the virtues of their spices. The effect of plasters and of what some call poultices prove these virtues, since they disperse tumours and abscesses and produce a distinct effect on the body and also its interior parts. If one lays a plaster on his abdomen and breast, he produces fragrant odours in his breath.

Perfumes, with their health-giving properties, were seen as gifts of the gods, and perfumes were in return offered on the altars of worship. At the temples of Venus and the Roman god of medicine, Aesculapius, the recipes of particularly effective essences were inscribed on marble plaques, so the attendants could easily refer to them when healing the sick. According to the Roman author, Pliny, in the first century, the plaster of the temple of Minerva at Elis had been mixed with saffron by Panaenus, with the result that 'even today, if one wets one's thumb with saliva and rubs it on the plaster, the latter still gives off the smell and taste of saffron.' Worship was fragrant indeed!

> The simple savin on the altars smoked,
> A laurel sprig the easy gods invoked,
> And rich was he whose votive wreath possessed
> The lovely violet with sweet flowers dress'd.

OVID

The Romans adopted the Greek practices of using incense in worship, bathing in fragrant water, and massaging with perfumed oils – and took them to the limits. Not only did they offer incense to their gods, but to their living god, the emperor. Their civic baths were of course legendary, comprising the tepidarium, calidarium, sudatorium and frigidarium: rooms and pools of varying temperature. There was also the unctuarium, where the body could be massaged with perfumed oils. In Rome, the use of rose oil became something of a cult.

The spiritual aspect of fragrance was not ignored, however. Cornelius Agrippa wrote, 'if of coriander, smallage, henbane, and hemlock, be made a fume, spirits do presently come together'.

THE VEDIC SCRIPTURES

There is a Spirit which is mind and
life, light and truth and vast spaces.
He contains all works and desires and
all perfumes and all tastes. He enfolds
the whole universe, and in silence is
loving to all.

CHANDOGYA UPANISHAD

The earliest sacred poetic writings of Hinduism are known as the Veda, which were completed around 900 BC. There are four groups of these prayers and hymns: the Rig-Veda, the Sāma-Veda, the Yajur-Veda and the Atharva-Veda. Other religious writings followed, including the Upanishads, Brahmanas and Puranas. Together, they form the religious writings of Hinduism.

Hinduism is monotheistic, not polytheistic. Although there appear to be many gods and goddesses, they are all aspects of the one god, Brahman, identified with the symbol OM, and conceptualized now less as a person than as a non-personalized divine principle. The Trimurti, or triad of gods, are the first layer of the manifestation of this principle, and comprised Brahma (the creator), Vishnu (the preserver) and Shiva (the destroyer). According to the Veda, their worship should involve burning fires of fragrant woods at the four cardinal points, onto which consecrated oils should be put, while a fragrant grass called *kusa* is scattered around (possibly *Cymbopogon jwarancusa*, known as 'karakusa'). This practice was mentioned in a poem written by Kalidasa 2,000 years ago, 'Sakoontala', in which the girl of the title is about to be married. Her father speaks:

Holy flames that gleam around
Every altar's hallowed ground;
Holy flames, whose frequent food
Is the consecrated wood,
And for whose encircling bed
Sacred Kusa-grass is spread;
Holy flames that waft to heaven
Sweet oblations daily given,
Mortal guilt to purge away;
Hear, oh, hear me, when I pray,
Purify my child this day!

The wives of the Trimurti are the goddesses Saraswati, Lakshmi and Sati respectively, although Shiva has another wife, who is known by several names – depending on the aspect of herself that is shown – including Parvati and Kali. An aspect of Brahman or OM could have many incarnations, and so we see the god Vishnu manifested as Rama, Krishna and Buddha. In this way, with ever increasing ripples of complexity – with spouses, sons, daughters, lifetimes, personality aspects and so forth – we arrive at the position where there are literally hundreds of Hindu gods, all manifestations of the one divine principle.

India, the home of Hinduism, is also a place where many fragrant plants abound. Fragrance is an integral part of worship, ritual and ceremony, and has been so for as long as written records can show. Sandalwood is mentioned, for example, in the oldest Vedic scripture, the Nirukta. India has produced certain fragrances for a very long time indeed – including sandalwood, aloeswood, cassia, costus, patchouli, cinnamon, spikenard, rose, jasmine, saffron, turmeric, ginger, camphor, vetiver, cypress, pine and aniseed – while long-established trade links to the West have ensured an ongoing supply of the Arabic gums. Also, benzoin was imported from Sumatra and Malaysia to the east. India produces many essential oils not generally used in Western aromatherapy, which derive from the many fragrant flowers growing there, such as *pandang*, *bookool* and *kurna*. Basil is considered a sacred herb in India, where it is known as *tulsi*.

The heavens and gods are fragrant, according to the Veda. There are said to be five heavens – presided over by Brahma, Vishnu, Shiva, Kuvera and Indra – each of which is full of flowers and redolent with fragrance. A blue champac flower is said to grow abundantly in Brahma's heaven, while in Indra's a flower called camalata has a delightful fragrance with the power to grant a person their wishes. Brahma emerged from a lotus flower which grew from the navel of Vishnu. Kama, the god of love, carries five arrows to pierce the five senses, all tipped with flower blossoms, while Indra is associated with sandalwood. Temples were often partly built of sandalwood, such as the thousand-year-old gates at Somnath.

Incense and essential oils are a central aspect of Hindu worship, with the fragrance of *dhoop* and *dhoona* emanating from countless public temples and private shrines. During the Krishna festivals, a red powder diluted in rose water is splattered over the participants, while during marriage ceremonies, scented oils are thrown into the sacred fire, the *oman*, along with sandalwood incense and other fragrant materials. Fragrant woods and incense are an integral part of the funeral pyre. On the last day of the Hindu year, Divali, some time during October or November, many rituals are carried out, including offering flowers to the gods and goddesses. In some places, impurities are symbolically washed away by throwing water at each other; in wealthy households, rose water and sandalwood are added. Indeed, as anyone who has visited India knows, fragrance is an integral part of daily life, as is spirituality itself.

> ... the worship of gods ... requires the use of auspicious perfumes and incense; it contributes to the pleasures of men; it leads to the attainment of the three ends of human life (that is, religious merit, worldly prosperity and sensual enjoyment) ...
>
> GANGADHARA, GANDHASARA, *c.* AD 750

ISLAM AND ARABIA

> It has been given to me to love three things in your base world: women, perfumes and prayer, but the apple of my eye is prayer.
>
> MOHAMMED (Hadith)

The prophet of Islam, Mohammed, was very fond of aromatics. Through his close association with traders, he had access to spices and resins and would have known about their healing and other properties. It is said, for example, that a pustule on his finger was cured by the application in a bandage of *Acorus calamus*, sweet flag – an aromatic perennial. In his time too, teeth were kept clean with *Salvadora persica*, the twigs of which are cut to make a natural brush with built-in toothpaste. According to the early eleventh-century Arabian doctor and philosopher, Avicenna, Mohammed appreciated 'excellent odours' because 'they fortify the senses. And when the senses are strong, the thoughts are precise and their conclusions upright. When, on the other hand, the senses become weak, thoughts become unbalanced and their conclusions confused.' Avicenna travelled a great deal and wrote many books, including *Canon Medicinae* – a huge reference book which was invaluable to many Arab and European medical students for centuries to come. He is also credited with inventing the first 'modern' distilling apparatus, capable of extracting essential oils from flower petals. A hundred years ago in France a still was called *al-embicm*, showing its Arabic origin.

Mohammed was born around AD 570, at which time the Arabs were already great traders. He moved from Mecca to Medina in 622, spreading the message of the Koran, and from 711 onwards, Islam was carried by the Umayyad caliphs to Spain to the west, along the North African coastal area, eastern Turkey, Persia, and as far east as the Indus valley. The Arab traders ventured even further, overland to China and across the Sahara desert to West Africa, and by sailing in dhows to East Africa and Zanzibar, and southeast Asia. All along the way, they traded in a great variety of aromatics.

The fragrances most associated with Mohammed are rose, myrtle, violet and henna-flower. Mohammed is reported to have said, 'When I was taken up to Heaven, some of my sweat fell on the earth, and from it sprang the rose, and whoever would smell my scent, let him have the rose.' The Arabs are said to have preserved roses by putting blooms in a pottery jar sealed with clay, burying it in the ground until wanted, then taking the blooms out and sprinkling them with water – at which point they sprung back to life.

Over the years a great deal has been written about the fragrances to be found in the Muslim paradise, which are said to be fabulous, although the Koran itself only refers to 'Gardens under which rivers flow'. No doubt the association of fragrance with Heaven has grown from the prophet's own appreciation of fragrance and, indeed, from the Arab people's love of perfumes in general. It is said, after all, that in Heaven you will find all that you most desire.

Centuries before Mohammed was born, Arab traders were supplying the great civilizations of Egypt and Mesopotamia with the fragrant materials that grew in their lands, such as frankincense, olibanum, myrrh, jasmine and rose. From the ancient Greeks they learnt the elements of chemistry and medicine, which they greatly further developed. Indeed, the Arabs between the sixth and eleventh centuries were the repository of much wisdom in medicine and science and can truly be called the cultural bridge between the old civilizations and the new one that grew from the Italian Renaissance period.

BUDDHA OF THE SACRED TREE

This supreme incense, the aroma of pure moral conduct,
We bless with meditation, mantra and mudra.
As this glorious fragrance pervades the Buddha realms,
May an ocean of Buddhas be delighted!

Tibetan prayer

Buddha was born as Prince Gautama Siddhartha in Nepal, in the sixth century BC. In the first century BC the first canonical texts were written, in Pali, an ancient Indian language, so for at least five hundred years the teachings of Buddha, and details of his life, were handed down orally. Buddha grew up in great royal luxury, unaware of the travails of life, married at sixteen, and thirteen years later had a son, an event which awakened in him thoughts of life, death and the meaning of it all. He determined to renounce his sheltered life with its attendant pleasures, and took to a wandering life, through which he hoped to find a panacea for the vicissitudes of life.

For six years he followed a course of great self-denial, fasting and meditating and seeking wisdom from the Hindu gurus he met along the way. Unsatisfied with this course of action, he decided on 'the Middle Way', neither indulgence nor denial. He decided the answer was to be found within his own consciousness, and settled under an Indian fig tree – a pipal or bodhi tree – and began to meditate. After four weeks, some say seven, he attained enlightenment. The Four Noble Truths of Buddhism are: life involves suffering; we suffer because we desire; to end desire means the end of suffering; this can be accomplished by following the Eightfold path – right views, right thought, right speech, right conduct, right livelihood, right effort, right mindfulness, right contemplation.

Buddhism spread southwards, to Sri Lanka, Burma, Vietnam, Cambodia, Thailand, Malaysia, Indonesia and the Philippines, and north and east to Tibet, China, Korea and Japan, while it declined in India itself. It has often taken on the flavour of other, older religious teachings encountered along the way, many of which also involved the offering of fragrant material. Today, at Buddhist shrines, huge amounts of incense are burnt before images of the Buddha, in the form of burning woods, resins or incense sticks. In China, the woods of camphor, pine and sandalwood are commonly used, along with fragrant spices. Camphor wood was once the material preferred to make the rosaries used by Buddhist monks and nuns, and also the boxes or chests which held the sacred texts, the sutras. Worshippers often light three incense sticks, which are held in their hands while the smoke is blown three times, before putting the incense down, and placing the palms of the hands together in prayer. In Japan, a small amount of ground incense is carried around in little boxes, from which a small amount can be placed on the hands and inhaled while making a prayer.

In Buddhist practice, incense is symbolic of several ideas. The sweetness of the aroma signifies pure moral conduct, delightful in the same way as is the practice of giving up those things which are damaging or hurtful. It metaphorically represents giving, the generosity of correct Buddhist practice, the overcoming of greed and selfishness. As the smoke rises and moves through the air, it can be seen as the Buddhist teachings spreading across the world. Incense is also appreciated as being simply pleasant for those offering it, and for others around.

In Tibet, Buddhism encountered, and became mingled with, the earlier folk religion, *Bon*, in which offerings and prayers were offered to ancestral spirits, family spirits and the deceased. Deities were seen to reside in mountains, plains, the soil, trees, rocks or rivers. According to Tucci in *The Religions of Tibet*, 'None of the local communities was ready to renounce its old protective gods ... Admitted into the new religion as guardians of the Law, they now punish each violation of the Law or transgression of the Buddhist vow.'

Each morning in Tibet incense is offered, most usually in the form of juniper, although other fragrant trees and shrubs such as *bu lu*, a rhododendron, and *stag pa*, birch, are also used. The smoke of the offering is said to be purifying and atoning. There are three types of juniper in Tibet: *Juniperus pseudosabina*, known as the central Asian juniper, *Juniperus squamosa*, a low shrub similar to *Juniperus communis*, and *Juniperus excelsa*, the pencil cedar tree which covers much of the Himalayan mountains and is considered sacred. This cypress-like tree produces berries (*shug 'bras*) which are burnt as incense and, in the earlier *Bon* tradition, were once used as a narcotic to help induce trance.

In every Tibetan home there is a small altar, possibly several, in which incense, juniper, tsampa, dried fruits and other offerings are burnt. Juniper branches are burnt in the high stone and earth stoves (*bsangs-thab*) kept on every flat Tibetan roof for that purpose. On special occasions, the ritual would be somewhat more elaborate, as described by Dorje Yudon Yuthok in *House of the Turquoise Roof*:

> *To make this special offering, slightly green juniper branches were burned along with two or three spoonfuls of barley mixed with butter, which were added before lighting the fire. When the fire was smouldering, another small juniper branch was dipped into a bowl of clean water and used to sprinkle the flames three times while the mantra, 'Om Ah Hum', was repeated each time. The ceremony purified the offering of incense and produced a very pleasant fragrance.*

TAOISM AND CHINESE TRADITION

Taoism is said to have started with Lao-Tzu in the sixth century BC, although the philosophy may in fact have developed 200 years later. Indeed, the origins of Taoism are uncertain, with Joseph Campbell referring to Lao-Tzu as 'a *complete* mirage' and a 'mythical sage'. Nevertheless, there are some very ancient texts referring to a Lao-Tzu, which means Old Master, and a philosophy, Taoism, which is about 'going with the flow' of nature, and recognizing the balance between the opposites, including yin and yang.

So deeply did the ancient Chinese wish to 'go' with nature, they spent a great deal of time trying to emulate it in the sense of being eternal. Immortality, or at least achieving a ripe old age, became something of a preoccupation, with the literature full of heroic journeys and adventures undertaken to find various herbs, fruits and fungi of 'immortality'. As well as many mythical plants, various real plants were considered to have 'soul substance', or the 'essence of life'; including cassia, pine, cypress and camphor.

The transformational aspects of nature were a source of great wonder, particularly the seasons. Incense, with its ability to change from one form to another – from fragrant material to smoke – came to be seen as representative of the Tao, and was a vital component in Taoist worship. Each service still begins with lighting the incense burner (*fa-lu*), and at the end of worship the incense burner is again replenished (*fu-lu*).

SHINTO AND THE JAPANESE TRADITION

> Plants are used in ceremony because
> God is invited to join us through the
> plant.

MIKINOSUKE KAKISAHA,
Shinto High-Priest,
Tenkawa Temple, 1997

Shinto is a uniquely Japanese religion and predates the arrival of Buddhism in the eighth century. Joseph Campbell describes it thus: 'Shinto, at root, is a religion not of sermons but of awe: which is a sentiment that may or may not produce words, but in either case goes beyond them. Not a "grasp of the conception of spirit", but a sense of its ubiquity.' Shinto does not follow a set moral code, but is moralistic in recognizing the difference between doing good and evil, of being pure and impure.

Perhaps because Shinto so deeply appreciates and venerates the intrinsic beauty in the living world, the Japanese have developed several unique art forms involving natural materials. There are stunning Zen Buddhist gardens which owe more to the Japanese reverence of nature than to Buddhism itself. The trees, shrubs and stones are arranged with quiet, purposeful reverence. Similarly in Japan, flower arranging has been elevated to an art form appreciative of every angle of every stem, highlighting the glorious radiance of every flower. Also, Japan has made the appreciation of incense into an art, known as *Koh-do*, the incense ceremony. A few fragrant woods are chosen, and by means of a guessing game, participants inhale the aroma of each in turn, slowly and purposefully appreciating each unique aroma. These three unique Japanese art forms are about the development of the senses, the awe of nature, and have Shinto at their heart.

Incense, *koh*, is widely used in Japan, in worship at home and at Buddhist shrines, although Japan itself does not produce most materials used, which have to be imported. The main ingredients of *koh* are *jinkoh* (aloeswood), of which there are several varieties including the very expensive *kyara*, sandalwood, ginger, cassia, cinnamon, benzoin, camphor, cloves, frankincense, star anise, patchouli, myrrh, *kansho*, an East Indian rhizome *rei-ryokoh*, an Asian mint, and the root of a Chinese plant *haiso*. One indigenous ingredient is the bark of *Cercidiphyllum japonicum*.

Incense comes in various forms. As well as the familiar incense sticks, there are long-burning incense coils, incense balls, incense cones, chopped mixtures for putting on hot ashes in altars, and *nioi-bukuro*, little cloth or paper sachets of ground incense used to fragrance clothing, rooms, drawers or hang around the neck. They were once widely believed to offer protection from bad luck. Ground incense is also carried in small boxes, from where it can be rubbed on the hands before prayer.

At Shinto shrines, incense or piles of fragrant wood and branches are burnt, so worshippers can direct the profuse smoke over themselves and others. This practice was once ubiquitous all over the world in ancient times, and is not unique to Shinto. But it is perhaps unusual today in being such an important part of organized official religious practice, and is indicative of Shinto's ancient roots.

Everything in the beginning had a good smell.
Even things today we consider bad smells, were
good. In ancient times everything smelt good –
all of life. All souls enjoyed the smells, every day.

For example, I make fire and I feel the smell
of fire. The smell of fire, not the wood. The
actual fire has a smell. The fire is a kind of
ceremony.

MIKINOSUKE KAKISAHA, Shinto High-Priest,
Tenkawa Temple, 1997

THE NATIVE AMERICAN NATIONS

To the Native American Nations, spirit resides not
only in people and animals but in the earth, sky, stars,
trees, herbs, flowers and rocks as well. The whole of
living nature has the same ultimate spiritual source
and is deserving of respect. Living in harmony with
nature brings out the best in it, and us.

In *Gift of Power*, Sioux medicine man Archie Fire
Lame Deer recounts an event he witnessed one day
involving his grandfather, a Lakota medicine man and
spiritual leader:

> *The stroke had left one of Grandma Lizzie's sides*
> *paralysed, and she had lost the power of speech.*
> *Grandpa had someone heat a rock over a fire*
> *while he and I went to pick certain herbs that were*
> *needed for the healing ... Grandpa took his*
> *buffalo horn, which was his most powerful*
> *medicine, and went into Lizzie's room. He*
> *wrapped her in a buffalo robe, put the heated rock*
> *under the small of her back, and purified her with*

cedar incense, using his eagle wing to fan the fragrant smoke toward her ... (he sang) sacred songs at Lizzie's bedside ... half an hour after the doctoring began, Grandma Lizzie came out of the house. She was walking around and chatting as if nothing had happened.

There are many spiritual practices among the Native American Nations and they differ from place to place, although common to many are smudging, the medicine wheel, the sacred pipe ceremony, the sweat lodge, vision-quest and sun-dance. The vision-quest is a personal journey of spiritual discovery involving meditation and fasting, while the sun-dance is a communal ceremony of giving thanks.

The sweat lodge is a tent-like building, with a roof made of bent branches covered with hides or other material. At its centre is a collection of red-hot rocks, on which water and herbs are placed, creating very hot steam. Some sweat lodges are single sex, and some are mixed. The one I attended on a Cree reservation was a mixed lodge of about sixteen people, men on one side, women on the other. It started around 10.30 at night, and, although a large fire was kept burning outside, because the flaps were kept tightly shut inside the lodge was completely dark. The darkness allows you to see, not with your eyes and logical mind, but with your spirit. To say it was hot would be a major understatement, but despite being uncomfortable at times, the heat was also releasing – you have to 'let go'. The smell of the sage burning on the hot rocks filled the humid atmosphere, and as each person in turn spoke their prayers out loud and gave thanks, the drums and rattles added their special tones. As Archie Fire Lame Deer has written, 'the sweat lodge becomes the

universe, the whole world concentrated in a tiny hut.'
In his Nation, three herbs are used during the *Inipi*,
the sweat lodge: sweetgrass, sage and cedar. A bundle
of sage might also be used to sprinkle water on the hot
stones.

It is difficult to overestimate the importance of
fragrant herbs and trees to the spiritual ceremonies of
Native American Nations. They are also a crucial
ingredient in personal 'medicine bundles', or spiritual
talismans. America is a vast continent, with such
varied landscape and flora, one would expect there to
be differences, from place to place, in the plant
materials used in ritual. Beside those already
mentioned, spruce, pine and juniper are also
important.

> I remain undaunted, for I dwell within my Spirit
> that is filled with the heady essence of Sage,
> Cedar and Sweetgrass, and with my head held
> high do I walk into the light that illuminates my
> new trail.

> MARY SUMMER RAIN

If you have difficulty finding pure essential oils suitable for the purposes outlined in *The Fragrant Heavens*, the following professional aromatherapy suppliers can be recommended. Essential oils can be obtained from Earth Garden by mail order and by calling into the shop. Aromatherapy treatments are also available as well as details of the author's workshops and seminars.

Earth Garden
Essential Oil and Herbal Dispensary
2, Fairview Parade, Mawney Road, Romford
RM7 7HH England

For information please enclose a stamped addressed envelope.

Bibliography

Abraham, Ralph; McKenna, Terence; Sheldrake, Rupert, *Trialogues at the Edge of the West*, Santa Fe: Bear and Co., 1992

Ackerman, Diane, *A Natural History of the Senses*, London: Chapmans, 1991

Adams, George, and Whicher, Olive, *The Plant Between Sun and Earth*, London: Steiner Press, 1980

Afnan, S. M., *Avicenna: His Life and Works*, London: Greenwood Press, 1958

Alder, Vera Stanley, *The Finding of the Third Eye*, London: Rider & Co., 1982

Ali, Abdullah Yusuf (ed.), *The Glorious Qur'an*, 1934

Alon, Azaria, *Flowers and Trees of the Holy Land*, Jerusalem: Palphot Ltd n.d.

Andrews, Ted, *Sacred Sounds*, St. Pail: Llewellyn Publications, 1993

Arcier, Micheline, *Aromatherapy, Health and Beauty Care with Massage and Essential Oils*, London: Hamlyn, 1990

Ash, David A., *The New Science of the Spirit*, London: The College of Psychic Studies, 1995

Avigad, Brakha, and Danin, Avinoam, *Flowers of*

409

Jerusalem, Tel Aviv: E. Lewin-Epstein-Modan Publishers, 1977

Babbitt, Edwin S., *The Principles of Light and Colour*, Secaucus: Citadel Press, 1967

Bach, Edward, *Heal Thyself*, Saffron Walden: C. W. Daniel, 1946

Bailey, Alice, *Esoteric Healing*, London: Lucis Press Ltd, 1967

Balfour, John Hutton, *The Plants of the Bible*, London: T. Nelson and Sons, 1885

Barker, Margaret, *The Lost Prophet*, London: S.P.C.K., 1988

Beattie, James Herries, *Traditional Lifeways of the Southern Maori*, Dunedin: University of Otago Press, 1994

Becker, Robert O. and Salden, Gary, *The Body Electric*, New York: William Morrow, 1987

Bennett, J. G., *Gurdjieff, A Very Great Enigma*, York Beach: Samuel Weiser, 1984

Benor, Daniel J., 'Survey of Spiritual Healing Research', *Complementary Medical Research*, 4:1, September 1990

Benor, Daniel J., 'Survey of Spiritual Healing Research', *Healing Research*, Vols 1–2, Munich: Helix Verlag GmbH, 1993 (Windeckstrasse 82, D81375, Munich)

Birren, Faber, *Colour Psychology and Colour Therapy*, Secaucus: Citadel Press, 1961

Boeser, Knut (ed.), *The Elixirs of Nostradamus*, London: Bloomsbury, 1995

Book of Mormon and the Doctrine of Covenants, Salt Lake City: The Church of Jesus Christ of the Latter-day Saints, 1981

Borghia, Anthony, *Life in the World Unseen*, London: Psychic Press Ltd, 1981

Brunton, Paul, *A Search in Secret Egypt*, London: Rider & Co., 1980

Bruyere, Rosalyn L., *Wheels of Light*, New York: Simon and Schuster, 1994

Budge, E. A. Wallace, *The Divine Origin of the Craft of the Herbalist*, New York: Dover Publications Inc., 1996

Buhner, Stephen Harrod, *Sacred Plant Medicine: Explorations in the Practice of Indigenous Herbalism*, Boulder: Roberts Rinehart, 1996

Burr, Harold Saxton, *Blueprint for Immortality: the Electric Patterns of Life*, Saffron Walden: C. W. Daniel, 1972

Callcott, Maria, *A Scripture Herbal*, London: Longman, Brown, Green and Longmans, 1842

Campbell, Joseph, *The Way of the Seeded Earth, Vol 2*, New York: Harper & Row, 1989

Campbell, Joseph, *Occidental Mythology*, London: Arkana/Penguin, 1991

Campbell, Joseph, *Oriental Mythology*, London: Arkana/Penguin, 1991

Case, E. M., *Odour of Sanctity*, Exeter (private publication, undated)

Charles, R. H. (ed.), *The Book of Enoch*, London: S.P.C.K., 1986

Classen, C.; Howes, D.; Synnot, A., *Aroma, the Cultural History of Smell*, London: Routledge, 1994

Coats, Callum, *Living Energies*, Bath: Gateway Books, 1996

Connolly, David, *In Search of Angels*, New York: Perigee Books, 1993

Copen, Bruce, *A Rainbow of Health*, Haywards Heath: Academic Publications, 1984

Cotterell, Arthur (ed.), *Penguin Encyclopedia of Ancient Civilizations*, London: Macmillan, 1983

Cowan, Eliot, *Plant Spirit Medicine*, Newberg: Swan Raven & Co., 1995

Culpeper, Nicholas, *Culpeper's Complete Herbal*, Manchester: J. Clere and Son, 1826

Davidson, Gustav, *A Dictionary of Angels*, New York: The Free Press, 1994

Davidson, John, *Radiation*, Saffron Walden: C. W. Daniel, 1986

Davidson, John, *Subtle Energy*, Saffron Walden: C. W. Daniel, 1987

Davidson, John, *The Web of Life*, Saffron Walden: C. W. Daniel, 1988

Davis, Richard H., *Ritual in an Oscillating Universe*, USA: Princeton University Press, 1991

Dawood, N. J. (trans.), *The Koran*, Harmondsworth: Penguin Books, 1983

Des Roches, Christian, *Tutankhamen*, London: Michael Joseph, 1969

Devereux, Paul, *The Long Trip: A Prehistory of Psychedelia*, New York: Penguin/Arkana, 1997

De Waal, M., *Medicinal Herbs in the Bible*, York Beach: Samuel Weiser Inc., 1984

Dossey, Larry, *Prayer is Good Medicine*, San Francisco: Harper, 1996

Dossey, Larry, *Healing Words*, San Francisco: Harper, 1997

Dudley, Martin, and Rowell, Geoffrey, *The Oil of Gladness*, London: S.P.C.K., 1993

Dumitrescu, Ion, and Kenyon, Julian, *Electrographic Imaging in Medicine and Biology*, Sudbury: Neville Spearman Ltd, 1983

Elliott, Maurice, *Spiritualism in the Old Testament*, London: Psychic Press Ltd, 1938

Endicott, K., *Batek Negrito Religion: The World-View and Rituals of a Hunting and Gathering People of*

Peninsular Malaysia, Oxford: Clarendon Press, 1979

Evans-Wentz, W. Y., *Cuchama and Sacred Mountains* (n.d. and publisher unknown)

Fire Lame Deer, Archie, *Gift of Power*, Santa Fe: Bear and Co., 1992

Fox, Matthew and Sheldrake, Rupert, *The Physics of Angels*, San Francisco: Harper, 1996

Frazer, Sir James George, *The Golden Bough*, London: Papermac, 1922

Gerber, Richard, *Vibrational Medicine*, Santa Fe: Bear and Co., 1988

Gerbert, Grohmann, *The Plant, Vols 1 & 2*, Kimburton: Biodynamic Farming and Gardening Association Inc., 1989

Gimbel, Theo, *Healing Through Colour*, Saffron Walden, C. W. Daniel, 1985

Ginzberg, Louis, *Legends of the Bible*, Philadelphia: The Jewish Publication Society of America, 1978

Gonen, Rivka, *Biblical Holy Places*, London: A. & C. Black, 1987

Gooch, Stan, *Cities of Dreams*, London: Aulis Books, 1995

Greber, Johannes, *Communication with the Spirit World of God*, Teaneck: Johannes Greber Memorial Foundation, 1979

Green, Celia and McCreery, Charles, *Apparitions*, Oxford: Institute of Psychophysical Research, 1977

Guirdham, Arthur, *A Foot in Both Worlds*, Saffron Walden: C. W. Daniel, 1991

'Gurudas', *Gem Elixirs and Vibrational Healing Vols 1 and 2*, Boulder: Cassandra Press, 1986

Halevi, Helen, *Reiki, Hawayo Takata's Story*, Olney: Archedign Inc., 1990

Halevi, Z'ev Ben Shimon, *Kabbalah*, London: Thames

and Hudson, 1992

Hareuveni, Nogah, *Ecology in the Bible*, Jerusalem: Neot Kedumim Ltd, 1974

Hareuveni, Nogah, *The Emblem of the State of Israel*, Jerusalem: Neot Kedumim Ltd, 1988

Hay, R. K. M. and Waterman, P. G. (eds), *Volatile Oil Crops: Their Biology, Biochemistry and Production*, London: Longman Group UK, 1993

Head, Joseph and Cranston, Sylvia (eds), *Reincarnation: An East-West Anthology*, Pasadena: Theosophical University Press, 1975

Hepper, F. Nigel, *Pharaoh's Flowers*, London: HMSO, 1990

Hepper, F. Nigel, *Planting a Bible Garden*, London: HMSO, 1991

Hepper, F. Nigel, *Illustrated Encyclopaedia of Bible Plants*, London: Three's Company, 1992

Herodotus, *The History* (trans. Cary, Henry), Buffalo: Prometheus Books, 1992

Hitti, P. K., *History of the Arabs*, London: Macmillan, 1951

Holy Bible, The, New International Version, London: Hodder & Stoughton, 1985

Holy Bible, The, London: Collins, 1958

Holy Scriptures, The, According to the Masoretic Text, Vols I and II, Philadelphia: The Jewish Publication Society of America, 1976

Howell, S., *Society and Cosmos: Chewong of Peninsular Malaysia*, Oxford: Oxford University Press, 1984

Hunt, Roland, *Fragrant and Radiant Healing Symphony*, Rochford: C. W. Daniel, n.d.

Hunt, Valerie V., *The Infinite Mind: The Science of Human Vibrations*, Malibu: Malibu Publishing Co., 1995

Hurnard, Hannah, *Mountains of Spices*, Eastbourne: Kingsway Publications, 1983

Hutchens, Alma R., *Indian Herbalogy of North America*, Windsor, Ontario: Merco, 1986

Jayjakar, Pupul, *The Earth Mother*, Harmondsworth: Penguin, 1989

Jigmenorbu, Thubten and Turnbull, Colin, *Tibet: Its History, Religion and People*, London: Penguin, 1983

Karagulla, Shafica and Kunz, Dora van Gelder, *The Chakras and the Human Energy Fields*, Wheaton: Quest Books, 1991

Kennett, Frances, *History of Perfume*, London: George G. Harrap & Co. Ltd, 1975

Khan, Hazratinayat, *The Mysticism of Sound and Music*, Boston: Shambhala, 1996

Leadbeater, C. W., *The Perfume of Egypt and Other Weird Stories*, Madras, India: 1911

Le Guerer, Annick, *Scent: The Mysterious and Essential Powers of Smell*, London: Chatto & Windus, 1992

Loehr, Revd, *The Power of Prayer on Plants* (details unknown)

Long, Asphodel, P., *In A Chariot Drawn by Lions*, London: The Women's Press Ltd, 1992

Lucretius, *Nature of Things, Book 3* (details unknown)

Mackenzie, Donald A., *China and Japan: Myths and Legends*, London: Senate/Studio Editions Ltd, 1994

Maclean, Dorothy, *To Hear the Angels Sing*, New York: Lindisfarne Press, 1980

Mallasz, Gitta, *Talking with Angels*, Einsiedeln: Diamon Verlag, 1992

Manniche, Lise, *An Ancient Egyptian Herbal*, London: British Museum Press Ltd, 1989

Mascaro, Juan (trans.), *The Bhagavad Gita*,

Harmondsworth: Penguin, 1970

Maury, Marguerite, *Guide to Aromatherapy, The Secret of Life and Youth*, Saffron Walden: C. W. Daniel, 1989

McKenzie, Dan, *Aromatics and the Soul*, London: William Heinemann, 1923

Mernissi, Fatima, *Women in Moslem Paradise*, New Delhi: Kali For Women, 1988

Miller, J. Innes, *The Spice Trade of the Roman Empire*, Oxford: Oxford University Press, 1988

Moldenke, H. N., and Alma, L., *Plants of the Bible*, New York: Dover Publications Inc., 1986

Moody, Raymond A. Jr., *Reflections of Life after Life*, New York: Bantam Books, 1978

Mookerjee, Ajit, *Kundalini: The Arousal of the Inner Energy*, London: Thames and Hudson Ltd, 1983

Moolenburgh, H. C., *A Handbook of Angels*, Saffron Walden: C. W. Daniel, 1988

Moolenburgh, H. C., *Meeting with Angels*, Saffron Walden: C. W. Daniel, 1993

Morita, Kiyoko, *The Book of Incense*, Tokyo: Kodansha International Ltd, 1992

Morris, Edwin T., *Fragrance: The Story of Perfume from Cleopatra to Chanel*, New York: E. T. Morris & Co., 1984

Moskvitin, Jirij, *Essay on the Origin of Thought*, Ohio: Ohio University Press, 1974

Mutma, Credo Vusamazulu, *My People: Writings of a Zulu Witchdoctor*, Harmondsworth: Penguin, 1977

Myss, Caroline, *Anatomy of the Spirit*, London: Bantam Press, 1997

Murphey, Edith van Allen, *Indian Uses of Native Plants*, Glenwood: Meyer Books, 1990

New Catholic Encyclopedia, New York: McGraw-Hill Book Company, n.d.

Neumann, Erich, *The Great Mother*, London: Routledge and Kegan Paul, 1963

Niazi, H. M., *The Egyptian Prescription*, Cairo: Elias Modern Press, 1988

Oldfield, Harry and Coghill, Roger, *The Dark Side of the Brain*, Shaftesbury: Element Books, 1988

Ono, Sokyo, *Shinto: The Kami Way*, Tokyo: Charles E. Tuttle Co., 1991

Ouseley, S. G. J., *The Power of the Rays*, Romford: L. N. Fowler & Co., 1976

Pagels, Elaine, *The Gnostic Gospels*, London: Penguin, 1982

Paulson, Genieve Lewis, *Kundalini and the Chakras*, St Paul: Llewellyn Publications, 1997

Pellant, Chris, *The Complete Book of Rocks and Minerals*, London: Dorling Kindersley, 1995

Pendell, Dale, *Pharmako-Poeia, Plant Powers, Poisons and Herbcraft*, Mercury House, 1995

Pert, Candace B., *Molecules of Emotions*, New York: Simon and Schuster, 1997

Piesse, G. W. Septimus, *The Art of Perfumery*, London: Longman Brown Green Longmans and Roberts, 1856

Plummer, Charles, *Lives of Irish Saints*, Oxford: Oxford University Press, 1997

Post, George E., *The Botanical Geography of Palestine*, private publication, 1888

Prabhupada, His Divine Grace A.A.C. Bhaktivedanti, Swami, *Coming Back: The Science of Reincarnation*, Sydney: ISKCON, 1982

Rain, Mary Summer, *Spirit Song*, Norfolk: Hampton Roads Publishing Co., 1985

Rain, Mary Summer, *Phantoms Afoot*, The Donning Co., 1989

Ratsch, Christian (trans. John Baker), *The Dictionary*

of Sacred and Magical Plants, Bridport: Prism Unity Press, 1992

Reed, A. W., *Aboriginal Myths*, French's Forest: Reed Books Aus, 1978

Rimmel, Eugene, *The Book of Perfumes*, London: Chapman and Hall, 1867

Rinpoche, Sogyal, *The Tibetan Book of Living and Dying*, London: Rider & Co., 1994

Roberts, Jane, *The Nature of the Psyche*, San Rafael: Amber Allen, 1996

Robinson, H. Wheeler, *The Christian Experience of the Holy Spirit*, London: Fontana, 1962

Ross, Hugh McGregor (trans.), *Thirty Essays on the Gospel of Thomas*, Shaftesbury: Element Books, 1990

Ross, Hugh McGregor (trans.), *The Gospel of St Thomas*, Shaftesbury: Element Books, 1991

Ross, Dr A. C., *Mitakuye Oyasin*, Denver: Bear & Co., 1993

Rossbach, Sarah, *Feng Shui*, London: Hutchinson, 1984

Ryerson, Kevin, *Gem Elixirs and Vibrational Healing, Vol 1*, Boulder, Colorado: Cassandra Press, 1995

Scott, Ian, *The Luscher Colour Test*, London: Pan Books, 1983

Shepsut, Asia, *Journey of the Priestess*, London: Aquarian/Thorsons, 1993

Shewell-Cooper, W. E., *Plants, Flowers and Herbs of the Bible*, Canaan: Keats Publishing Inc., 1988

Shrii Shrii Ananda Murti, *Beyond the Superconscious Mind*, Calcutta: Ananda Marga, 1987

Snellgrove, Brian, *The Unseen Self*, Saffron Walden: C. W. Daniel, 1996

Smith, E. Lester, Slater, V. Wallace, Reilly, Gerard, *The Field of Occult Chemistry*, London:

Theosophical Publishing House, 1934

Stein, R., *Tibetan Civilization*, London: Faber & Faber, 1972

Steiner, Rudolph, *Manifestations of Karma*, London: Rudolph Steiner Press, 1995

Steiner, Rudolph, *Nature Spirits*, London: Rudolph Steiner Press, 1995

Stone, Robert B., *The Secret Life of Your Cells*, Atglen: Schiffer Publishing Ltd, 1989

Stonehouse, Julia, *Idols to Incubators: Reproduction Theory through the Ages*, London: Scarlet Press, 1994

Sylvia, Claire, and Novak, William, *A Change of Heart*, London: Little, Brown, 1997

Szekely, Edmond Bordeaux (trans.), *The Gospel of the Essenes*, Saffron Walden: C. W. Daniel, 1993

Talbot, Michael, *Mysticism and the New Physics*, London: Arkana/Penguin, 1993

Tansley, David V., *The Raiment of Light*, London: Routledge & Kegan Paul, 1984

Thiering, Barbara, *Jesus the Man*, London: Corgi Books, 1993

Thompson, C. J. S., *The Mystery and Lure of Perfume*, London: John Lane, Bodley Head, n.d.

Thompson, Richard, *The Brain: A Neuroscience Primer* (2nd edition), New York: W. H. Freeman & Company, 1993

Tompkins, Peter, *The Secret Life of Nature*, San Francisco: Thorsons, 1997

Tucci, G., *The Religions of Tibet*, London: Routledge & Kegan Paul, 1980

Valnet, Jean, *The Practice of Aromatherapy*, Saffron Walden: C. W. Daniel, 1982

Vogel, Virgil J., *American Indian Medicine*, Norman: University of Oklahoma Press, 1986

Von Hagen, Victor W., *The Ancient Sun Kingdoms of the Americas*, 1957

Walker, Barbara G., *The Woman's Encyclopaedia of Myths and Secrets*, San Francisco: Harper and Row, 1983

Watson, Lyall, *The Biology of Death*, London: Hodder and Stoughton, 1987

Weiss, Brian L., *Many Lives, Many Masters*, New York: Simon and Schuster, 1988

Weiss, Brian L., *Through Time into Healing*, London: Piatkus, 1995

White, John, *The Meeting of Science and Spirit*, New York: Paragon House, 1990

Whitman, John, *The Psychic Power of Plants*, London: Star Books/W. H. Allen, 1975

Wilkinson, Sir J. Gardner, *The Ancient Egyptians: Their Life and Customs*, London: Bracken Books, 1988

Wilson, Michael, *What is Colour?*, Stourbridge: Goethean Science Foundation, 1983

Woolger, Roger J., *Other Lives, Other Selves*, Wellingborough: Thorsons Publishing Group, 1990

Worwood, Valerie Ann, *The Fragrant Pharmacy*, London: Macmillan, 1990, Bantam, 1991, as *The Complete Book of Essential Oils and Aromatherapy*; Novato, USA: New World Library, 1991

Worwood, Valerie Ann, *The Fragrant Mind*, London: Doubleday, 1995, Bantam, 1997; Novato, USA: New World Library, 1996

Worwood, Valerie Ann, *Fragrant Sensuality*, London: Bantam, 1996

Wright, Ruth V., and Chadbourne, Robert L., *Crystals, Gems and Minerals of the Bible*, New Canaan: Keats Publishing, 1988

Yang-Chang, Li, *Lao-Tzu's Treatise on the Response of*

the Tao, New York: Harper Collins, 1994

Yewchnode Two Wolves and Grandmother Twylah Hurd Nitsch, *The Living Circle Teaching Manual*, private publication, 1990

Yewchnode Two Wolves and Grandmother Twylah Hurd Nitsch, *Mythological Philosophy*, private publication, 1995

Yuthok, Dorje Yudon, *House of the Turquoise Roof*, Ithaca: Snow Lion, 1990

Ziegler, John J., *Let Them Anoint the Sick*, Minnesota: The Liturgical Press, 1987

INDEX

Aaron 31, 48, 380, 382
Abraham 379
absent healing 238–41
absolutes 276
acacia 229
addiction 70–1
  see also individual names
Adonis 5, 355
Aeone 390
Aesculapius 392
Afghanistan 161, 329
Africa 189, 310, 359
Ahmose, Queen 5
alchemy 375
alcohol addiction 71
Alexandria 375–6
allergic reactions 71
almond, bitter 71
almond oil 59–60, 62, 68, 229, 276
aloeswood 59, 382, 394, 404
amber 5, 382
  spiritual profile 280
ambergris 7, 382
ambrette 251, 258, 263
amethyst 248
Amon Ra 5
Amun 302
amyris 99, 250, 263
Anacreon 142
angelica 72
angelica root 251, 263
  spiritual profile 281
angelica seed 117, 212, 249, 256, 263
  spiritual profile 282
angels 2, 3, 4, 94, 101–28, 132, 143, 252
  dark 113; fragrance of 105–7, 115–28
aniseed 70, 195, 249, 263, 394

spiritual profile 283
anointing 52–6, 62, 374–6, 380, 386
  royal 7, 52
Aphrodite/Venus 4, 355, 372, 390, 392
Apollonius of Herophilia 391
apricot kernel oil 68
Arab countries 59, 353, 380, 396–8
aroma
  evoking emotions 8; evoking memory
    9, 233; as regression tool 151–6;
    using different 214–15
aroma molecules 8, 9, 35, 148–9, 187
  vibration rate 193
Aroma-Genera 117, 149, 150–3
Artemis 4
artemisia 195
'ascended masters' 252, 254
ash 21
Asperges me 323
Assyria 20, 377
Astarte 370
astral bodies 180, 184
Athene 370
Augustus, Emperor 373
aura imaging 184
auras 180, 182–92, 203, 247
  fluffing 189
auric colours 198
auric field 148–9, 163, 173–4, 180, 198,
    203, 235–8
Australia 114, 161, 359
Avicenna 397

babies 150, 155
Babylon 48, 377
Bacchus 4
Bach, Edward 21

Bach Flower Remedies 21
Backster, Cleve 26, 42
balanos, oil of 391
balm 382
balsam 93
balsam de Peru 93, 195, 213, 228, 251, 263
    spiritual profile 284
balsam fir 249
baptism 57–8, 387
Baric, Arnaud 160
bark, aromatic 49, 161, 380, 403–4
barley 401
basil 250
    and angels 117; in auric field 197; for
        chakras 212; colour 250, 263; evapo-
        ration rate 195; and fear 70; in
        Greece 286; in India 286, 395; for
        prayer 92; and pregnancy and lacta-
        tion 70; and skin irritation 63;
        spiritual profile 285–6
Basil, St 286
Batek Negrito 5
bath, use of oils in 57, 62, 276, 392
bathing, ritual 57–8
baths 95
    energy-cleansing 168–71; Roman 392
bay
    in ancient Greece 391; and angels 118;
        at Delphi 372; for channelling 256;
        colour 250, 263; evaporation rate
        195; and pregnancy and lactation 70
bay laurel, spiritual profile 287–8
Beall, Daphne 28
Becker, Robert 184
Bell, John Stewart 77
Benares 143
Benedicta of Notre Dame du Laus,
    Venerable 134
Benor, Daniel 76
benzoin 97
    and angels 118; in anointing 7; blending
        229; for chakras 213; for channelling
        256; cleansing 167; colour 251, 264,
        382; evaporation rate 195; and guilt
        86; in incense 143, 173–5, 374, 404;
        in India 395; spiritual profile 288–9;
        staining 42
bereavement 129–30
bergamot
    and angels 118; blending 228; for
        chakras 212; colour 251, 264;
        evaporation rate 195; and fear 85;
        and sensitive skin 72; spiritual
        profile 290–1
Bible 104, 323, 384
    King James version 246; Masoretic text
        246, 384; New Internationalist ver-

sion 246, see also New Testament;
    Old Testament
bio-plasma 184
birch 18, 70, 118, 401
    white 250, 273; spiritual profile 292
black pepper
    and angels 118; for chakras 212; cleans-
        ing 167; colour 250, 264; evaporation
        rate 195; for prayer 92; and preg-
        nancy and lactation 70; spiritual
        profile 293
blackcurrant 118
blending 43, 69, 96, 217, 222, 230
    spiritual 60–1
Blu-u Kayans 161
body oils 59–60, 63, 95, 381–2
body scanning 203, 215–16
body-work 147, 154, 201
boldo leaf 71
Bon 401
The Book of Mormon 110
bookool 395
Borneo 161, 294
boronia 251
    absolute 264
bottles 62
bowls 62
    water 65
Brahma 5, 393–4
Brahman 393–4, 395
Brahmanas 393
Brahmandapurana 58
breastplate of judgement 246
British Columbia, Ministry of Forests 18
broom 119
bu lu 401
buchu 251, 264
Buddha 6, 20, 31, 89, 294, 363, 394,
    398–401
Buddhism 2, 31, 47, 97, 147, 398–401, 403
Buhner, Stephen Harrod 26
Burma 399
Burr, Dr Harold 184
Byzantine rite 55

Cairo 159
Cajetan, St 134
cajuput 195
calamus 71, 228, 377, 381
California, University of, Los Angeles 232
    Mu and Anechoic rooms 33, 182–4
camalata 395
Cambodia 399
camomile see chamomile
Campbell, Joseph 402, 403
camphor
    blending 229; in China 400, 402; colour

camphor *(cont.)*
249, 382; in incense 400, 404; in
India 394; spiritual profile 294; white
264; yellow 71
camphor wood 6
Canaan 379
Canaanites 371, 379
Canada 18
cananga 250, 264
candles 59, 64, 91, 172, 174, 215, 236
caraway 195, 264
seed 119, 251
cardamom
in ancient Greece 390; and angels 119;
for chakras 213; colour 250, 264;
evaporation rate 195; in incense 373;
and letting go 88; in meditation 97;
spiritual profile 295; and unworthiness 87
carnation 93
absolute 264; spiritual profile 296
and angels 119; blending 228; for channelling 256; colour 251; and letting
go 88; spiritual use 277
carrier oils 59–60, 68
carrot seed 250, 264
and tops 119
Case, E. M. 132
cassia 372
in ancient Greece 390; in China 402;
for embalming 374; in incense 49,
380, 404; in India 394
cassie 250, 265
castor oil 228, 391
Catherine, St 134
Catholic Church 52, 53–4, 387
cedarwood 407
and angels 119; for chakras 212–13; for
channelling 256; for cleansing 167;
colours 250, 265; for embalming
374; evaporation rate 195; and fear
85; forest 18–19; in incense 377; in
Lebanon 5; and pregnancy and lactation 70; in purification 2; smudge
sticks 173–9; spiritual profile 297–8;
spiritual uses 31, 93, 158; as tree of
life 20; and unworthiness 87
cedrat (lemon) 228
celery seed 250, 265
cellular memory 145
censers 143, 173, 375, 378
Central America 304
Ceylon (Sri Lanka) 359, 399
chakras 180, 183, 185, 193, 202–13,
222–7, 261
base 222; brow 226–7; crown 227;
essential oils for 212–13; heart 225;

and related vertebrae and body areas
(table) 207–11; sacral 223; solar
plexus 224; throat 225, *see also* auras
chamomile 93, 171, 204, 212
chamomile blue 66
chamomile german 195, 251, 265
spiritual profile 299
chamomile maroc *see* ormenis flower
chamomile roman 86, 88, 120, 195, 249,
256, 265
spiritual profile 300
champaca 256
Chandogya Upanishad 393
channelling 251–6
charcoal 174, 175
Charles I, King 7
Cheops' pyramid, King's Chamber 29, 245
Chewong 5
ch'i energy 32, 164
China 2, 5, 20, 47, 143, 174, 289, 302,
326, 352, 397, 399, 400, 402
chrism rite 53–5, 387
Christian Scientists 110
Christianity 2, 6, 48–50, 113, 147, 158,
384–9
Christopher, St, medal 158
Church of England 34, 387
Church of Jesus Christ of Latter-day Saints
110
cinnamon 372, 394
in ancient Greece 390; and angels 120;
for anointing 7; bark 302; blending
228; for cleansing 167; colour 265,
382; definition 380; and fear 85; in
incense 49, 160, 372, 403; leaf 195,
250, 251; and pregnancy and lactation 70; and skin irritation 63;
spiritual use 93; spiritual profile
301–2
Circe 261
cistus 70, 93, 120, 195, 197, 251
cistus labdanum 265
citronella 195, 228, 251, 265
citrus oils 72, 277
civet 7, 228
clary sage 70, 86, 120, 171, 177, 195, 197,
213, 250, 265
spiritual profile 303
cleanliness 165
cleansing 161–2
blends for 167; energy-cleansing baths
168–72; spiritual 166
clematis 228
Cleopatra 373
clothing, use of oils on 59, 66, 381, 404
clove
and angels 120; blending 229; for

clove *(cont.)*
 cleansing 160, 167, 179; colour 266;
  and guilt 86; in incense 160, 403;
  and pregnancy and lactation 70; and
  skin irritation 63; spiritual use 93
clove bud 195
 spiritual profile 304
Coghill, Roger 34
cold pressing 276
cologne 161
colour 193, 198, 214, 249–51, 257–62,
 263–73, 382
companion gardening 25
Constantine, Emperor 147
copal 97, 174
Coptic church 2, 173
coriander 195
 in ancient Rome 392; and angels 120;
  for chakras 212–13; for cleansing
  167; colour 250, 266; and fear 86;
  and letting go 88; spiritual profile
  305–6
Cornelius Agrippa 392
coronation oil 7
costus 49, 380, 391, 394
Cree 406
Crete 328
Criton 391
crocus 372
cross (worn for protection) 158
Crow, Gillian 388
crystals 172, 179, 191–2, 215, 245–8
cubeb 251, 266
cucumber seed 382
cumin 70, 249, 266
curtains, opening 172
cypress
 and angels 121; for bereavement 121;
  for chakras 212–13; for channelling
  256; in China 402; for cleansing 167;
  colour 250, 266; evaporation rate
  195; and fear 86; and goddess worship 371; for healing 158; hinoki
  243–4; in incense 373, 377; in India
  394; and letting go 88; for meditation
  97; in rooms 234; for smudge sticks
  177; spiritual profile 307–8; spiritual
  use 92–4
Czech Republic 352

Dalai Lama 6
dance 29
date 20
David, King 247
Davidson, Gustav 113
Dawood, N. J. 110
De Waal, M. 302

deadly nightshade 71
death
 and astral body 185; fragrance associated with 129–32; preparation for
  136–8; rituals after 355, 372–5
decorative bundles 179
Defoe, Daniel 160
Delphi 372
Delphi, oracle 288, 372
Demeter 4, 372
Demetrius, St 133
dhoona 395
dhoop 395
diffusers 51, 62, 64, 91, 94, 140, 172, 236,
 239, 244
dill 121, 249, 266, 391
 spiritual profile 309
distant healing 238–41
distillation 379
distillation unit 11, 397
Divali 395
Divine, idea of 1, 73
DNA 41, 147, 247
dolmens 245
Douglas fir 18
dragon 352
Drokpa Tibetans 6
Dudley, Martin 53

East Africa 397
Eddy, Mary Baker 110
Edfu, temple of Horus 374
Egforth, King of Mercia 8
Egypt 159, 223, 253
 ancient 4–5, 20, 48, 89, 94, 159, 245,
  298, 302, 336, 338, 372–6, 379–80
Eisenhofer and Lechner 387
electrical equipment 231, 234, 239
electrocardiogram 181
electroencephalography 181
electromagnetic energy in body 181–3, 203
elements 170, 172
elemi 213, 249, 266
 spiritual profile 310
Elijah 326
Eliphas Levi 382
Elis, temple of Minerva 392
Elisha 45
Elizabeth II, Queen 7
Ely Cathedral 104
Elysium 3, 390
embalming 359, 373–6
emotions 9, 151
energetic aromatherapy 201, 231–73
energy fields 32–4, 148, 180–4, 185, 231
energy work 244
enfleurage 276

Eros 4
etheric bodies 180, 184, 248
eucalyptus 171, 197
eucalyptus citriodora 35, 97, 250, 266
eucalyptus globulus 195, 250, 266
eucalyptus piperata 63
eucalyptus radiata 249, 266
    spiritual profile 311
Euphrates, River 376
Europe 94, 104, 159, 199–200, 326, 355
exorcism 173–4
fear 85
feet, washing 65
feng shui 158, 164–6, 215
fennel
    and angels 121; in auric field 195; for
        chakras 212–13; for cleansing 167;
        colour 250, 267; and pregnancy and
        lactation 70; sweet 195; spiritual pro-
        file 312
fir
    in auric field 197; balsam 267; for
        channelling 256; for cleansing 167;
        evaporation rate 195; in incense 377;
        for meditation 97; needle 197; in
        rooms 234; as tree of life 20; (white
        spruce), spiritual profile 313
Fire Lame Deer, Archie 405–6
fires 67
flower arranging 403
flowers 91, 94, 141, 215, 276
forgiveness 86
fountains 172
Four Noble Truths of Buddhism 399
fragrance, spiritual 135
Francis of Assisi, St 134
frangipani 229
frankincense 97, 384
    and angels 121; in Arab world 398; in
        auric field 197; for chakras 212–13;
        for channelling 256; for cleansing
        167; colour 250, 267; for embalming
        374–5; and energy field 35; evapora-
        tion rate 195; and fear 86; in incense
        2, 5, 49, 94, 159, 174–5, 377, 380,
        404; spiritual profile 314–15; spiri-
        tual uses 93; in spritzer 140; unguent
        391
Frazer, J. G. 161, 378
freesia 106
French National Centre for Scientific
    Research 187
fruits 93, 99, 401
Fungus of Immortality 352

Gabriel (angel) 111
galangal 250, 267

galbanum
    in ancient Egypt 375; in auric field 197;
        for channelling 256; colour 251, 267;
        evaporation rate 195; in incense 49,
        380; spiritual profile 316; spiritual
        use 93
Galen 373, 391
Galilee 321
gamut of odours 228–9
gandhakuti 5
gandhamadana 3
Gangadhara, Gandhasara 396
Ganges, River 57, 143
gardenia 250
    absolute 267
garlic 160
Garrison, Omar 295
Garudas 247
gems 245–8
Geneva 232
geranium
    and angels 121; in auric field 197;
        blending 228; for chakras 212–13;
        colour 251, 267; evaporation rate
        195; spiritual profile 317; and
        unworthiness 87; varieties 274
Ghazipur 143
Gilgamesh, Epic of 376, 378
gillyflower 391
ginger 3
    and angels 122; in auric field 197; and
        cleansing 167; colour 250, 267; evap-
        oration rate 195; and fear 86; in
        incense 402; in India 394; spiritual
        profile 318; spiritual uses 93
ginger-grass 391
Ginzberg, Louis 3
Gloucester, Bishop of 7
Goddard Space Flight Center 32
goddess worship 20, 370–2
gods and goddesses 2, 3, 370, 373, 389,
    393–6
Gold Medicine 144
grains of paradise 382
granite 245
grapefruit 63, 97, 122, 167, 251, 267
    spiritual profile 319
grapeseed oil 68
'Great Mother' 353
Greece, ancient 3, 4, 159, 288, 348, 355,
    372, 389–92
Greek Orthodox Church 50, 387
Gregor, St 4
guaiacwood 97
Guarani 298
guides 249
guilt 86

Guitemea, Cachora 22–3
gum arabic 174
gum mastic 374
gums 143, 395
Gurdjieff, George 81

hadass (spice box) 383
Hahnemann, Samuel 218
haiso 404
hands
    rubbing oils into 65, 95, 203, 237;
        washing 65, 66, 244
hands-on therapy 203
Hangzhon, China, Spiritual Grove Temple
    5
Hasidic sect 147
Hatshepsut, Queen 5
havdallah 2, 383
healing lists 241
heavens 3, 4, 398
Hebrew tradition 31, 48, 379–83
Hebron 379
Helen, St 286
helichrysum (Italian everlasting) 122, 195,
    251, 267
    spiritual profile 320
heliotrope 228
hemlock 392
henbane 392
henna-flower 397
Henry IV, King 7
herb bundles 167–8, 177–9
herbal smoke bowls 179
Hezekiah 382
Hinduism 47, 57, 104, 147, 286, 289,
    393–7, 399
Hippocrates 391
ho-wood 93, 97
Holy Spirit 4, 387
homeopathy 70, 218
Homer 3, 4, 141
    Odyssey 141
hops 70
horseradish 71
Horus 374, 375
houses, cleansing 162–5
Howser Creek 19
Hunt, Dr Valerie 33, 180–3, 232
hyacinth 93
    absolute 268
        spiritual profile 321;
    in ancient Greece 391; and angels 106,
        122; for chakras 212–13; for chan-
        nelling 256; colour 251; and death
        139; spiritual uses 276
hydrolats 140
hypnosis 147

hyssop 5, 70, 93, 122, 159, 167, 195, 212,
    250, 268, 380
    spiritual profile 322–3

I Ching 367
imagery 183
immortality, herb of 378, 402
incense
    and Aaaron 31; ceremony of 403; for
        cleansing 173–5; and death 141–3;
        dishes 175; energy of 163; forms of
        400; for fumigation 378, 381; and
        goddess worship 48, 371; in India 2;
        ingredients 49, 159–60, 315, 338,
        378; in Mesopotamia 377; methods
        of use 50; and resins 93; spiritual
        uses 67, 374, 386; and Taoism 402;
        for worship 371, 390, 392, 400
India 2, 5, 31, 57–8, 89, 94, 186, 289, 298,
    318, 343, 353, 359, 363, 393–7
Indonesia 399
Indra 395
Indus Valley 377, 397
Innocent I, Pope 53
International Federation of Aromatherapists
    71
inula 251, 268
Inyushin, Vladimir M. 184
ions, positive and negative 232, 244
Iran 329
Iraq 376
iris 391
iron 248
Ishtar 48, 378
Isidore, St 133
Islam 48, 111, 113, 396–8, *see also*
    Muslims
Israel 6
    tribes 247, *see also* Hebrew tradition
Israel, Dr Martin 113

jaborandi leaf 71
Jacob 111
Japan 45, 94, 143, 173–5, 243–5, 334, 352,
    399, 400, 403–4
jasmine 268
    and angels 106, 123; in anointing 7, 59;
        and Arab world 398; in auric field
        197; blending 228; for chakras
        212–13; for channelling 256; for
        cleansing 167; colour 251; and death
        139; evaporation rate 195; and guilt
        86; in India 394; for meditation 98;
        spiritual profile 324; spiritual uses 93
jasmine sambac 251, 268
Java 94, 289
Jerusalem 57

427

Mosque of Omar 162; Temple Institute museum 246, 380; Temple of Solomon 5, 31, 49, 248, 380, 383
Jesus Christ 5, 6, 53, 74, 89, 96, 112, 129, 315, 338, 360, 384
cross of 286
jinn 162
John Paul II, Pope 104
jonquil 228
Joseph 111
Judaism 2, 6, 20, 48–9, 111, 113, 147
Juliana, St 133
juniper
in ancient Egypt 159, 374; and angels 123; in auric field 197; berry 93; central Asian 401; in chakras 212–13; for cleansing 167; colour 250, 268; definition 176; evaporation rate 195; and goddess worship 370; and guilt 86; in incense 374, 377; and letting go 88; and Native Americans 407; and pregnancy and lactation 70; and Reiki 244; spiritual profile 325–6; spiritual uses 93; in Tibet 6, 159, 244, 401

Kabbalah 20, 111, 147, 382
Kakisaha, Mikinosuke 405
Kali 394
Kalidasa, *Sakoontala* 393
Kama 395
Kanchenjunga 104
kansho 404
karakusa 393
Kashmir 6
Kent, William and Elizabeth 16
Kenya 18
Kirlian, Semyon and Valentina 184
Kirlian photography 9, 184
Kish 377
Ko Hung 143
Koh-do 403
Koran 57, 104–5, 111, 397–8
Korea 245, 399
Krishna 89, 286, 363, 394, 395
kurna 395
kusa 393
Kuvera 395
kyara 404
Kyogen theatre 352
Kyoto 243
kyperion 391
kyphi 374

labdanum (rock rose), spiritual profile 327–8
lactation, use in 70

Ladakh 6
Lagash 376
Lakota 41, 405
Lakshmi 286, 394
Lao-Tzu 402
lavender
and angels 123; in auric field 197; blending 228; for chakras 212–13; for cleansing 171; colour 250, 268; evaporation rate 195; hydrolat 140; for protection 160; and receiving love 88; and smudge sticks 177; spiritual profile 328–9
Le Guerer, Annick 187
leaf people 5
Lebanon 5, 31, 298, 351
lemon
and angels 123; in auric field 197; blending 228; for chakras 212–13; for cleansing 167, 171; colour 251, 268; evaporation rate 195; and herb bundles 179; and letting go 88; for meditation 97; and skin irritation 63; spiritual profile 330; spiritual uses 93
lemon verbena 250, 268
lemongrass 123, 195, 251, 269
spiritual profile 331
Lethe, River 3
letting go 88
Lhasa 6
life fields 183
life force 375
light interference 259–61
light particles 186–7
lighting 215
lillies (susinon) 391
lily 106
lily of the valley 321
lime 63, 97, 212, 250, 269
linden blossom
absolute 269
spiritual profile 332–3
and angels 124; in auric field 197; for chakras 212–13; for channelling 256; for cleansing 167; colour 251; and guilt 86; for meditation 98
linseed oil 391
litsea cubeba 97, 250, 269
Loehr, Revd 76
logging 18
Lot 379
lotus 5, 391
oil 374
love, as spiritual experience 30
Lucian 3
Lucretius 141
Luther, Martin 49

428

Lutheran Church 55
Lydwyne, St 134

macadamia oil 68
mace 70, 382
maceration 276
McIntyre, Gladys 19–20
Mackenzie, Donald A. 333
magic eye pictures 186
magnolia 96, 228
Malaysia 5, 94, 289, 343, 363, 395, 399
Malevi, monastery of 134
Mali 289
Manchester, New York State 110
mandarin
    and angels 124; in auric field 197; for
        chakras 212–13; for cleansing 171;
        colour 250, 269; evaporation rate
        195; for meditation 97; spiritual
        profile 334; and unworthiness 87
Manniche, Lise 302
manuka 250
Marah 302
Maria the Jewess 375
marigold 179
marjoram 70, 93, 124, 212, 250, 269
    sweet 195, 269, 391
        spiritual profile 335–6
marriage ceremony 59–60
Mary Magdalene 6, 53, 384
Mary, mother of James 384
Mary, Virgin 89, 111, 333, 355
massage 199–201, 392
mastic 251, 269
Maury, Marguerite 199
May Day festival 356
maya 295
Mazatec 358
medication, people on 70
medicine wheel 406
meditation 73–4, 97–100
    position for 99
melissa 124, 160, 195, 212, 250, 269
    spiritual profile 336
memory 145–56, 2313, 232–3
menorah 6, 383
mental bodies 180, 186
Mesopotamia 52, 159, 162, 376–8
metal 172
Mexico 22–3, 358
miasms 218
Michael (angel) 110
microtubules 248
Milburga, St 133
Milky Way 32
mimosa 124, 256
    leaf 251, 269

minerals 179, 248, 258
mint 228, 373, 391
Minthe 348
mirrors 172, 215
misters and sprayers 165, 167, 172, 196–7,
    238, 239–40, 244
Mohamet II 162
Mohammed 48, 111, 396–8
Moolenburgh, H. C. 107
Moriah, Mount 6
moriah plant 383
Mormons 110
Moroni (angel) 110
Morris, Revd Allen 50, 55, 387
Moses 15, 48, 57, 302, 315, 338, 380
Moskvitin, Jirij 186
mugwort 71
Muir Woods 16
multidimensional bodies 180–98
mummification 298, 372–3
muscular sites, emotional 217
music 90, 166, 170, 172, 213, 228, 406
musk 3, 7, 228
Muslims 2, 3, 48, 57, 80, 111, 113, 143,
    162
mustard 71
myrrh 3, 384
    in ancient Egypt 373–4; and ancient
        Greece 391; and angels 124; and
        Arab world 398; for chakras 212–13;
        for cleansing 167; colour 251, 269;
        for embalming 374; evaporation rate
        195; in incense 5, 49, 159, 175, 378,
        381, 404; in India 2; for meditation
        97; and pregnancy and lactation 70;
        spiritual uses 93, 94; staining 66;
        unsuitable use 237; spiritual profile
        337–8
myrrh gushing 134
myrtle 88, 93, 125, 167, 172, 256, 269,
    378, 383, 391, 397
    spiritual profile 338–9

Nabonnedos, King 378
Nanderuvuzu 298
narcissus 93, 125, 251, 256, 270, 391
    absolute 270
        spiritual profile 340
Narcissus (flower-god) 340
NASA 32, 192
Native Americans 2, 22, 27, 31, 41, 68,
    104, 109, 150, 159, 162, 173, 175, 189,
    298, 358, 366, 405–7
    spiritual practices 405–6
nature, harmony with 406–7
near-death experiences 129–30
negativity 158, 163, 232

Neot Kedumim 323
Nepal 104, 286
Nepelle 114
Nero, Emperor 142
neroli (orange blossom)
    and angels 125; in anointing 7, 59; in
        auric field 197; blending 228; for
        chakras 212–13; for channelling 253;
        for cleansing 171; colour 250, 270;
        for distant healing 238; and energy
        fields 35; evaporation rate 195;
        hydrolat 140; for meditation 98; spir-
        itual properties 252–3; and
        unworthiness 87; spiritual profile
        341–2
Network First 113
New Testament
    Epistles of Paul 112, 385; James 385;
        John 6, 53, 129; Luke 80, 112; Mark
        53, 384; Matthew 74, 348;
        Revelations 4, 20, *see also* Bible
niaouli 195, 348, 356
Nile, River 373
Nippur 377
Nirukta 359, 394
non-local quantum thought phenomena 40
Norse myths 20–1
North Africa 397
North America 94, 173, 326
Novali Cori 370
Nurunderi 114
nutmeg 70, 93, 125, 195, 249, 270
    spiritual profile 343

oakmoss 125, 251, 270
odic force 184
odour of sanctity 133
oils, essential 2
    in auric field of client 237; for chakras
        212–13; and channelling 252–6; and
        colour healing 257–73; colours 193,
        249–51; definition 275; for dying
        person 139–40; energy field of
        190–1; for energy-cleansing baths
        171; etheric colour 259–60, 263–73;
        evaporation rate 193–6; on feet 6,
        238, 244; in funerary rites 141–4;
        grounding 194; handling and storage
        46; on healer 238; in herb bundles
        178–9; methods of use 61–8; and
        prayer 80–2; profiles 234; sacramen-
        tal use 387; spiritual effects 9–12; for
        spiritual healing 221–2, 231–73; spir-
        itual profiles 274–368; therapeutic
        and medicinal properties 276, 369,
        389, 390–2; in treatment or waiting
        room 233–5; and use of smoke

173–5; using in auric field 196–8;
    vibrations of 34–7, 41–3, 219, 257;
    viscosity 193, *see also* blending;
    individual names
Old Testament 30, 111, 160
    Chronicles 141; Esther 338; Exodus 48,
        52, 246–7, 302, 315, 338, 361, 380;
        Ezekiel 48; Genesis 141, 328, 379;
        Isaiah 339, 351, 382; Jeremiah 370;
        Kings 45, 326; Leviticus 330;
        Nehemiah 339; Psalms 50, 298,
        385–6; Song of Solomon 321, 338;
        Zachariah 339, *see also* Bible
Oldfield, Harry 34, 190, 231
olibanum 398
    see also frankincense
olive oil 59–60, 62, 385, 391
Olympus, Mount 3
onycha 49, 380
oodsoz 143
opoponax 250, 270
oracles 372
orange
    and angels 125; blending 229; for
        cleansing 167, 171, 176; colour 250,
        270; evaporation rate 195; for medi-
        tation 97; spiritual profile 344;
        spiritual uses 93; to receive love 88
orange blossom *see* neroli
oregano 70, 177, 196, 250, 270
organ transplants 145, 148–9
orgone dots 186
ormenis flower (chamomile maroc)195, 250
    spiritual profile 345
orris 228, 372
    root 195
Orthodox churches 2, 50, 173, 387
Osiris 298
osmanthus 256
oud (aloeswood) 59
Ovid 392

Paiutes 358
Pakistan 48, 143
palma rosa 126, 196, 250, 270
    spiritual profile 346
Panaenus 392
pandang 395
paradises 3–4, 398
parsley seed 70, 196
Parvati 394
past-life memories 145–56
patchouli
    and angels 126; blending 229; for
        chakras 212–13; colour 251, 270;
        evaporation rate 195; in incense 143,
        394; spiritual profile 347

430

Patrick, St 133
Paul, St 112, 385
peach 20
pendulums 242
pennyroyal 71
peppermint
    and angels 126; in auric field 197;
        blending 228; for chakras 212–13;
        colour 250, 270; evaporation rate
        196; and pregnancy and lactation 70;
        and skin irritation 63; spiritual pro-
        file 348
perfume
    oils used as 55, 68; origin of word 82
pergalaria 228
Pergamus 391
Persia 52, 161, 397
Pert, Candace 37
petitgrain
    and angels 126; in auric field 197; for
        chakras 212–13; for channelling 256;
        for cleansing 171; colour 250, 271;
        evaporation rate 196; spiritual profile
        349
Philippines 399
Phoenicians 380
photo-sensitivity 71
Piesse, G. W. Septimus 228–9
piezoelectric effect 247
Pilkington, James, Bishop 386
pillows, use of oil on 67, 95
pimento berry 70, 256, 271
    spiritual profile 350
pine
    and angels 126; aroma 2; in auric field
        197; for chakras 212–13; for chan-
        nelling 256; in China 400, 402; for
        cleansing 167; colour 250, 271; evap-
        oration rate 196; and goddess
        worship 370–2; and guilt 86; hinoki
        93, 243–4, 250, 267; in incense
        159–60, 378, 400; in India 394; and
        letting go 88; for meditation 97; and
        Native Americans 407; needles 277;
        in rooms 234; Scotch 94; smudge
        sticks 175, 177; spiritual uses 93, 94;
        Virginia 94; spiritual profile 351–2
pineapple 228
pinks (carnation) 228, 277
pipe, sacred 406
pirs 162
plants
    effect of prayer on 76; experiments with
        26, 76; functions of 13–14; human inter-
        action with 21–6, 41; sanctity of 29–31;
        for spiritual use 277
Plato 4

plehiding bark 161
Pliny 376, 392
Plutarch 3, 373
Pluto 348
Poland 352
Polycontrast Interface Photograph (PIP)
    190, 231, 260
Polynesia 3, 21
pomegranate 20
Poppaea 142
portugal (orange) 229
prairie lavender 176
prayer 61, 73–100, 172
    blocks to 85–8; fragrance for use in
        89–97; Newsweek survey 75, 79;
        position for 84; space for 89–92;
        sung 82; unanswered 78–9; written 82
pregnancy, use in 69–70
priests and priestesses 370–2, 373
protection, fragrance as 157–61
psycho-neuro-immuno-endocrinology, 10,
    148
Ptah Du-Auu 374
Ptolemies 373
Punt 5
Puranas 393
purification 44–5, 90, 162–6, 173
Pythagoras 390
Pythia 372

Ra 338, 373
Rama 394
Rameses II 301
Rameses III 302
Raphael (angel) 111
Ratsch, Dr Christian 298
receiving and accepting 88
red sanders 382
Redwood National Park, California 14
redwoods 16, 17, 18
referred pain syndrome 189
Reformation 49
rei-ryokoh 404
Reich, Wilhelm 186
Reichenbach, Karl von 183
Reiki 243–5
reincarnation 146–7
resins 4, 93, 94, 143, 162, 173–5, 177, 328,
    352 369, 373, 380
rhododendron 401
Rimmel, Eugene 52, 142, 372, 390
Rinpoche, Sogyal 97, 138
rites of passage 173
Rohutu noanoa 3
rolfers 183
Rome, ancient 4, 49, 159, 355, 358, 386,
    392

room sprays 67
roots 93
rosaries 6
  Buddhist 400
rose 43
  in ancient Egypt 375; and angels 106, 127; in anointing 7, 52; in Arab world 398; in auric field 197; blending 228; for chakras 212–13; for cleansing 162, 167, 171; herb bundles 177; hydrolat 140; in incense 382, 390; in India 394; and meditation 98; for protection 173–5
rose bulgar 231, 240
rose maroc
  absolute 271
    spiritual profile 352–3
  for chakras 212; for channelling 256; colour 251; and death 139; evaporation rate 196; for meditation 98; staining 66; and unworthiness 87
rose otto 86, 98, 196, 271
  spiritual profile 354–5
Rose, St 134
rose 'Turk' 353
rose water 2, 162, 394
rosemary 196
  and angels 127; for chakras 212–13; for cleansing 171; colour 249, 271; and pregnancy and lactation 70; for protection 173–5; smudge sticks 177; spiritual profile 355–6; spiritual uses 93
rosewood 93, 196, 213, 250, 271
Rowell, Geoffrey 53
rubies 245–7
rue 71, 160
rush, fragrant 374
Russell, George W. 114
Russian Orthodox Church 388
Ryerson, Kevin 247

Sabbath 383
sacraments 387
Sacred Tree 378
safety and precautions 71
saffron 372
  in ancient Greece 391; and gods 4; in incense 49, 380, 382; in India 394
sage 2
  and angels 127; Californian white 177; for channelling 256; for cleansing 167; colour 250, 271; evaporation rate 196; and healing 159–60; human interaction 24; and menorah 6, 383; and Native Americans 2, 159, 175–6, 358, 407; and pregnancy and lacta-

tion 70; smudge sticks 175–6; spiritual profile 357–8; spiritual uses 93
sage brush 176
saints 3, 4
  fragrance of 133–4
Saladin 162
Salome 384
salt 45, 63, 90, 166, 168, 170, 172, 239
saltpeter 380
Salvadora persica 396
Salvia 6
Sancta Sophia, Constantinople 162
sandalwood 43
  in ancient Egypt 374; and angels 127; blending 228; for chakras 212–13; in China 400; evaporation rate 195; and fear 86; in incense 143, 374, 400; in India 6, 94, 143, 394; in Japan 404; and meditation 97; spiritual profile 358–9; spiritual uses 93; and unworthiness 87
Santa Ana winds 232
santal (sandalwood) 229
Saqqâra 374
Sarah 379
Saraswati 394
sassafras 71
Sati 394
savin 71
'savour', as fragrance 384
sesame oil 7, 391
Shakespeare, William 7
shamans 5, 30, 189, 289, 298, 326
Shewell-Cooper, W. E. 301
Shinto 47, 82, 243–4, 368, 403–5
Shiva 89, 286, 363, 393–4, 395
showers 66
Shu 373
Shumann resonance 27
Siberia 30, 326
Sikkim 97, 104
silver fir 93, 250, 272
skin irritation 71–2
sleep 100
smallage 392
smelling strips 190, 193, 195, 234
Smith, Joseph 110
smoke
  as message to gods 369; for purification 173–9, 189, 389, 401, 402; to drive away witches 352; to induce trances 370–2; for visions 327
smudge sticks 68, 173–9, 189, 406
Sobek 336
Sodom 379
solvent extraction 276
Somnath 395

sound 213, 228
memories 213; spiritual use of 30, 170, *see also* music
southernwood 71, 229
Spain 397
spearmint 196, 250, 272
spices 93, 143
see also individual names
spikenard
and ancient Egypt 375; in ancient Greece 391; and angels 127; for cleansing 167; colour 272; in incense 49, 374, 380; in India 394; Jesus and 6, 53; and pregnancy and lactation 70; spiritual profile 360; spiritual uses 93
spirit guides 256
spiritual crisis, healing 219
spray method *see* misters and sprayers
spritzers 140
spruce 93, 97, 197, 234, 256, 407
Sri Lanka (Ceylon) 359, 399
stacte 49, 261, 380
star anise 250, 272, 404
steam distillation 276
Steiner, Rudolph 199
stinging nettle 71
stocks 228
storax (styrax) 97, 195, 229, 251, 272, 382, 391
spiritual profile 361
styrax *see* storax
styrax balsam 93
substance addiction 70
subtle bodies 183–6, 203
Sukkot 330
Sumatra 294, 395
Sumeria 371, 376
Summer Rain, Mary 407
sun dance celebration 358, 406
sweat lodges 2, 68, 176, 406–7
Swedenborg, Emanuel 110
sweet flag 391, 396
sweet gum bark 374
sweet pea 228
sweetgrass (vanilla grass) 2, 159, 175, 176, 407
sycamore 20
Sylvia, Claire 145, 148
Syria 52, 376
syringa (mock orange flower) 228

tagetes 196, 251, 272
Tammuz 48, 378
tangerine 97, 212
Tanio, Bruce 231
tansy 71

Tantrists 98
Taoism 47, 141, 289, 402
tarragon 70
Taylor, Arnold 200
tea tree 250, 272
Tefnet 373
Tepe Gawra 379
Thailand 399
Theophrastus 390
theosophy 184, 186
Theresa of Avila, St 133
Theresa, Mother 137
Thessaloniki 134
Thompson, Richard 41
thuja 71
thyme
and ancient Greece 391; and angels 128; for chakras 212–13; colour 251, 272; evaporation rate 196; and pregnancy and lactation 70; and skin irritation 63; smudge sticks 177; spiritual profile 362
Tibet 2, 6, 136, 243–4, 326, 399, 400–1
Tigris, River 376
tissue or handkerchief use of oils 66
tolu 228
tonka bean 228, 250, 272
tranquilliser addiction 70
Tree of Life 352
trees 15–21, 93, 234
communication with 19–20, *see also* individual names
Trimurti 393–4
tsampa 401
tuberose
absolute 272
spiritual profile 363
and angels 128; blending 229; for channelling 256; colour 251; and letting go 88; spiritual uses 93, 251
Tucci, G. 400
tulsi (basil) 286, 395
tun fu 159
Turin, Dr Luca 192
Turkey 161, 162, 353, 376
turmeric 196, 250, 272, 394
Tutankhamen 302, 306
Tyndale, John 258
Tyrol 356

Umayyads 397
unfragranced products 234
United Arab Emirates 144
unworthiness 87
Upanishads 393
Ur 376
Uriel (angel) 111

433

Uruk 376
Urutaete 3
usnea 26
Usui, Dr Mikao 243

valerian 6, 70, 195, 251, 273
Valhalla 326
vanilla 97, 229, 251, 273
Vedic scriptures 359, 393–6
Venezuela 5
verbena 128, 159, 228
vernal grass (new hay) 229
vetiver 93, 167, 195, 251, 273, 394
    spiritual profile 364
vibrational aromatherapy 199–230
    treatment 213–16
vibrations 32–7, 41–3, 96, 107–8
Vietnam 399
violet 106, 229, 382, 391, 397
violet leaf 196, 251, 256
    absolute 273
        spiritual profile 365
Vishnu 286, 393–4, 395
vision pillows 67, 95
vision quest 406
vitality globules 186–7
vivification 274
Vogel, Marcel 27

wallflower 229
Warao 5
Washoe 358
water
    bowls 167; for cleansing and purifying

57–9
Weiss, Dr Brian 145
West Africa 397
West Indies 359
White, John 255
white sandal 382
wind chimes 272
wine 374, 391
wintergreen 70, 71
witches 159
woods 99, 172
    fragrant 175, 179
wormseed 71
wormwood 71, 175, 176

xenoglossy 146

Yaquis 22
yarrow 128, 196, 251, 273
    spiritual profile 366
Yehoshua Ben-Levi, Rabbi 379
Yezdijird, King 141
yin and yang 402
ylang ylang 87, 128, 196, 212, 250, 273
    spiritual profile 367
Yom Kippur 49
Yuthok, Dorje Yudon 401
Yuwipe 162
yuzu 93, 243, 250, 273
    spiritual profile 368

Zanzibar 397
Zen Buddhism 403
Zeus 4, 370

434